GREAT BRITAIN & IRELAND

TOURIST and MOTORING ATLAS
ATLAS ROUTIER et TOURISTIQUE
STRASSEN- und REISEATLAS
TOERISTISCHE WEGENATLAS
ATLANTE STRADALE e TURISTICO
ATLAS DE CARRETERAS y TURÍSTICO

Contents / Sommaire / Inhaltsübersicht
Inhoud / Sommario / Sumario

Inside front cover: Key to map pages
Intérieur de couverture : Tableau d'assemblage
Umschlaginnenseite: Übersicht
Binnenzijde van het omslag: Overzichtskaart
Copertina interna: Quadro d'insieme
Portada interior: Mapa índice

IV-XXI

Route planning / Grands itinéraires / Reiseplanung
Grote verbindingswegen / Grandi itinerari / Información general
1 inch = 15.8 miles - 1:1 000 000 - 1cm = 10km

XIV

Unitary Authorities

XXII

Distances / Distances / Entfernungen
Afstandstabel / Distanze / Distancias

XXIII

Shipping Services / Liaisons maritimes / Schiffsverbindungen
Scheepvaartverbindingen / Collegamenti marittimi / Enlaces marítimos

2-87

Great Britain / Grande-Bretagne / Großbritannien
Groot-Brittannië / Gran Bretagna / Gran Bretaña
1 inch = 4.75 miles - 1:300 000 - 1cm = 3km

88-119

Ireland / Irlande / Irland / Ierland / Irlanda - 1 inch = 4,75 miles - 1:300 000 - 1cm = 3km

120-121

Greater London - 1 inch = 3.16 miles - 1:200 000 - 1cm = 2km

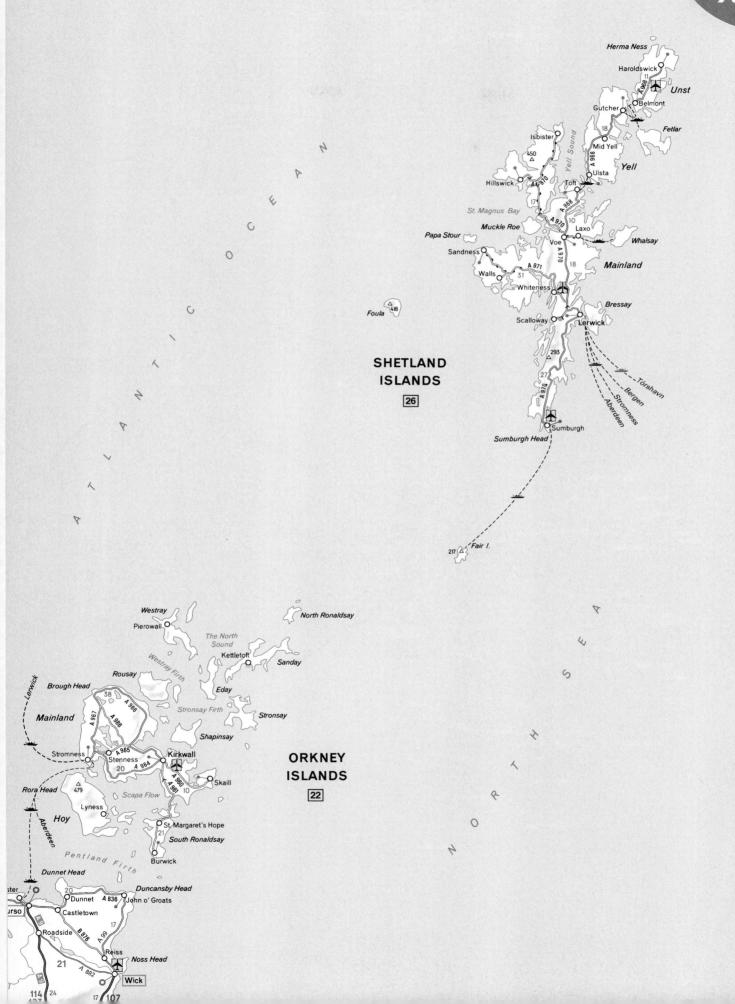

ATLANTIC OCEAN

Herma Ness
Haroldswick
A 968
Unst
Gutcher ○ ○ Belmont
Fetlar
Isbister
18
Mid Yell
450 △
A 970
A 968
Yell
Hillswick ○ Ulsta
17 Toft
A 968
St. Magnus Bay 10
A 970
Muckle Roe
Laxo
Papa Stour 7 Voe
Whalsay
Sandness ○
A 971 A 970
Mainland
Walls 31 18
Whiteness
Bressay
Foula △418 293 △ Scalloway ○ Lerwick

**SHETLAND
ISLANDS**

26

27
A 970

Sumburgh Head Sumburgh

─ ─ ─ Tórshavn
─ ─ ─ Bergen
─ ─ ─ Stromness
─ ─ ─ Aberdeen

217 △ *Fair I.*

N
O
R
T
H

S
E
A

Westray
Pierowall
North Ronaldsay
*The North
Sound*
Kettletoft
Sanday
Eday
Brough Head *Rousay* *Stronsay Firth* *Stronsay*
38 *Westray Firth*
A 967 A 966 *Shapinsay*
Mainland
A 966
15
A 965
Stromness ○ Stenness Kirkwall
20 A 964 **ORKNEY
ISLANDS**
A 961
479 △ 10 Skaill 22
Scapa Flow A 961
Hoy Lyness
St. Margaret's Hope
Rora Head 21
South Ronaldsay
Burwick
Pentland Firth

Lerwick
Aberdeen

Dunnet Head
Duncansby Head
20 Dunnet
─ster ○ A 836 John o' Groats
urso ○ Castletown 17
Roadside ○ B 876 A 99
21 A 882 Reiss *Noss Head*
114 24 **Wick**
127 17 107

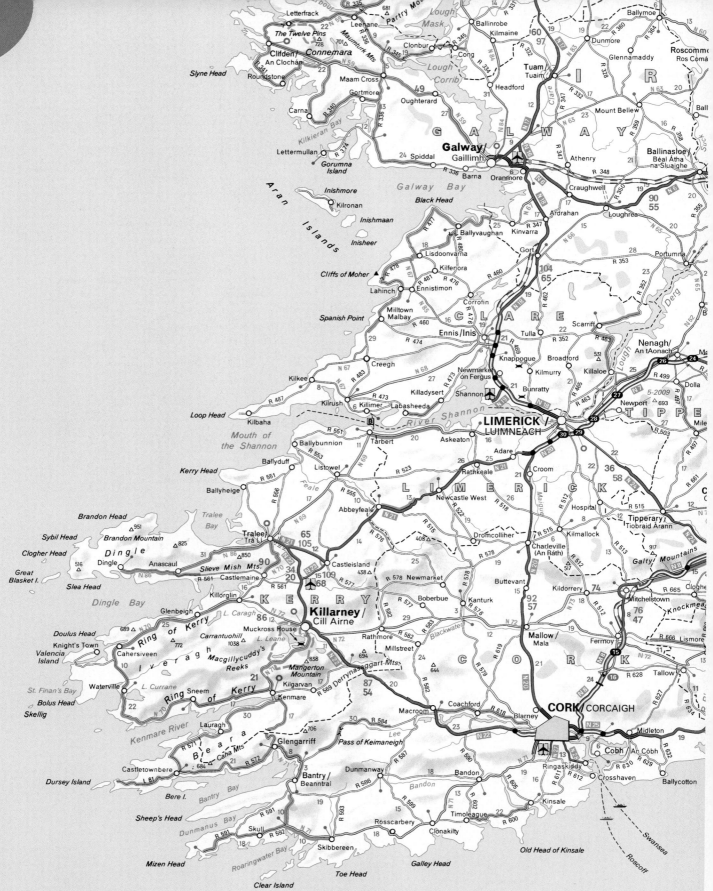

Longford / An Longfort
Granard
Lanesborough
Edgeworthstown / Meathas Troim
Castlepollard
Oldcastle
Kells
Monasterboice
Old Mellifont
Slane
Clogherhead

Drogheda / Droichead Átha
Newgrange
Duleek
Balbriggan
Athlone / Baile Átha Luain
Ballymahon
Ballymore
Mullingar / An Muileann gCearr
Delvin
Athboy
Trim
Navan / An Uaimh
Dunshaughlin
Ashbourne
Naul
Skerries
Rush
Lusk
Swords
Malahide
Portmarnock
Howth

Moate
Kilbeggan
Kinnegad
Enfield
Kilcock
Maynooth
Clara
Tullamore / Tulach Mhór
Edenderry
Lucan

DUBLIN / BAILE ÁTHA CLIATH
Dún Laoghaire
Clondalkin
Dalkey

Ferbane
Clonmacnoise
Clonfert
Banagher
Cloghan
Kilcormac
Birr
Kinnitty
Portarlington
Newbridge (An Droichead Nua)
Naas
Russborough
Kippure
Enniskerry
Powerscourt
Bray
Greystones

Kildare
Monasterevin
Mountmellick
Slieve Bloom Mts.
Portlaoise
Kilcullen
Hollywood
Poulaphouca Resr.
Glendalough
Laragh
Rathnew
Wicklow / Cill Mhantáin
Wicklow Head

Roscrea
Mountrath
Abbeyleix
Athy
Baltinglass
Lugnaquillia Mountain 924
Rathdrum
Wicklow Mountains

Templemore
Rathdowney
Durrow
Castledermot
Tullow
Aughrim
Arklow / An tInbhear Mór

Thurles / Durlas
Holy Cross
Freshford
Castlecomer
Carlow / Ceatharlach
Tinahely
Carnew
Gorey
Courtown

Urlingford
Callan
Kilkenny / Cill Chainnigh
Ballingarry
Killenaule
Fethard
Thomastown
Jerpoint
Graiguenamanagh
Bagenalstown (Muine Bheag)
Borris
Kiltealy
Bunclody
Enniscorthy / Inis Córthaidh
Blackstairs Mts.
Cahore Point

Cashel / Caiseal
Cahir
Clonmel / Cluain Meala
Carrick-on-Suir / Carraig na Siúire
New Ross
Wexford / Loch Garman
Blackwater

Comeragh Mts.
Slievenamon △719
Waterford / Port Láirge
Arthurstown
Wellington Bridge
Rosslare

Cappoquin
Dungarvan / Dún Garbhán
Bunmahon
Tramore
Dunmore East
Kilmore Quay
Saltee Islands
Rosslare Harbour / Calafort Ros Láir
Carnsore Point

Youghal / Eochaill
Youghal Bay
Ardmore
Helvick Head
Dungarvan Harbour
Waterford Harbour
Hook Head

ST. GEORGE'S CHANNEL
Pembroke
Roscoff
Cherbourg-Octeville

Douglas (I. of Man)
Liverpool
Cardi...
Aber...
Newport
Strumble Head
Pembrokeshire Coast National Park
Fishguard / Abergwaun
St. David's Head
St. David's
PEMBROKESHIRE
St. Bride's Bay
Haverfordwest / Hwlffordd
Narberth
Milford Haven / Aberdaugleddau
Neyland
Pembroke Dock / Doc Penfro
Pembroke
St. Govan's Head
Rosslare

L. Derravaragh
Lough Ree
River Shannon
Grand Canal
Royal Canal
Nore
Barrow
R. Suir
Slaney
Bann

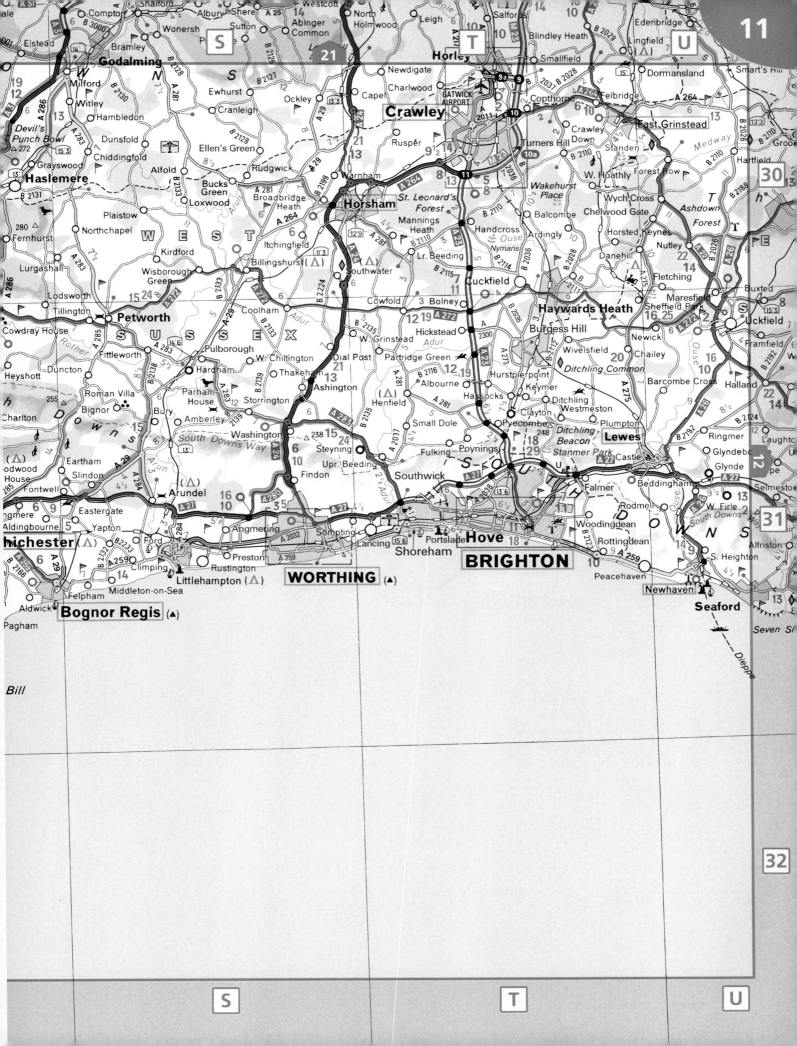

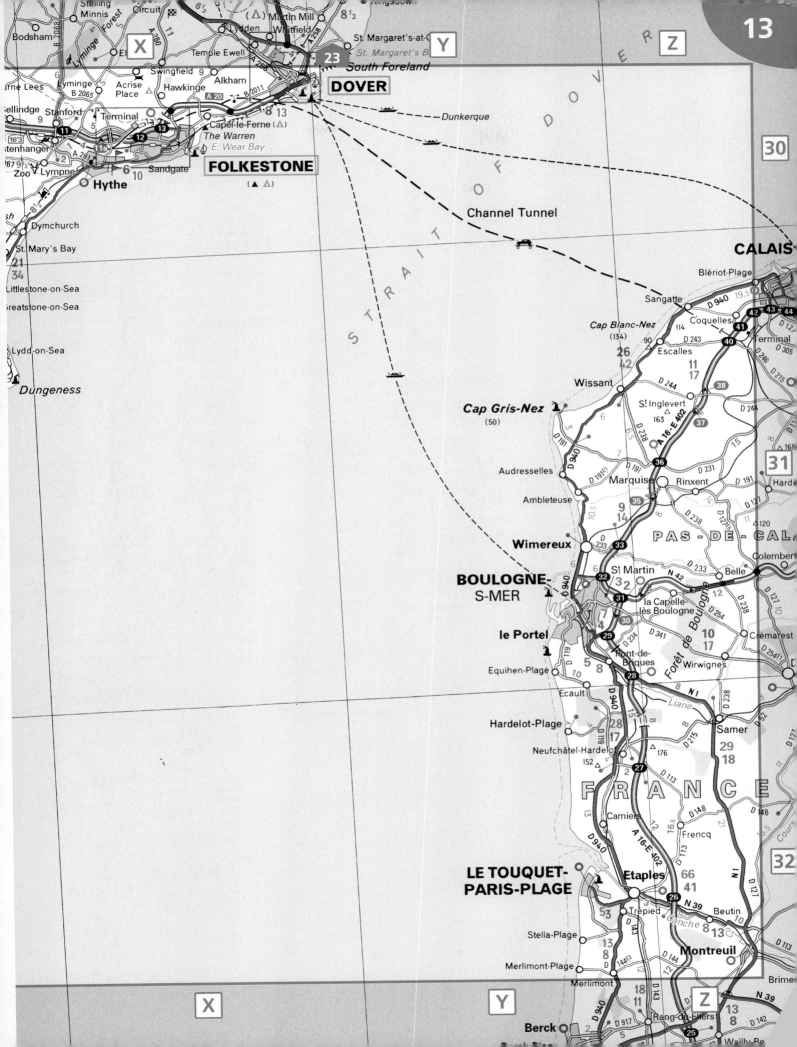

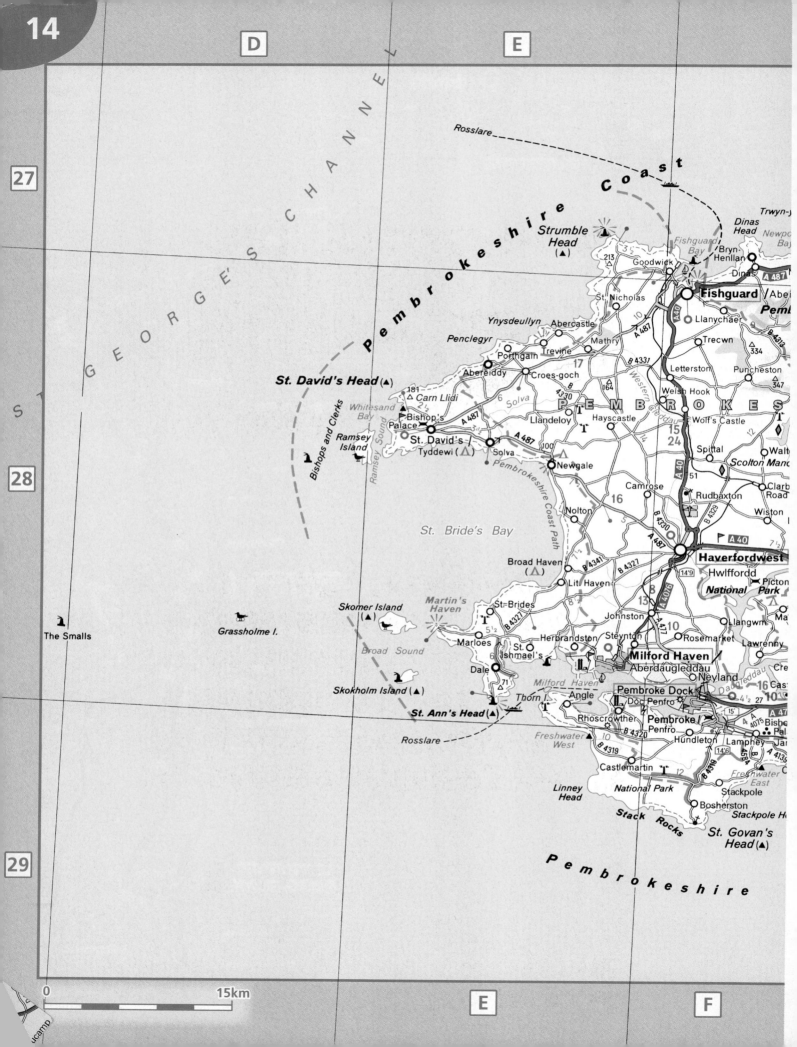

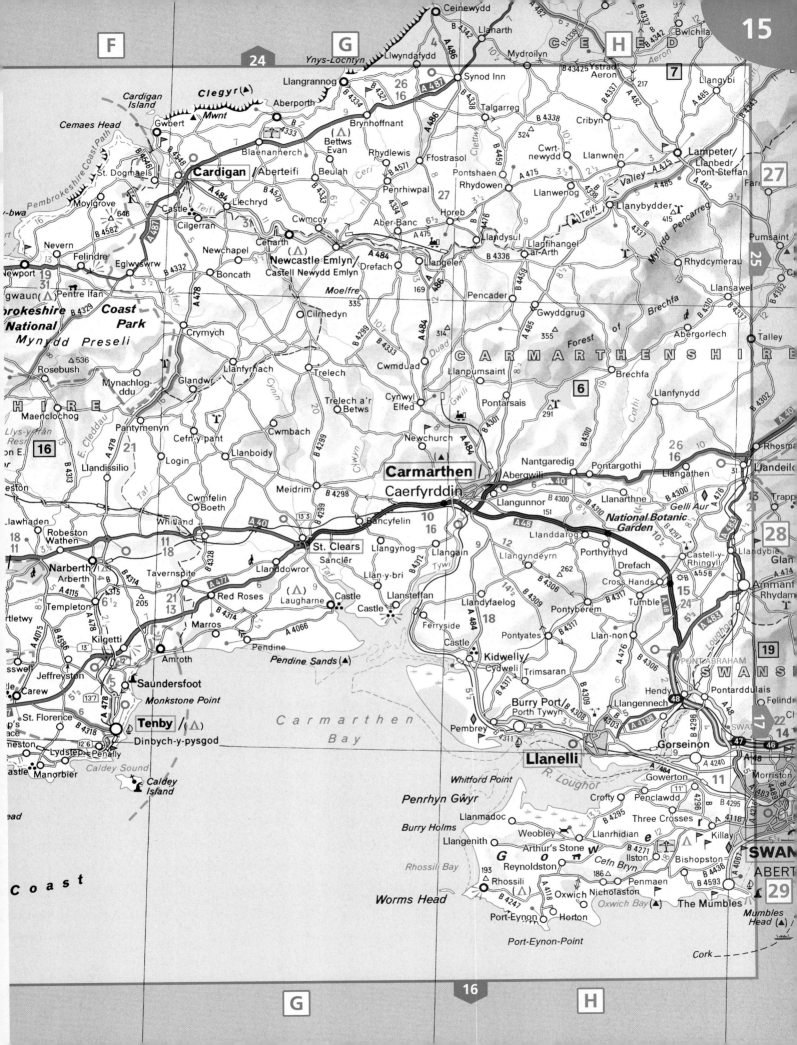

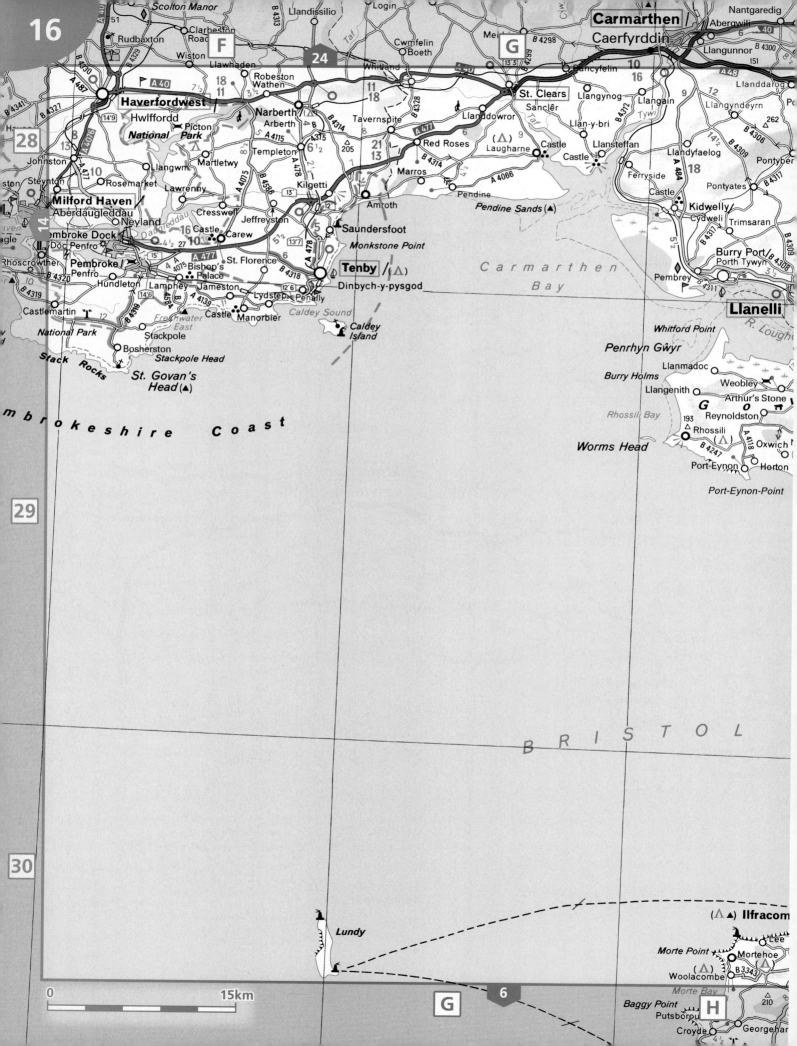

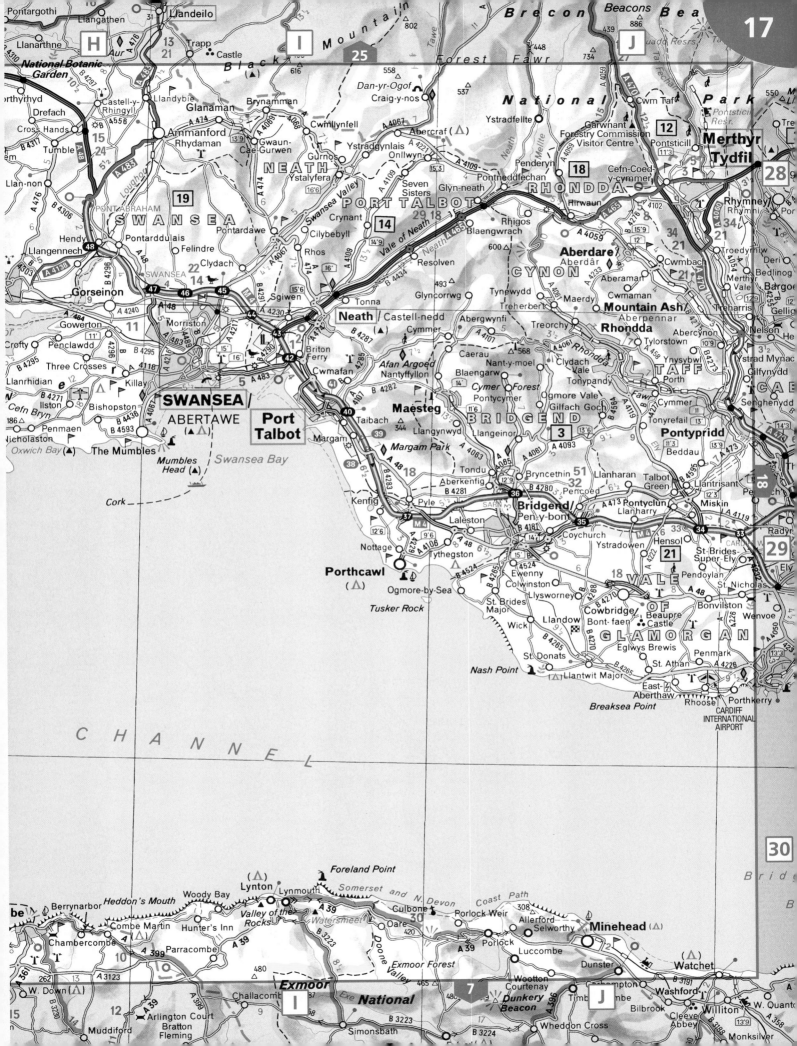

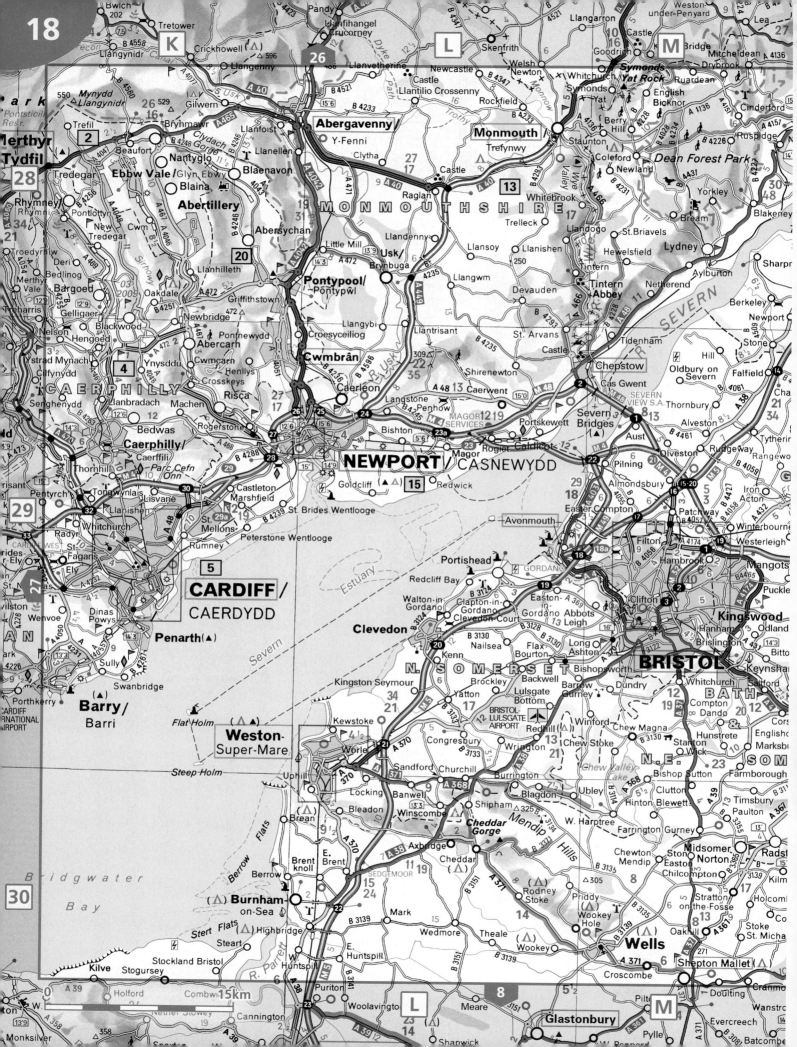

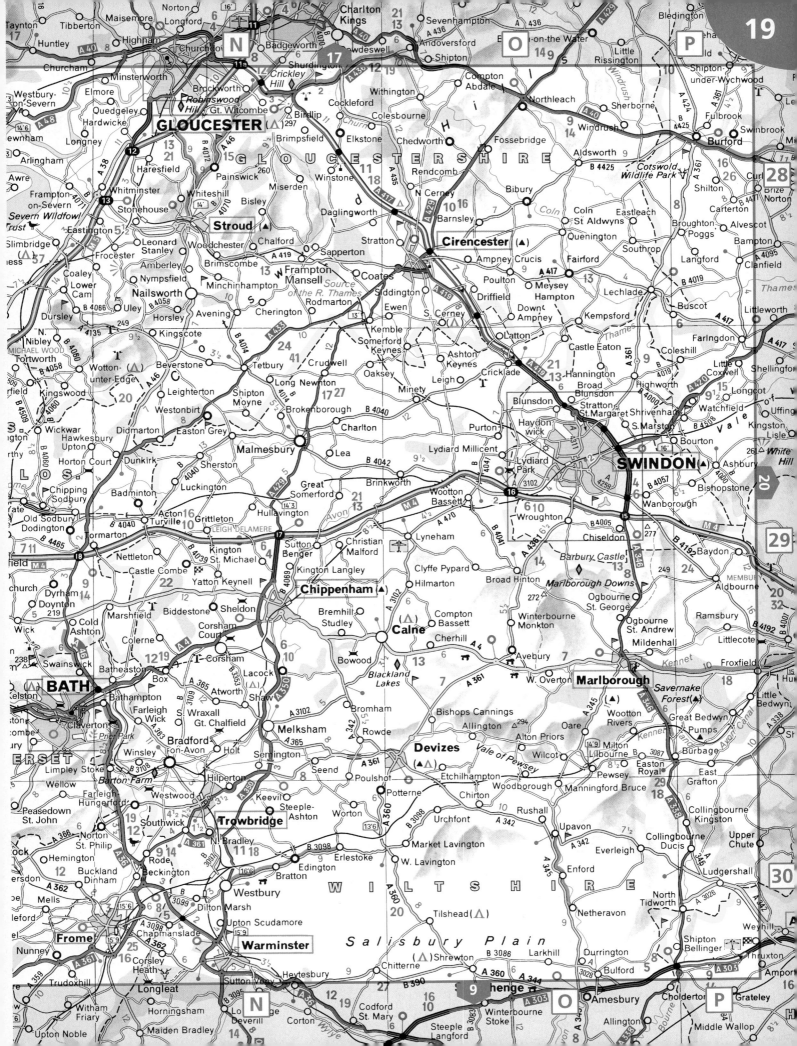

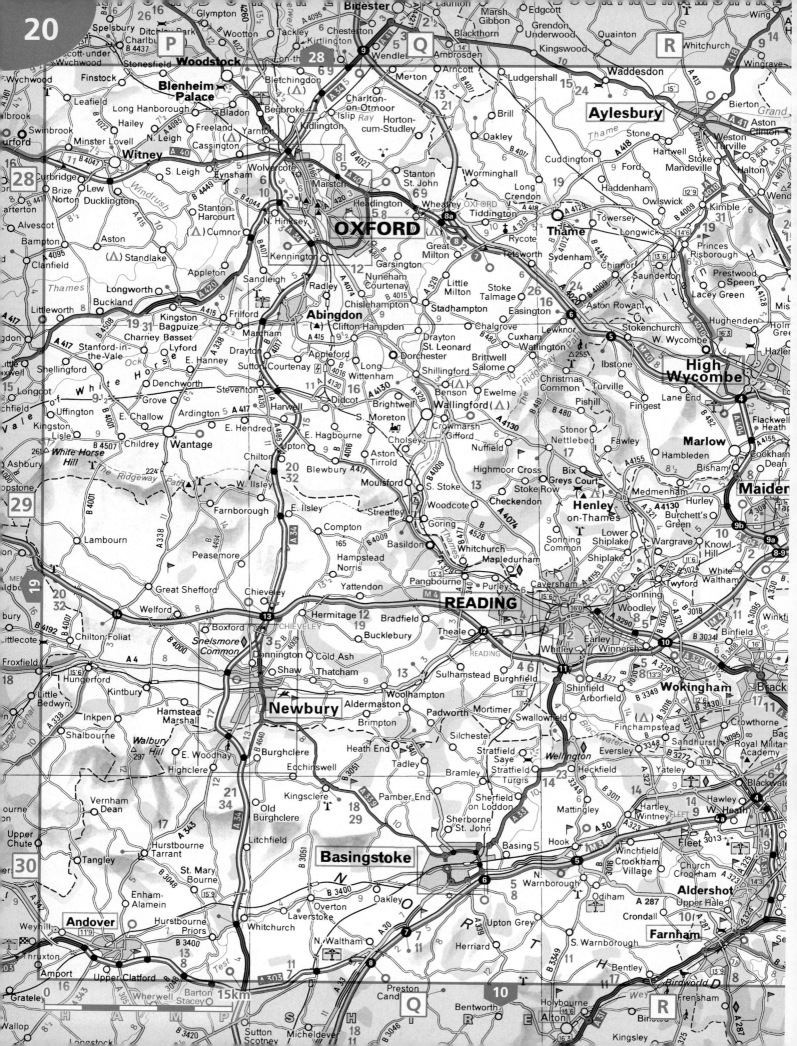

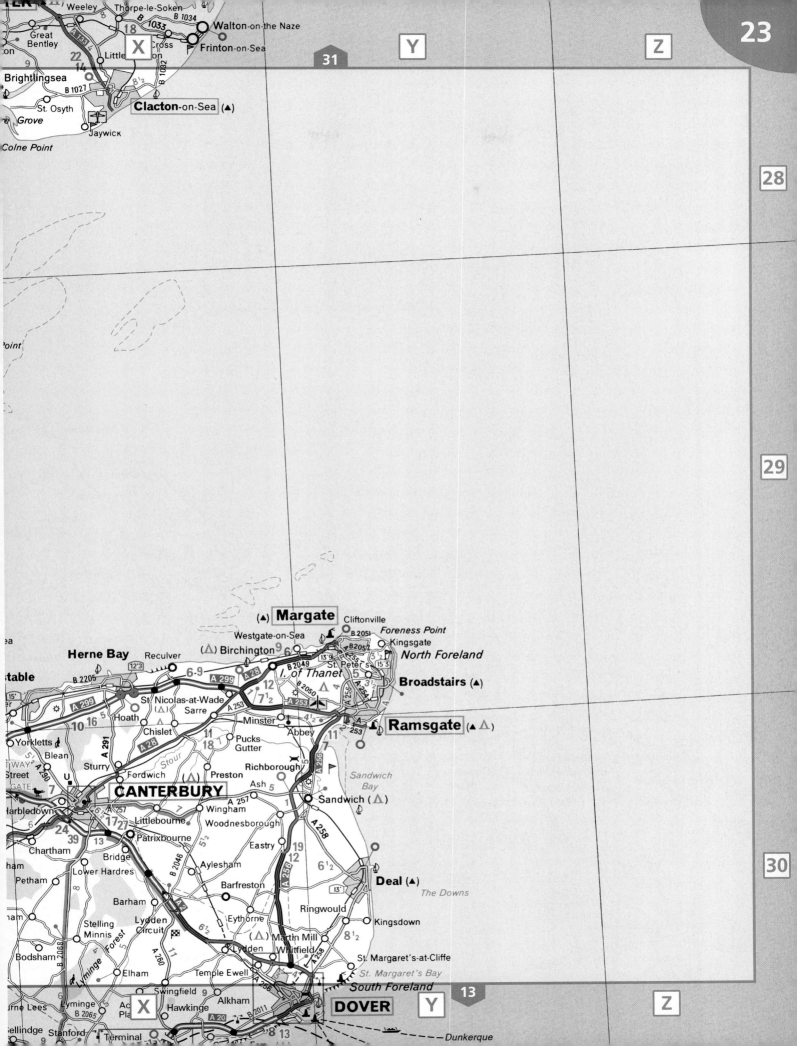

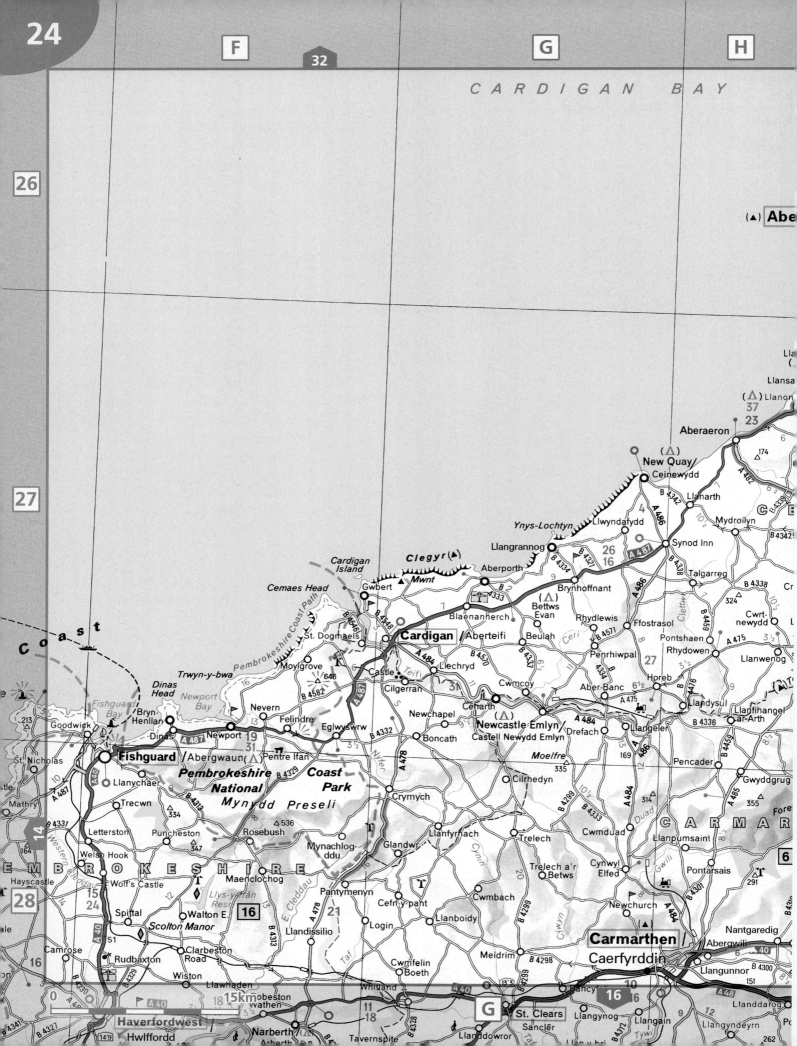

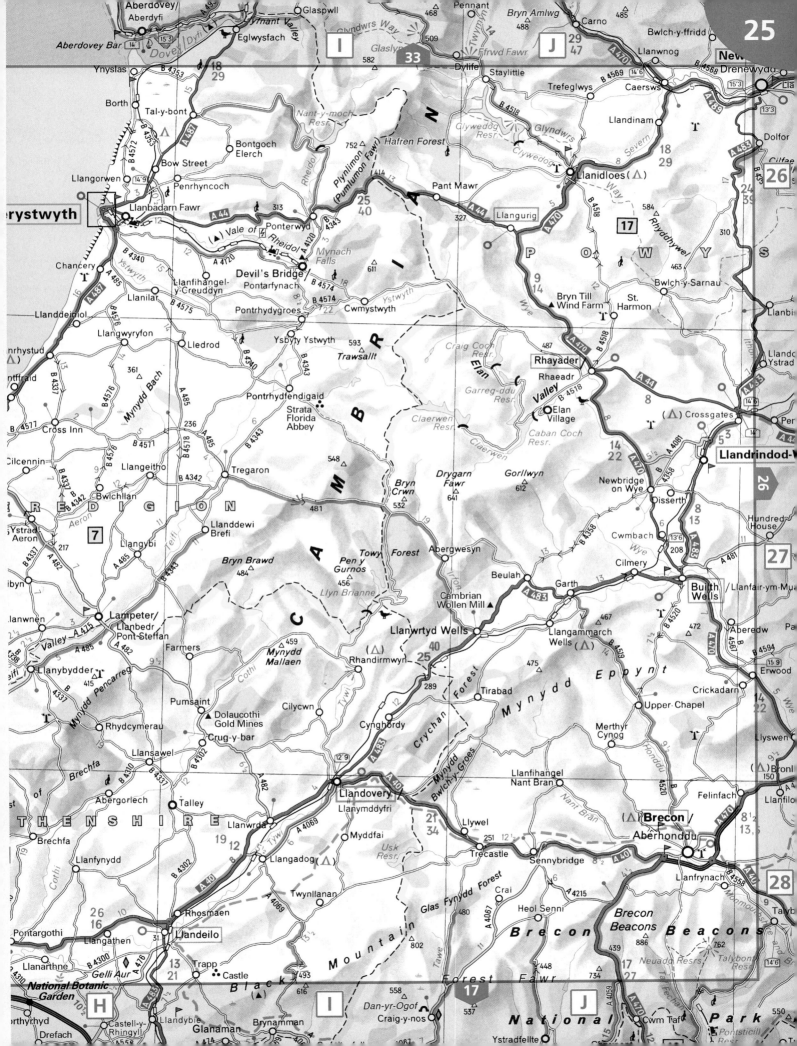

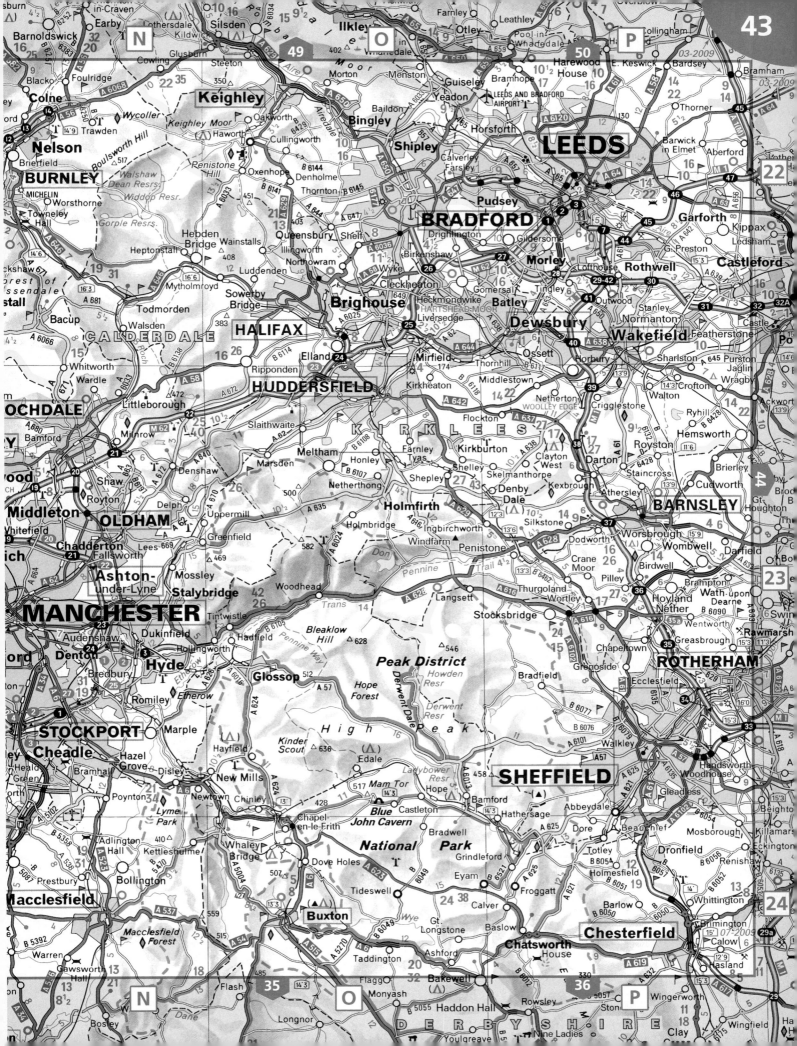

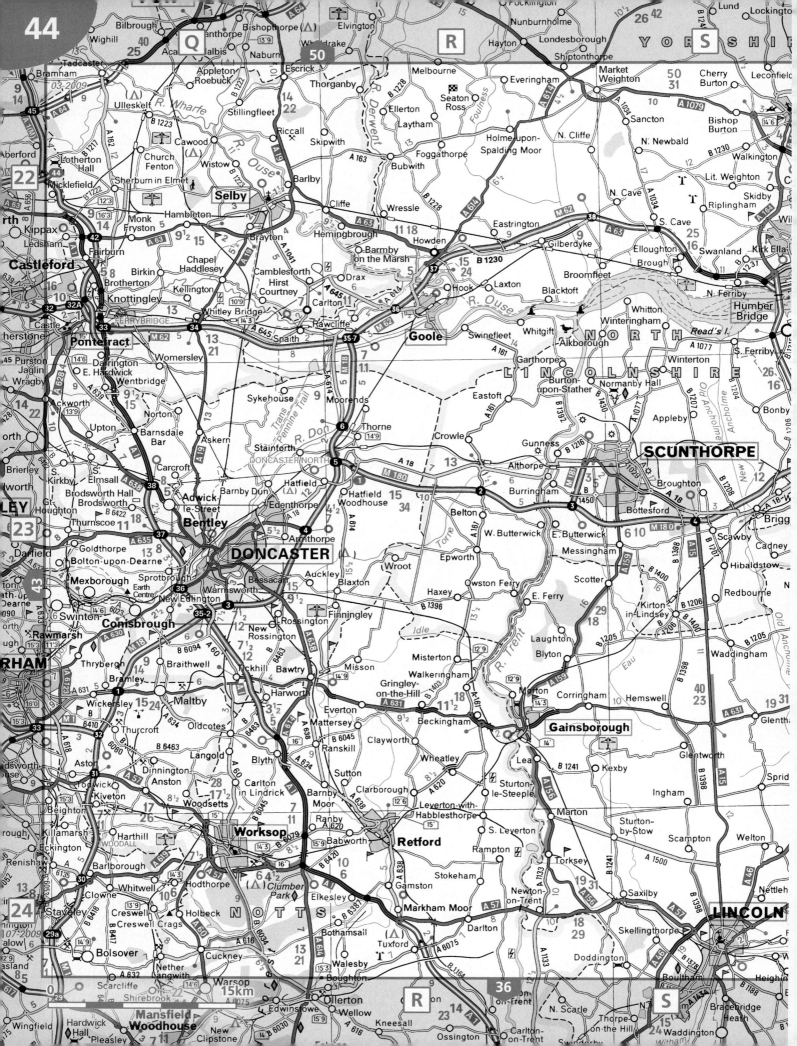

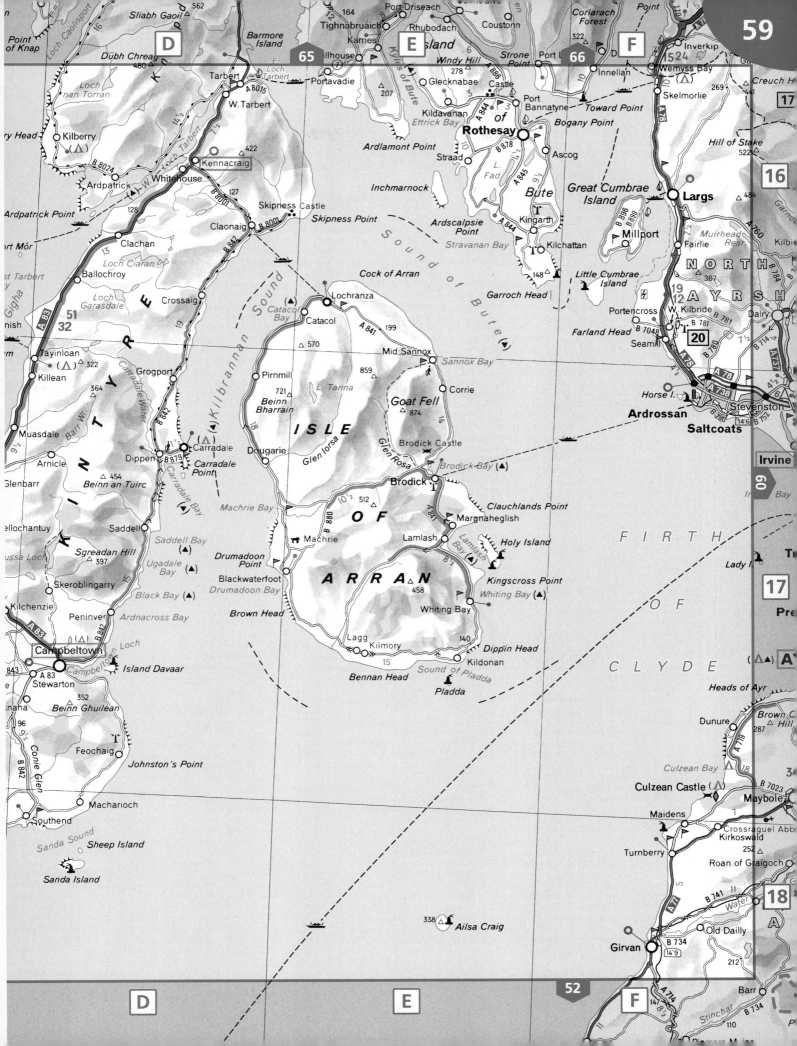

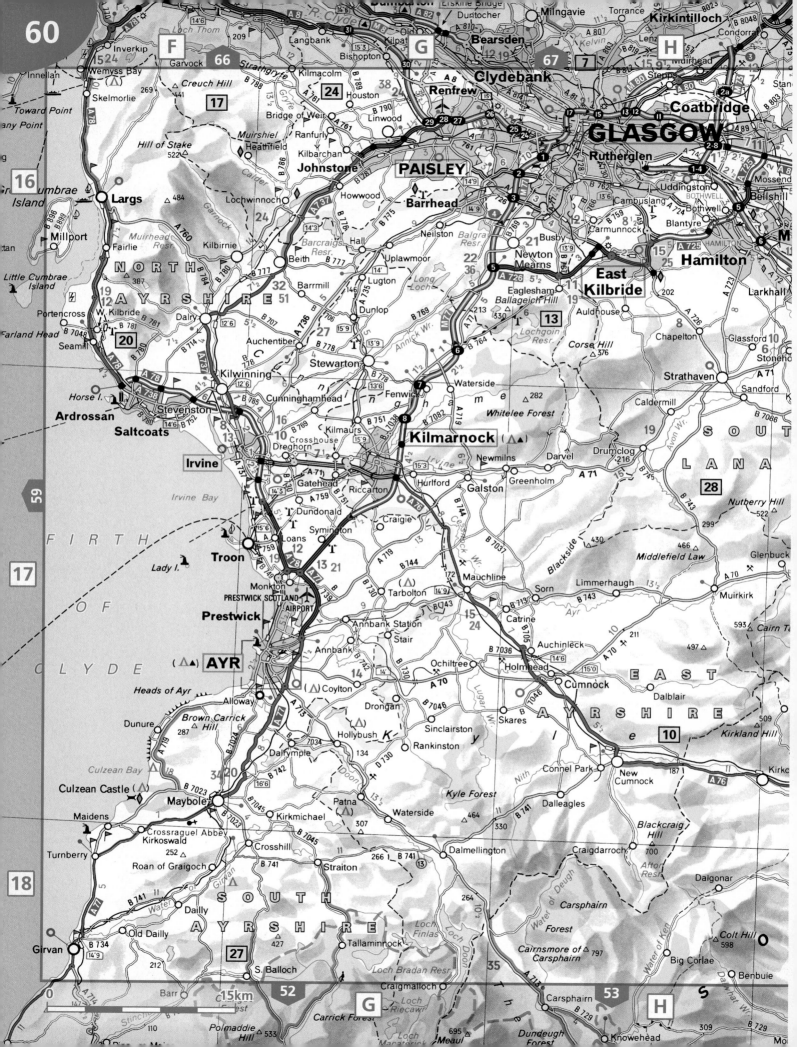

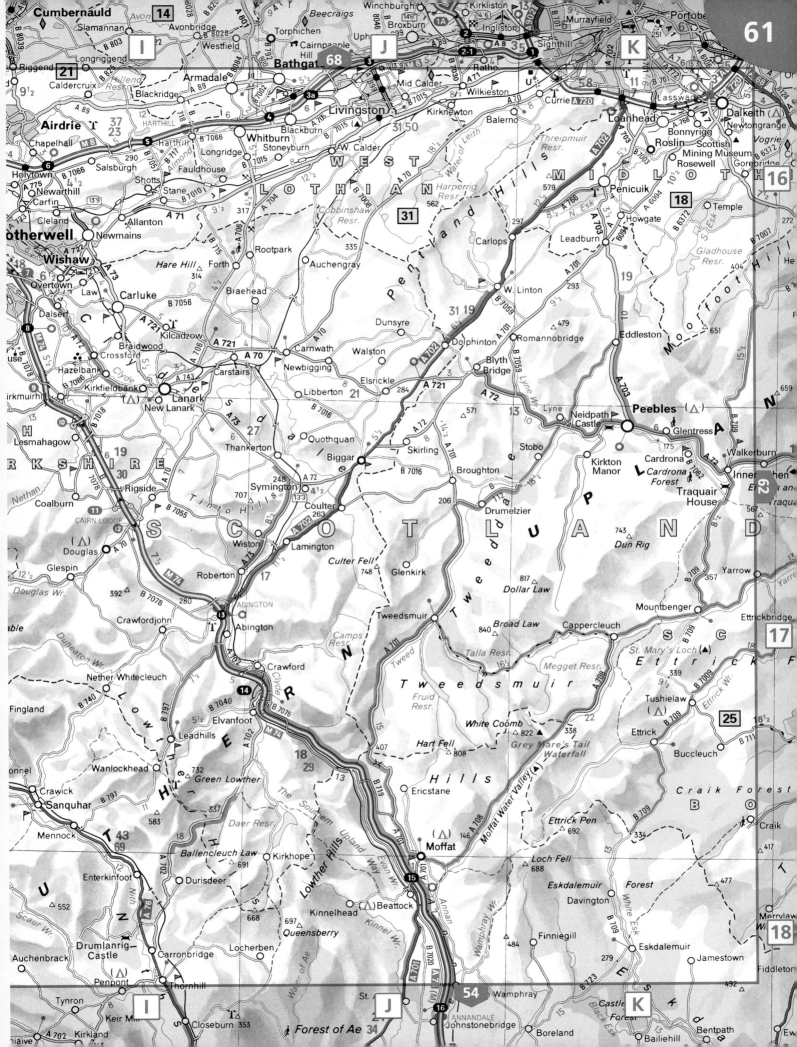

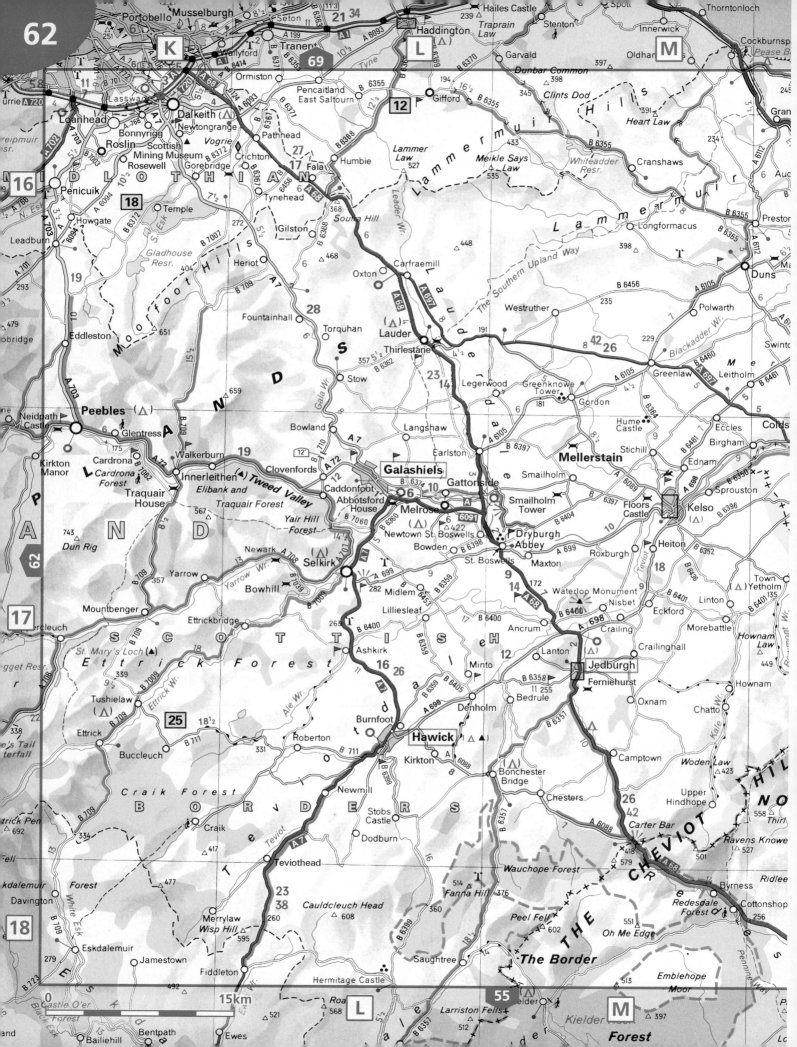

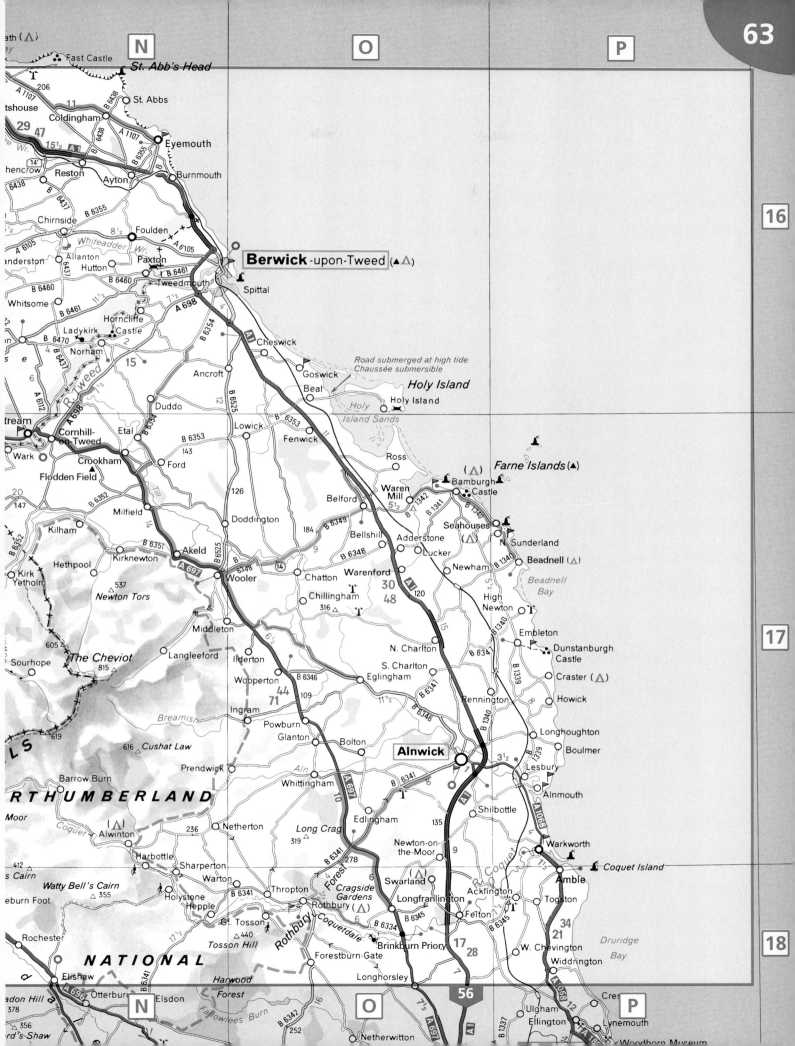

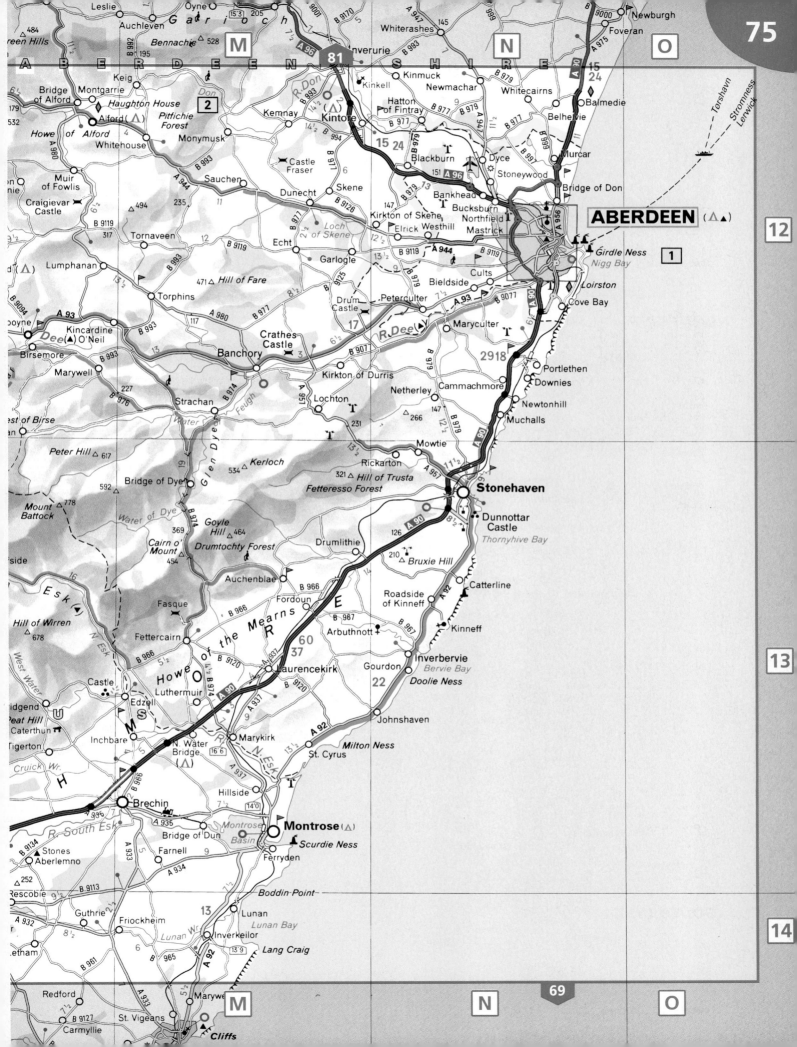

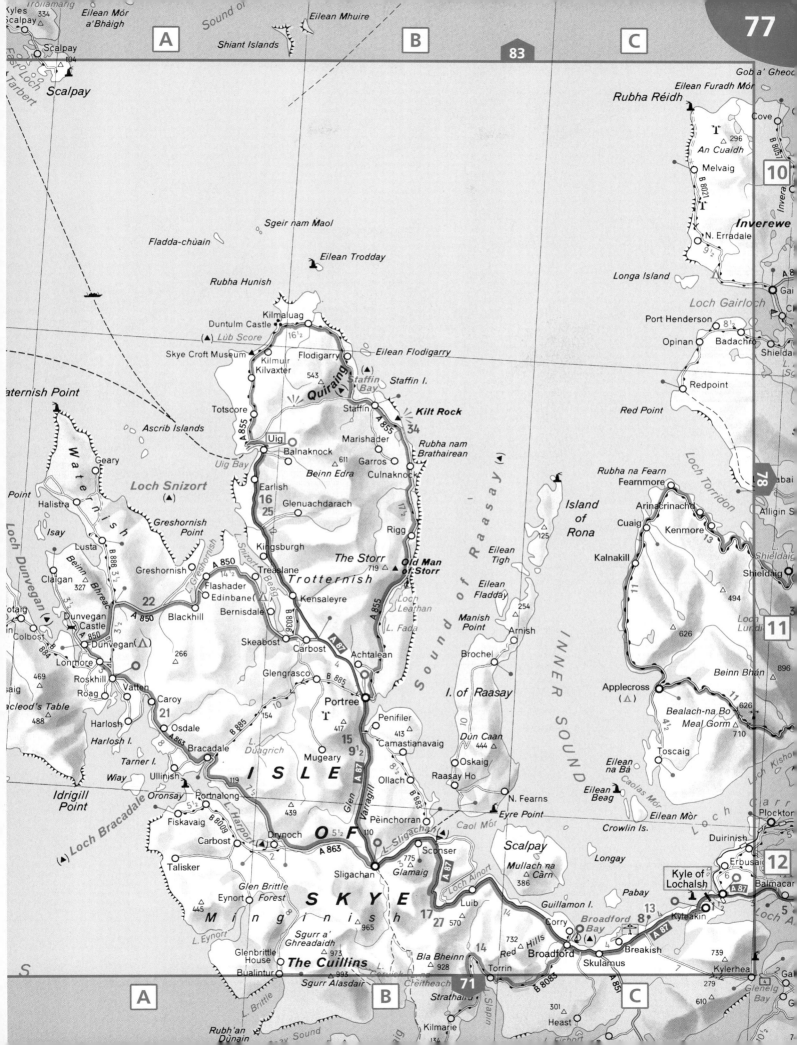

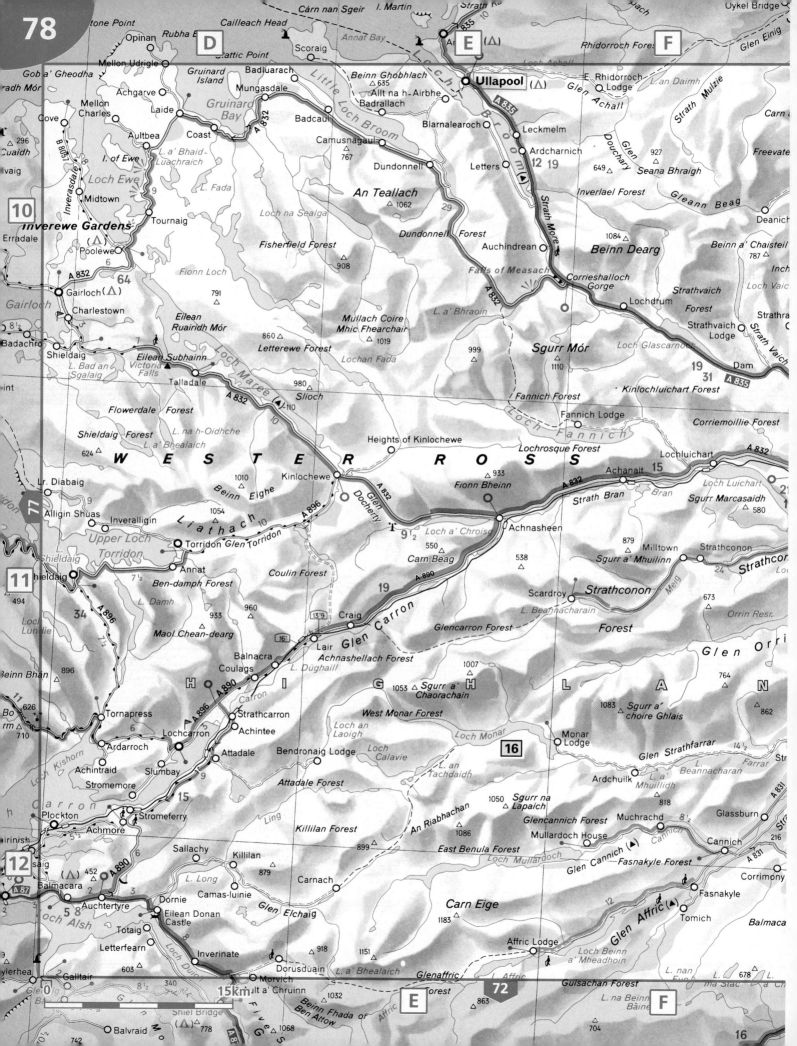

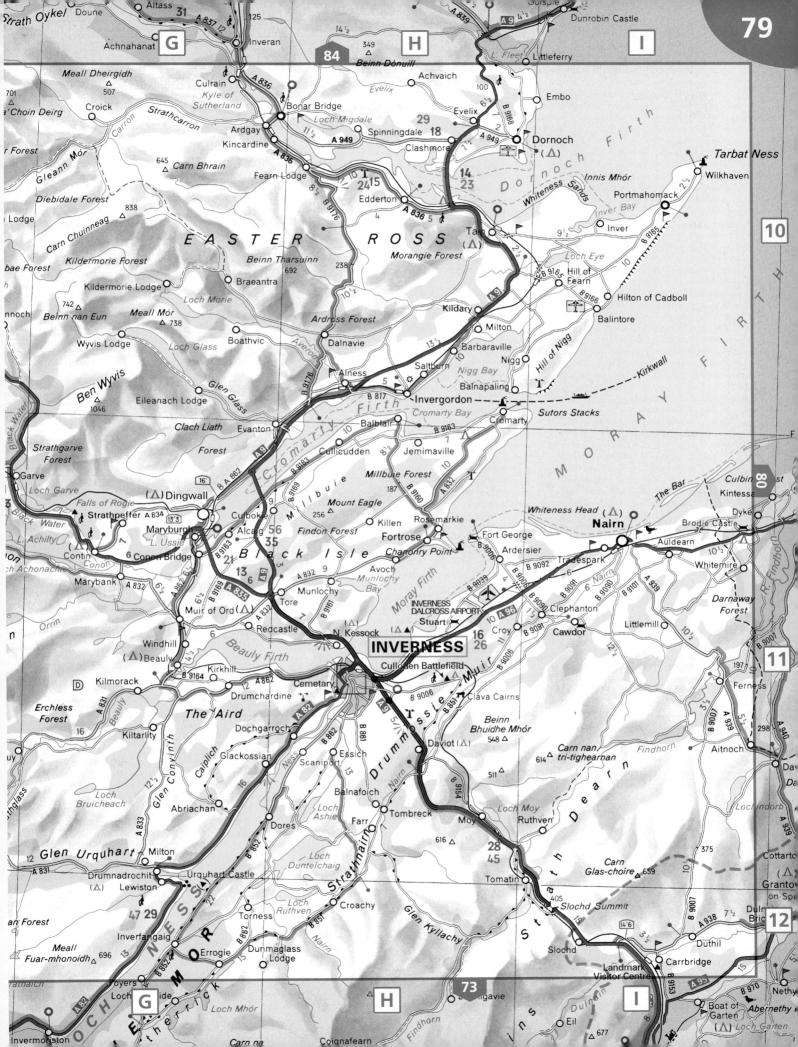

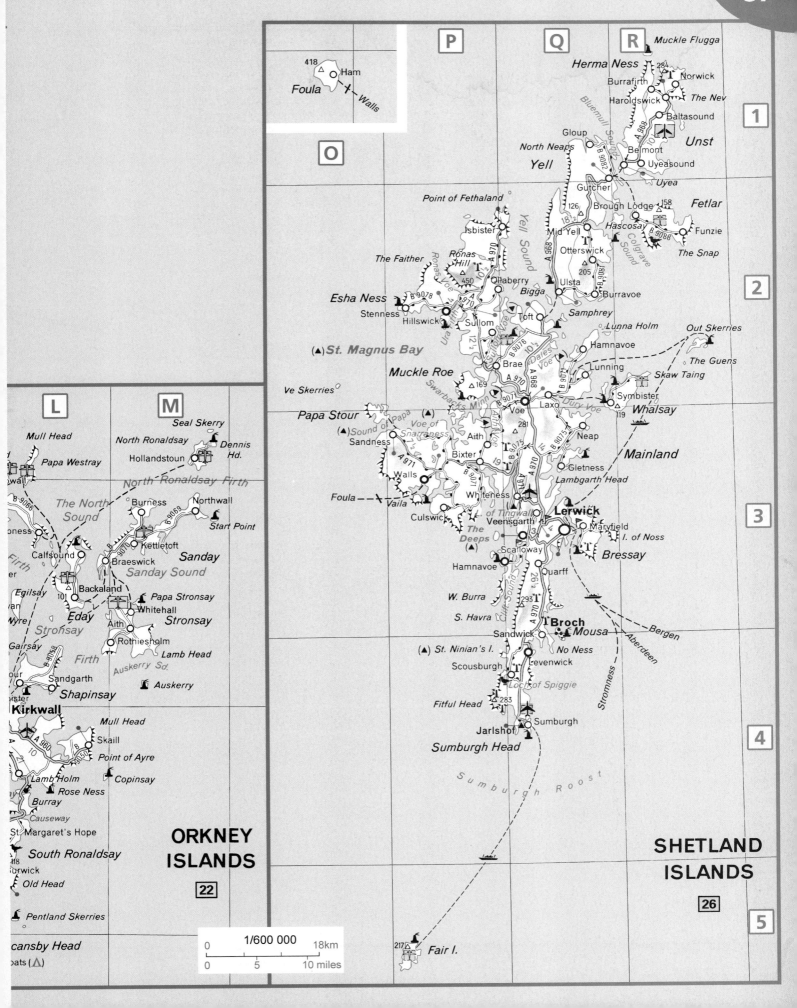

Foula inset (O / P)

Foula
418
△ Ham
Walls

Shetland Islands

Muckle Flugga
Herma Ness
Burrafirth
Haroldswick — 284 — Norwick — The Nev
Baltasound
Bluemull Sound
A 968
Unst
Gloup
North Neaps
Belmont
B 9082
Uyeasound
Uyea
Yell
Gutcher
126
Brough Lodge — 158
Point of Fethaland
Isbister
Mid Yell
Hascosay
Fetlar
181½
Funzie
The Faither
Ronas Hill
A 970
B 9088
The Snap
450 — 102½
Ollaberry
205
Ulsta
180½
Esha Ness
B 9078
Bigga
A 970
Samphrey
Burravoe
Stenness
A
12½
Sullom
Toft
Lunna Holm
Hamnavoe
Out Skerries
Hillswick
A 970
Sullom Voe
The Guens
(▲)St. Magnus Bay
Muckle Roe
Brae
Dales Voe
Lunning
Skaw Taing
101¾
A 968
B 9071
Ve Skerries
Swarbacks Minn
A 970
Symbister
Whalsay
Papa Stour
169
B 9071
B 9074
119
(▲)Sound of Papa
Laxo
Dury Voe
Voe of Snarraness
(▲)
Voe
281
Mainland
Sandness
Aith
Neap
B 9075
A 971
Bixter
14
B 9075
Gletness
Walls
19
B 9071
A 970
Lambgarth Head
Whiteness
Foula —
Vaila
Culswick
of Tingwall
Lerwick
3½
Veensgarth
Maryfield
I. of Noss
The Deeps
Scalloway
Bressay
(▲)
Hamnavoe
Quarff
W. Burra
26½
293
Cliff Sounds
S. Havra
Broch
Mousa
Sandwick
No Ness
Bergen
(▲) St. Ninian's I.
Levenwick
Aberdeen
Scousburgh
Loch of Spiggie
Stromness
Fitful Head
283
Jarlshof
Sumburgh
Sumburgh Head
Sumburgh Roost

SHETLAND ISLANDS

26

Orkney Islands

Mull Head
Seal Skerry
North Ronaldsay
Dennis Hd.
Papa Westray
Hollandstoun
North Ronaldsay Firth
B 9066
The North Sound
Burness
Northwall
B 9069
Start Point
Kettletoft
Sanday
Calfsound
Braeswick
Sanday Sound
Egilsay
Backaland
Papa Stronsay
101
Whitehall
Stronsay
Eday
Aith
Gairsay
Rothiesholm
Lamb Head
Firth
Stronsay
Auskerry Sd.
B 9058
Auskerry
Sandgarth
Shapinsay
Kirkwall
Mull Head
A 960
Skaill
B
10
Point of Ayre
Lamb Holm
Copinsay
Rose Ness
Burray
Causeway
St. Margaret's Hope
South Ronaldsay
Old Head
Pentland Skerries
cansby Head
oats (△)

ORKNEY ISLANDS

22

1/600 000
0 — 18km
0 — 5 — 10 miles

217
Fair I.

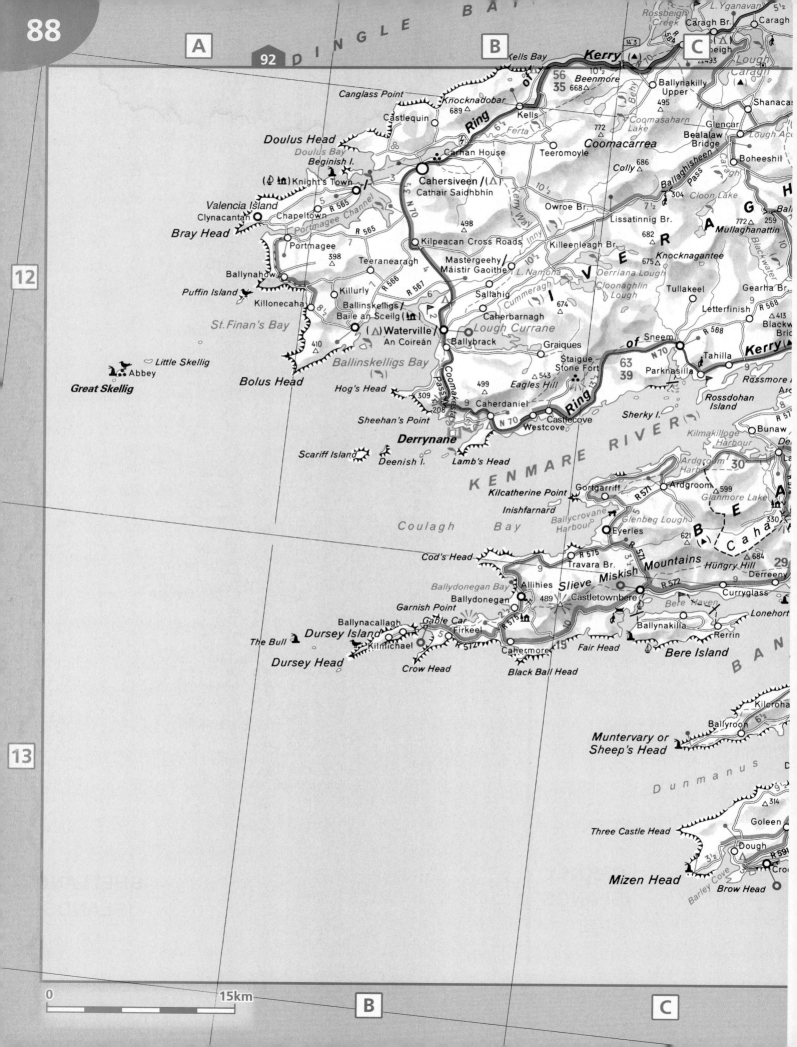

DINGLE BAY

Rossbeigh Creek
L. Yganavan
Caragh Br.
Caragh
Kells Bay
Kerry
Ballynakilly Upper
Shanaca
Lough Caragh

A
92
B
C

Canglass Point
Knocknadobar 689
Beenmore 668
Coomasaharn Lake
Glencar
Lough Ac

Castlequin
Kells
Coomacarrea
Bealalaw Bridge
Boheeshil

Doulus Head
Doulus Bay
Beginish I.
Carhan House
Teeromoyle
Colly 686
Ballaghisheen Pass
772

Knight's Town
Cahersiveen / Cathair Saidhbhín
304 Cloon Lake

Valencia Island
Clynacantan
Chapeltown
Portmagee Channel
Owroe Br.
Lissatinnig Br.
V E R A G
Mullaghanattin 772 259

Bray Head
R 565
498
Killeenleagh Br.
682
Knocknagantee
Blackw
Bri

Portmagee
R 565
Kilpeacan Cross Roads
N 70
675

Teeranearagh 398
R 566
Mastergeehy Máistir Gaoithe
L. Namona
Derriana Lough
Tullakeel
Gearha Br.

Ballynahow
Killurly
R 567
Sallahig
Cummeragh
Cloonaghlin Lough
Letterfinish
R 568

Puffin Island
Killonecaha
Ballinskelligs / Baile an Sceilg
Caherbarnagh
674
413
Blackw

St. Finan's Bay
Waterville / An Coireán
Ballybrack
Lough Currane
Sneem
Kerry
R 568

Little Skellig
410
Graiques
Staigue Stone Fort
63 39
Tahilla
Parknasilla

Abbey
Great Skellig
Bolus Head
Hog's Head
499
Eagles Hill 543
Ring
Rossmore
Ar

Sheehan's Point
309 208
9 Caherdaniel
Sherky I.
Rossdohan Island

Derrynane
N 70
Castlecove Westcove
Kilmakilloge Harbour
Bunaw
De

Scariff Island
Deenish I.
Lamb's Head
KENMARE RIVER
Ardgroom Harb
30

Kilcatherine Point
Gortgarriff
R 571
Ardgroom
599
Glanmore Lake
330

Inishfarnard
Ballycrovane Harbour
Glenbeg Lough
Eyeries
621
B
Caha

Coulagh Bay
Cod's Head
Travara Br.
Miskish Mountains
Hungry Hill 684
Derreeny 29

Ballydonegan Bay
Allihies
Slieve
R 572
Curryglass

The Bull
Dursey Island
Ballynacallagh
Garnish Point
Ballydonegan 489
Castletownbere
Bere Haven
Ballynakilla
Lonehort

Kilmichael
Gable Car
Firkeel
R 575
Rerrin

Dursey Head
Crow Head
R 572
Cahermore
Black Ball Head
Fair Head
Bere Island
B

Kilcroha
Ballyroon

Muntervary or Sheep's Head

DUNMANUS

Three Castle Head
Goleen

Dough
R 591

Mizen Head
Barley Cove
Brow Head
314
Croo

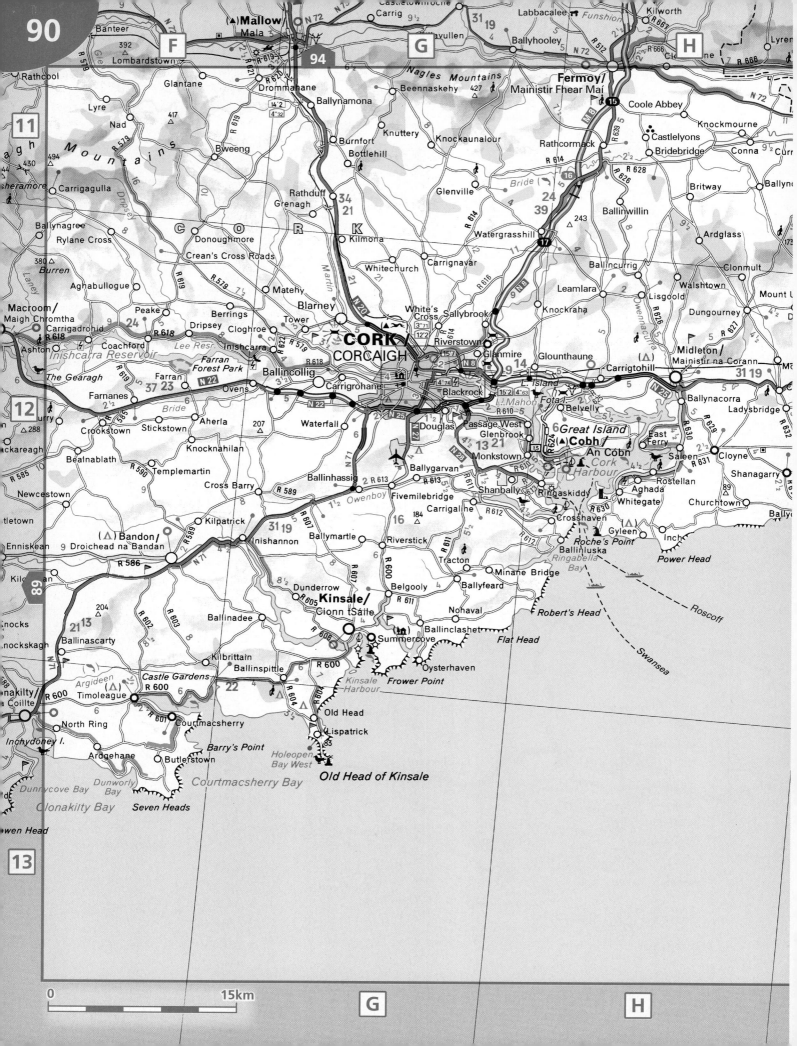

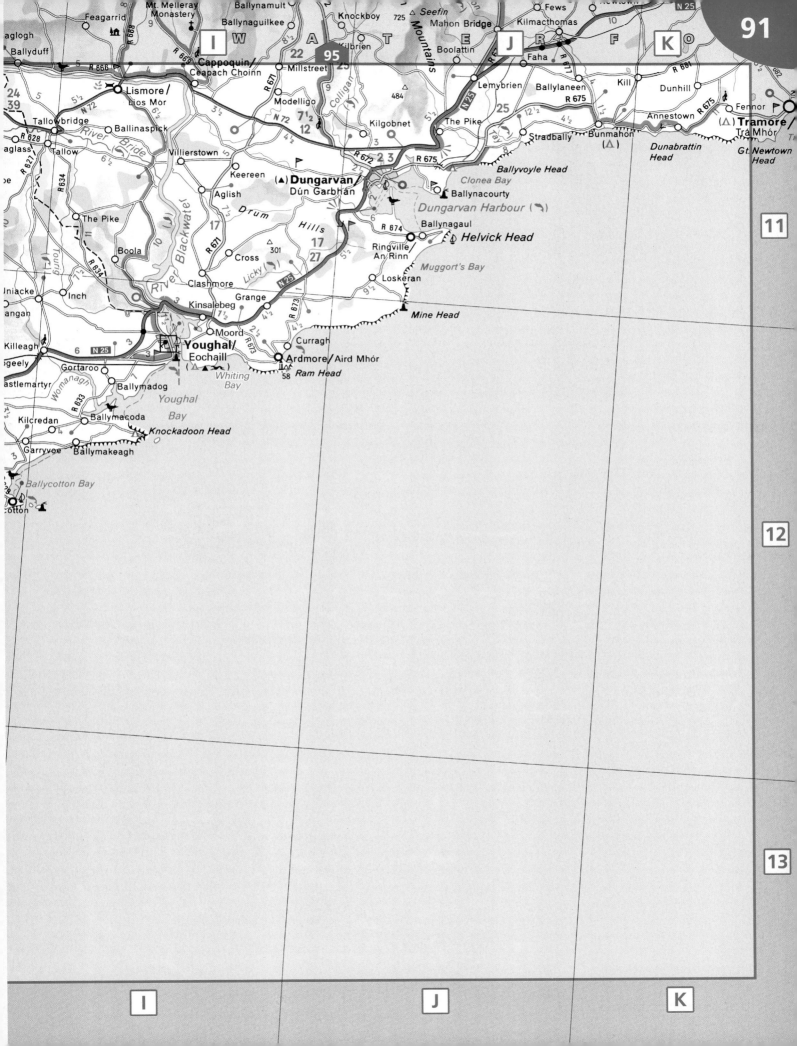

Feagarrid
Ballyduff
aglogh
R 688
Mt. Melleray Monastery
Ballynaguilkee
Ballynamult
Knockboy 725
△ Seefin
Mahon Bridge
Fews
Kilmacthomas
Newtown
N 25

R 666
Cappoquin/
Ceapach Choinn
Millstreet
Kilbrien
Mountains
Boolattin
Faha
R 671
10

I **W** **A** **T** **E** **J** **R** **F** **K** **O**

22
95
25
Modelligo
9
484
Lemybrien
Ballylaneen
Kill
Dunhill
N 25

Lismore/
Lios Mór
N 72
5½
7½
12
Kilgobnet
R 675
R 675

Tallowbridge
Ballinaspick
River Bride
6½
4½
Kilgobnet
3
The Pike
25
12½
4½
Annestown
R 675
Fennor
Tramore/
Trá Mhór

Tallow
R 828
R 627
aglass
Villierstown
N 72
Keereen
R 672
2 3
R 675
Stradbally
Bunmahon
(△)
Dunabrattin
Head
Gt. Newtown
Head

The Pike
R 634
Aglish
(△) **Dungarvan**
Dún Garbhán
Ballyvoyle Head

Boola
17
Drum
Ballynacourty
Clonea Bay

Inch
R 671
301
Cross
Licky
17
27
R 674
Dungarvan Harbour
Ballynagaul
Helvick Head

Uniacke
angan
Clashmore
Grange
N 25
1
Ringville
An Rinn
Muggort's Bay

Killeagh
N 25
6
Kinsalebeg
R 673
4½
Loskeran
9½

Gortaroo
Moord
2½
Curragh
Mine Head

astlemartyr
R 633
Youghal/
Eochaill
Ardmore/Aird Mhór
Ram Head
58

Ballymadog
Whiting Bay

Kilcredan
Ballymacoda
Youghal Bay

Garryvoe
Ballymakeagh
Knockadoon Head

Ballycotton Bay

cotton

11

12

13

I **J** **K**

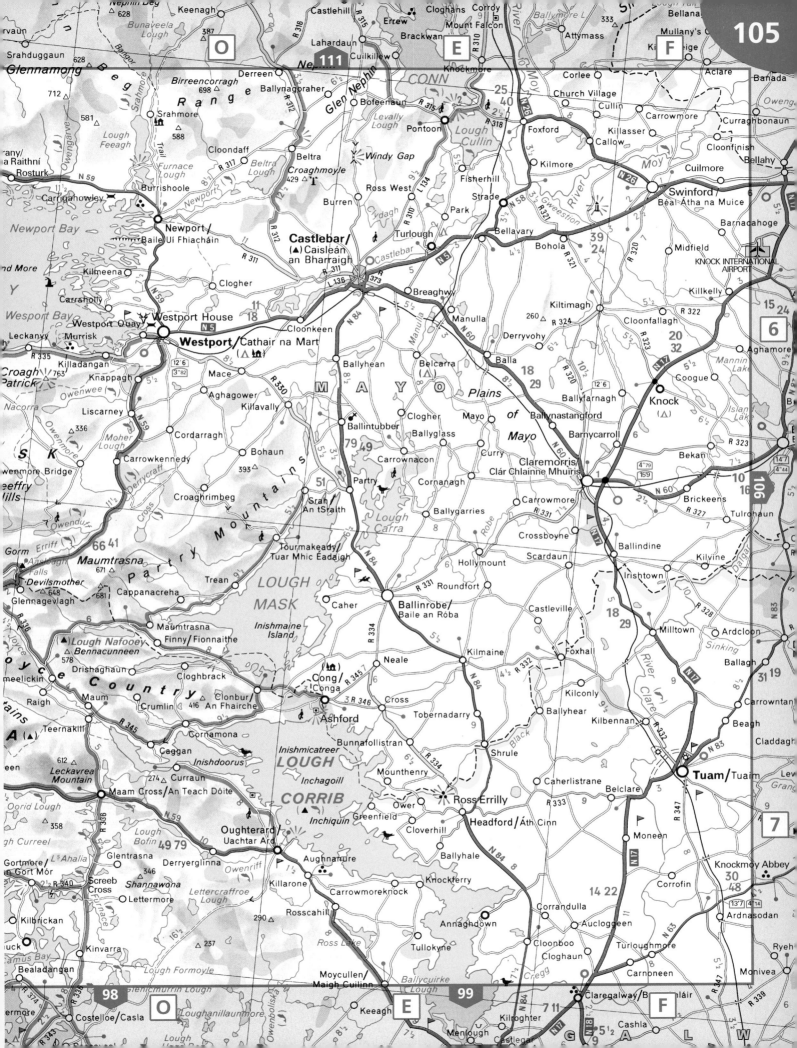

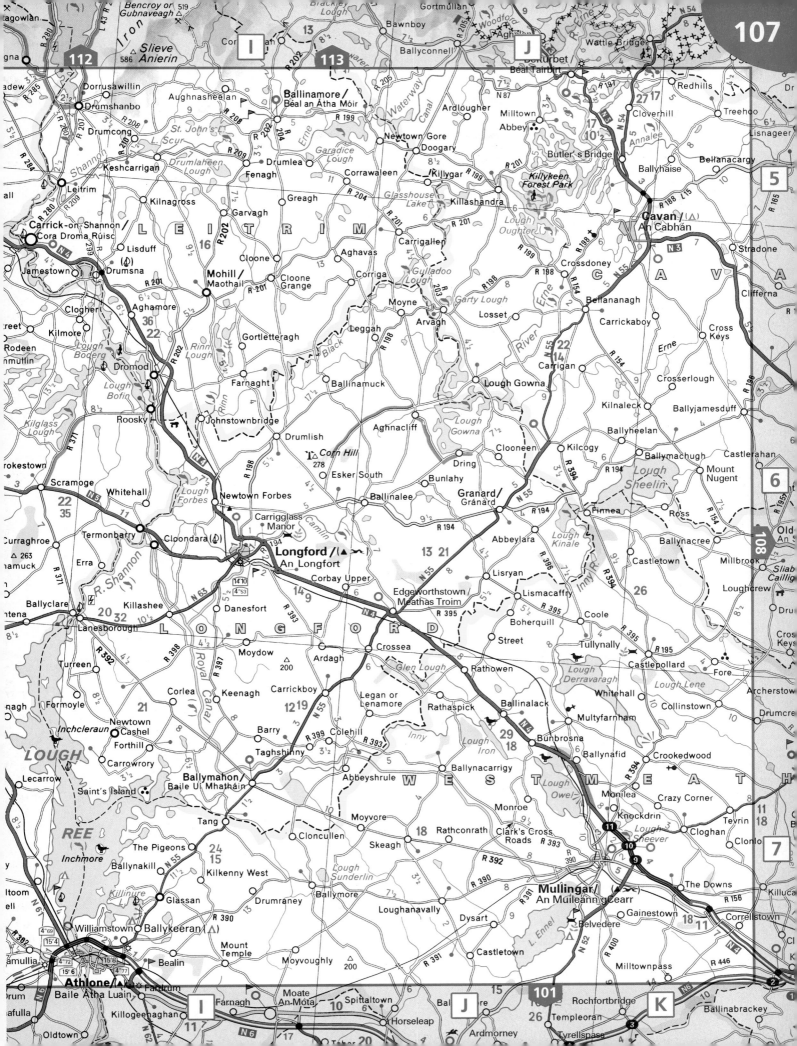

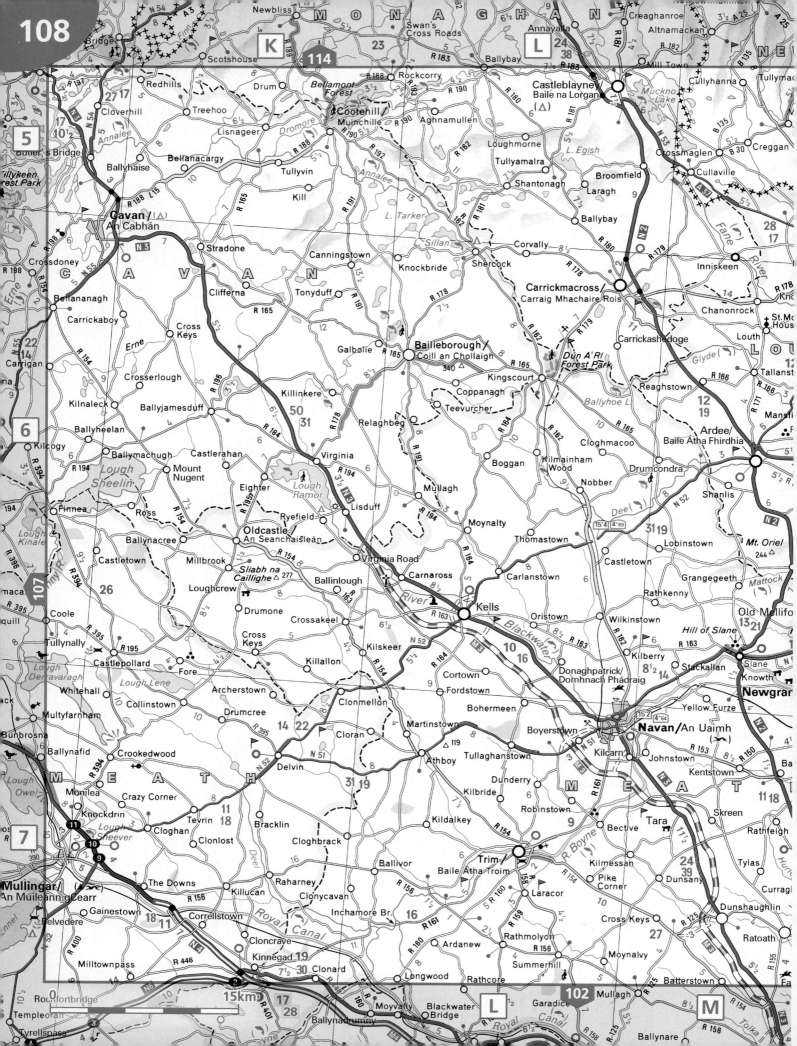

M Bernish Rock
Lislea
Camlough 2
Mayobridge 4
Hilltown
B 27
B 180
Tollymore Forest Park
Newcastle (▲ ᵐ △)
114
Newry
N M O U R N E
Spelga Dam (▲)
Slieve Donard
M
708
Killeen
Churches
Cloghoge
B 25
Ulster Way
350
115
Slieve Gullion
Killevy
Narrow Water Castle
626
B 27
Dunmore
Glasdrumman
573
Donaghaguy
Shannagh
Silent Valley
Mullartown
Warrenpoint
Rostrevor
A 2
Attical
40
Annalong
Drumintee
Omeath
Killowen
25
Jonesborough
1912
509
Lisnacree
Ballymartin
Forkill
B 113
Windy Gap
R 173
Ballygowan
A 2
Kilkeel
Ravensdale
Carlingford Mt.
Castle
Kilcurry
Proleek Dolmen
587
Greencastle
5
Dowdallshill
R 175
Carlingford
Greenore
Cranfield Point
R 173
Grange
Ballagan Point
DUNDALK/
DÚN DEALGAN (▲ ✈)
11
The Bush
Whites Town
Giles Quay (△)
Rathcor
Cooley Point
Blackrock
18 11
Dundalk
16
Dromiskin
Bay
R 132
15
R 166
Castlebellingham
Kilsaran
Annagassan
R 132
R 166
Dunany Point
14 N 33
Drumcar
Dunany
11
Dromin
Togher
Port
13
Dunleer
R 170
Grangebellew
12 R 169
R 132
Clogher Head
Monasterboice
Clogherhead
11
Ballymakenny
R 188
Collon
R 168
Termonfeckin
13 8
DROGHEDA DROICHEAD ÁTHA (▲)
Tullyallen
Baltray
10
R 167
R 151
Dowth
Mornington
Boyne
R 150
Donacarney
9
Donore
8
Bettystown (△)
Julianstown
Laytown
R 150
Nanny
9
R 150
R 132
Mosney (△)
Duleek
14
Gormanston
Bellewstown
Stamullin
7 N 1
7
Greenanstown
Balscaddan
R 152
11
Balbriggan/Baile Brigín
Ardcath
Fourknocks
R 122
Clonalvy
6
Rockabill
Garristown
Naul
17
R 130
178
32
Balrothery
Skerries/Na Sceirí
5
20
R 127
R 126
Damastown
Loughshinny
R 108
R 122
Oldtown
Ballyboghil
Lusk
Ashbourne
R 130
Corduff
R 128
Rush/An Ros (△)
R 125
Donaghmore
R 129
Portrane
Kilsallaghan
F I N G A L
R 126
Donabate
Lambay Island
103
Swords
N
Malahide/Mullach Íde
Kilbride
St. Margaret's
R 106
M
S E A

6

7

Alpheton 30 W27
Alphington 4 J31
Alpraham 34 M24
Alresford 30 X28
Alrewas 35 O25
Alsager 35 N24
Alsh (Loch) 78 D12
Alston 55 M19
Alstonefield 35 O24
Alswear 7 I31
Altadnduin 85 H9
Altandhu 83 D9
Altarnun 3 G32
Altass 84 G10
Alternative Technology Centre 33 I26
Altham 42 M22
Althorne 22 W29
Althorpe 44 R23
Altnabreac Station 85 I8
Altnacealgach 84 F9
Altnaharra 84 G9
Alton (Hants.) 10 R30
Alton (Staffs.) 35 O25
Alton Pancras 9 M31
Alton Priors 19 O29
Alton Towers 35 O25
Altrincham 42 M23
Alum Bay 10 P31
Alva 67 I15
Alvaston 36 P25
Alvechurch 27 O26
Alvediston 9 N30
Alves 80 J11
Alvescot 19 P28
Alvie 73 I12
Alvingham 45 U23
Alwinton 63 N17
Alyth 74 K14
Amberley 11 S31
Amble 63 P18
Amblecote 27 N26
Ambleside 48 L20
Ambrosden 28 Q28
Amersham 21 S29
Amesbury 9 O30
Amhuinnsuidhe 82 Y10
Amisfield 53 J18
Amlwch 40 G22
Ammanford / Rhydaman 15 I28
Amotherby 50 R21
Ampleforth 50 Q21
Amport 20 P30
Ampthill 29 S27
Amroth 15 G28
Amulree 67 I14
An Riabhachan 78 E11
An Socach 74 J13
An Teallach 78 E10
Anchor 26 K26
Ancroft 63 O16
Ancrum 62 M17
Andover 20 P30
Andoversford 27 O28

Andreas 46 G20
Angle 14 E28
Anglesey (Isle of) 40
Anglesey Abbey 30 U27
Angmering 11 S31
Annan 54 K19
Annan (River) 61 J18
Annat 78 D11
Annat Bay 83 E10
Annbank 60 G17
Annbank Station 60 G17
Anne Hathaway's Cottage 27 O27
Annesley-Woodhouse 36 Q24
Annfield Plain 56 O19
Ansley 28 P26
Anstey 36 Q25
Anston 44 Q23
Anstruther 69 L15
Anthorn 54 K19
Antony House 3 H32
Appin 72 E14
Appleby (Eden) 55 M20
Appleby (North Lincolnshire) 44 S23
Appleby Magna 36 P25
Applecross 77 C11
Appledore (Devon) 6 H30
Appledore (Kent) 12 W30
Appleford 20 Q29
Appleton 20 P28
Appleton Roebuck 44 Q22
Appleton Wiske 50 P20
Appletreewick 49 O21
Aran Fawddwy 33 I25
Arberth / Narberth 15 F28
Arbigland 53 J19
Arbirlot 69 M14
Arbor Low 35 O24
Arborfield 20 R29
Arbroath 69 M14
Arbury Hall 28 P26
Arbuthnott 75 N13
Archiestown 80 K11
Ard (Loch) 67 G15
Ardanaiseig 66 E14
Ardarroch 78 D11
Ardcharnich 78 E10
Ardchiavaig 64 B15
Ardchuilk 78 F11
Ardchyle 67 G14
Ardechive 72 E13
Arden 66 G15
Ardentallan 65 D14
Ardeonaig 67 H14
Ardersier 79 H11
Ardery 72 C13
Ardfern 65 D15
Ardgartan 66 F15
Ardgay 79 G10
Ardgour 72 D13
Ardhasaig 82 Z10
Ardingly 11 T30
Ardington 20 P29
Ardivachar 76 X11

Ardleigh 30 W28
Ardley 28 Q28
Ardlui 66 F15
Ardlussa 65 C15
Ardmair 84 E10
Ardminish 58 C16
Ardmore Point (Isle of Skye) 77 A11
Ardnacross 71 C14
Ardnamurchan 71 B13
Ardnastang 72 D13
Ardnave 64 A16
Ardnave Point 64 B16
Ardpatrick 59 D16
Ardrishaig 65 D15
Ardrossan 59 F17
Ardshealach 71 C13
Ardslignish 71 C13
Ardtalla 58 B16
Ardtalnaig 67 H14
Ardtoe 71 C13
Ardvasar 71 C12
Ardverikie Forest 73 G13
Ardvorlich 67 H14
Ardwell 52 F19
Argyll 65 D15
Argyll Forest Park 66 F15
Arichastlich 66 F14
Arienas (Loch) 71 C14
Arileod 71 A14
Arinacrinachd 77 C11
Arinagour 71 A14
Arisaig 71 C13
Arivruaich 82 Z9
Arkaig (Loch) 72 E13
Arkendale 50 P21
Arkengarthdale 49 O20
Arkholme 48 M21
Arklet (Loch) 66 G15
Arley 27 P26
Arlingham 19 M28
Arlington Court 7 I30
Armadale (Highland) 85 H8
Armadale (West Lothian) 61 I16
Armadale Bay 71 C12
Armitage 35 O25
Armthorpe 44 Q23
Arnabost 71 A14
Arncliffe 49 N21
Arncott 20 Q28
Arncroach 69 L15
Arne 9 N31
Arnesby 28 Q26
Arnicle 59 D17
Arnisdale 72 D12
Arnish 77 B11
Arnol 82 A8
Arnold 36 Q25
Arnprior 67 H15
Arnside 48 L21
Aros 65 B14
Arram 45 S22
Arran (Isle of) 59 E17
Arreton 10 Q31

Arrochar 66 F15
Arscaig 84 G9
Arundel 11 S31
Ascog 59 E16
Ascot 21 R29
Ascott House 29 R28
Ascott-under-Wychwood 28 P28
Ascrib Islands 77 A11
Asfordby 36 R25
Ash (Kent) 23 X30
Ash (Surrey) 20 R30
Ash Mill 7 I31
Ashbourne 35 O24
Ashburton 4 I32
Ashbury 19 P29
Ashby de la Zouch 36 P25
Ashby Magna 28 Q26
Ashcott 8 L30
Ashdon 30 U27
Ashford (Kent) 12 W30
Ashford (Surrey) 21 S29
Ashford-in-the-Water (Derbs.) 43 O24
Ashie (Loch) 79 H11
Ashill (Breckland) 38 W26
Ashill (South Somerset) 8 L31
Ashingdon 22 W29
Ashington (Northumb.) 56 P18
Ashington (West Sussex) 11 S31
Ashkirk 62 L17
Ashleworth 27 N28
Ashley (East Cambridgeshire) 30 V27
Ashley (Newcastle-under-Lyme) 35 M25
Ashley (Torridge) 7 I31
Ashley Green 21 S28
Ashmore 9 N31
Ashover 36 P24
Ashperton 26 M27
Ashreigney 7 I31
Ashtead 21 T30
Ashton 34 L24
Ashton-in-Makerfield 42 M23
Ashton Keynes 19 O29
Ashton-under-Lyne 43 N23
Ashton-upon-Mersey 42 M23
Ashurst 10 P31
Ashwell (North Hertfordshire) 29 T27
Ashwell (Rutland) 36 R25
Ashwellthorpe 39 X26
Askam in Furness 47 K21
Askern 44 Q23
Askernish 76 X12
Askerswell 5 L31
Askham 55 L20
Askrigg 49 N21
Askwith 49 O22
Aslacton 31 X26
Aslockton 36 R25
Aspatria 54 K19
Aspley Guise 29 S27
Assynt (Loch) 84 E9
Astley 34 L25
Aston (Vale Royal) 44 Q23

Aston (West Oxfordshire) 20 P28
Aston Clinton 20 R28
Aston Magna 27 O27
Aston Rowant 20 R28
Aston Tirrold 20 Q29
Astwood Bank 27 O27
Atcham 34 L25
Athelhampton Hall 9 N31
Athelney 8 L30
Athelstaneford 69 L16
Atherington 7 H31
Athersley 43 P23
Atherstone 36 P26
Atherton 42 M23
Atholl (Forest of) 73 H13
Attadale 78 D11
Attleborough (Breckland) 38 X26
Attleborough (Nuneaton and Bedworth) 28 P26
Attlebridge 39 X25
Atwick 51 T22
Atworth 19 N29
Aucharnie 81 M11
Auchavan 74 K13
Auchenblae 75 M13
Auchenbowie 67 I15
Auchenbrack 61 I18
Auchenbreck 65 E16
Auchencairn 53 I19
Auchencrosh 52 F18
Auchencrow 63 N16
Auchengray 61 J16
Auchenmalg 52 F19
Auchentiber 60 G16
Auchindrean 78 E10
Auchinleck 60 H17
Auchleven 81 M12
Auchlyne 67 G14
Auchnafree 67 I14
Auchnagallin 80 J11
Auchnagatt 81 N11
Aucholzie 74 K12
Auchronie 74 L13
Auchterarder 67 I15
Auchteraw 73 F12
Auchterderran 68 K15
Auchterhouse 68 K14
Auchtermuchty 68 K15
Auchtertyre 78 D12
Auckengill 86 K8
Auckley 44 Q23
Audenshaw 43 N23
Audlem 34 M25
Audley 35 N24
Audley End 30 U27
Aughton (near Lancaster) 48 L21
Aughton (near Ormskirk) 42 L23
Auldearn 79 I11
Auldgirth 53 I18
Auldhouse 60 H16
Ault a' Chruinn 72 D12
Aultbea 78 D10
Aust 18 M29
Austrey 35 P26

Austwick 49 M21
Avebury 19 O29
Aveley 22 U29
Avening 19 N28
Aveton Gifford 4 I33
Aviemore 73 I12
Avoch 79 H11
Avon (Glen) 74 J12
Avon (River) (R. Severn) 28 Q26
Avon (River) (Wilts.) 9 O31
Avonbridge 67 I16
Avonmouth 18 L29
Avonwick 4 I32
Awe (Loch) 65 E15
Awliscombe 8 K31
Awre 19 M28
Axbridge 18 L30
Axminster 8 L31
Axmouth 5 K31
Aylburton 18 M28
Aylesbury 20 R28
Aylesford 22 V30
Aylesham 23 X30
Aylsham 39 X25
Aylton 26 M27
Aymestrey 26 L27
Aynho 28 Q28
Ayr 60 G17
Aysgarth 49 O21
Ayside 48 L21
Ayton (Scarborough) 51 S21
Ayton (Scottish Borders) 63 N16

B

Bà (Loch) 65 C14
Babbacombe Bay 4 J32
Babcary 8 M30
Babell 41 K23
Babworth 44 R24
Back 83 B9
Backaland 87 L6
Backmuir of New Gilston 69 L15
Backwater Reservoir 74 K13
Backwell West Town 18 L29
Baconsthorpe 39 X25
Bacton (Mid Suffolk) 30 X27
Bacton (North Norfolk) 39 Y25
Bacup 43 N22
Bad a' Ghaill (Loch) 84 E9
Bad an Sgalaig (Loch) 78 D10
Badachro 77 C10
Badanloch (Loch) 85 H9
Badanloch Lodge 85 H9
Badcaul 78 D10
Baddesley Ensor 35 P26
Baddidarach 84 E9
Badenoch 73 H13
Badenscallie 83 E9
Badenyon 74 K12
Badlipster 86 K8
Badluarach 78 D10
Badminton 19 N29

Badrallach 78 E10
Bae Colwyn / Colwyn Bay 41 I23
Bagh nam Faoileann 76 Y11
Bagillt 41 K23
Bagley 34 L25
Bagshot 21 R29
Bagworth 36 P25
Bagwyllydiart 26 L28
Baile Mór 64 A15
Bailiehill 54 K18
Bainbridge 49 N21
Bainton 51 S22
Bakewell 35 O24
Bala 33 J25
Balallan 82 A9
Balbeggie 68 J14
Balblair 79 H10
Balcary Point 53 I19
Balchrick 84 E8
Balcombe 11 T30
Balderton 36 R24
Baldock 29 T28
Baldrine 46 G21
Baldwin 46 G21
Balemartine 64 Z14
Balephetrish Bay 70 Z14
Balephuil 64 Z14
Balephuil Bay 64 Z14
Balerno 61 J16
Baleshare 76 X11
Balevulin 65 B14
Balfour 87 L6
Balfron 67 H15
Balgray 69 L14
Balintore (Angus) 74 K13
Balintore (Highland) 79 I10
Balivanich 76 X11
Balk 50 Q21
Ballabeg 46 F21
Ballachulish 72 E13
Ballajora 46 G21
Ballamodha 46 G21
Ballantrae 52 E18
Ballasalla 46 G21
Ballater 74 K12
Ballaugh 46 G21
Ballevullin 70 Z14
Balliemore (near Dunoon) 65 E15
Balliemore (near Oban) 65 D14
Ballig 46 G21
Ballingry 68 K15
Ballinluig 74 J14
Ballochan 75 L12
Ballochroy 59 D16
Ballyhaugh 71 A14
Balmaclellan 53 H18
Balmaha 67 G15
Balmedie 75 N12
Balminnoch 52 F19
Balmoral Castle 74 K12
Balmullo 69 L14
Balnacra 78 D11
Balnafoich 79 H11
Balnaguard 74 I14

Balnahard 64 B14
Balnakeil Bay 84 F8
Balnaknock 77 B11
Balnapaling 79 H10
Baltonsborough 8 M30
Balvicar 65 D15
Balvraid 72 D12
Bamburgh Castle 63 O17
Bamford 43 O23
Bampton (Cumbria) 48 L20
Bampton (Devon) 7 J31
Bampton (Oxon.) 20 P28
Banavie 72 E13
Banbury 28 P27
Banchory 75 M12
Bancyfelin 15 G28
Bandenscoth 81 M11
Banff 81 M10
Bangor 40 H23
Bankend 53 J18
Bankfoot 68 J14
Bankhead 75 N12
Banks 42 L22
Bankshill 54 K18
Banniskirk 85 J8
Bannockburn 67 I15
Banstead 21 T30
Banwell 18 L30
Bapchild 22 W30
Bar Hill 29 U27
Barbaraville 79 H10
Barbon 48 M21
Barcaldine 65 E14
Barcombe Cross 11 U31
Bardney 45 T24
Bardsea 48 K21
Bardsey 43 P22
Bardsey Island 32 F25
Barford 39 X26
Barford-St. Martin 9 O30
Barfreston 23 X30
Bargoed 18 K28
Bargrennan 52 G18
Barham 23 X30
Barking 30 X27
Barking and Dagenham (London Borough) 21 U29
Barkston 37 S25
Barkway 29 U28
Barlaston 35 N25
Barlborough 44 Q24
Barlestone 36 P26
Barley (North Hertfordshire) 29 U27
Barley (Pendle) 42 N22
Barlow 43 P24
Barmby on the Marsh ...44 R22
Barming 22 V30
Barmouth / Abermaw ...33 H25
Barmouth Bay 33 H25
Barmston 51 T21
Barnack 37 S26
Barnard Castle 49 O20
Barnby Dun 44 R22
Barnby Moor (East Riding of Yorks.) 50 R22

Barnby Moor (Notts.) ...44 Q23
Barnet (London Borough) ..21 T29
Barnetby-le-Wold 45 S23
Barney 38 W25
Barnham 30 W26
Barnham Broom 38 X26
Barnhill 80 J11
Barnhills 52 E18
Barningham 49 O20
Barnoldswick 49 N22
Barnsley 43 P23
Barnstaple 7 H30
Barnton 42 M24
Barnwell 29 S26
Barr 52 F18
Barra 70 X13
Barra (Sound of) 70 X12
Barra Head 70 X13
Barregarrow 46 G21
Barrhead 60 G16
Barrhill 52 F18
Barrington 8 L31
Barrisdale 72 D12
Barrisdale Bay 72 D12
Barrmill 60 G16
Barrock 86 K8
Barrow 30 V27
Barrow Burn 63 N17
Barrow Gurney 18 L29
Barrow-in-Furness 47 K21
Barrow-upon-Humber ...45 S22
Barrow-upon-Soar 36 Q25
Barrowby 36 R25
Barrowford 43 N22
Barry (Angus) 69 L14
Barry / Barri (Vale of Glamorgan) 18 K29
Barsham 31 Y26
Barston 27 O26
Bartestree 26 M27
Barton (Eden) 49 P20
Barton (Lancs.) 42 L22
Barton in the Clay 29 S28
Barton le Willows 50 R21
Barton Mills 30 V26
Barton-on-Sea 9 P31
Barton-under-Needwood 35 O25
Barton-upon-Humber ...44 S22
Barvas 82 A8
Barwell 36 P26
Barwick-in-Elmet 43 P22
Baschurch 34 L25
Bashall Eaves 42 M22
Basildon (Berks.) 20 Q29
Basildon (Essex) 22 V29
Basing 20 Q30
Basingstoke 20 Q30
Baslow 43 P24
Bass Rock 69 M15
Bassenthwaite 54 K19
Bassingham 37 S24
Baston 37 S25
Bastwick 39 Y25

Batcombe 8 M31
Bath 19 M29
Bathampton 19 N29
Batheaston 19 N29
Bathgate 61 J16
Batley 43 P22
Battle 12 V31
Baumber 45 T24
Bawburgh 39 X26
Bawdeswell 38 X25
Bawdsey 31 Y27
Bawtry 44 Q23
Bayble 83 B9
Baycliff 48 K21
Baydon 19 P29
Bayhead 76 X11
Bayston Hill 34 L25
Beachampton 28 R27
Beachy Head 12 U31
Beacon (The) 2 E33
Beacon End 30 W28
Beaconsfield 21 S29
Beadlam 50 R21
Beadnell Bay 63 P17
Beaford 7 H31
Beal 63 O16
Beaminster 8 L31
Beamish Hall 56 P19
Beamsley 49 O22
Bearsden 67 G16
Bearsted 22 V30
Beattock 61 J18
Beauchief 43 P24
Beaufort 18 K28
Beaulieu 10 P31
Beauly 79 G11
Beauly Firth 79 G11
Beaumaris 40 H23
Beaumont 54 K19
Beaupré Castle 17 J29
Bebington 42 L23
Beccles 31 Y26
Beckfoot 54 J19
Beckingham 44 R23
Beckington 19 N30
Beckley 12 V31
Beckton 21 U29
Bedale 50 P21
Beddau 17 J29
Beddgelert 33 H24
Beddingham 11 U31
Bedford 29 S27
Bedgebury Pinetum 12 V30
Bedlington 56 P18
Bedlinog 17 K28
Bedrule 62 M17
Bedwas 18 K29
Bedworth 28 P26
Bee (Loch) 76 X11
Beer 5 K31
Beeston 36 Q25
Beeswing 53 I18
Begbroke 20 Q28
Beguildy 26 K26

Beighton 44 P23
Beinn a' Ghlò 74 I13
Beinn a' Mheadhoin (Loch) 78 F12
Beinn Dearg (Highland) ..78 F10
Beinn Dearg (Perthshire and Kinross) 73 I13
Beinn Heasgarnich 67 G14
Beinn Ime 66 F15
Beith 60 G16
Belbroughton 27 N26
Belchford 45 T24
Belford 63 O17
Belhelvie 75 N12
Bellabeg 74 K12
Bellingham 55 N18
Bellshill (Berwick-upon-Tweed) 63 O17
Bellshill (North Lanarkshire) 60 H16
Belmont 87 R1
Belnacraig 74 K12
Belnahua 65 C15
Belper 36 P24
Belsay 56 O18
Belstead 31 X27
Belstone 4 I31
Belton (Lincs.) 37 S25
Belton (Norfolk) 39 Y26
Belton (North Lincs.) ..44 R23
Belton (Rutland) 36 R26
Belvoir 36 R25
Bembridge 10 Q31
Bempton 51 T21
Ben Alder 73 G13
Ben Alder Lodge 73 G13
Ben Armine Forest 85 H9
Ben Armine Lodge 85 H9
Ben Chonzie 67 I14
Ben Cruachan 65 E14
Ben-damph Forest 78 D11
Ben Hope 84 G8
Ben Klibreck 84 G9
Ben Lawers 67 H14
Ben Ledi 67 H15
Ben Lomond 66 G15
Ben Loyal 84 G8
Ben Macdui 74 I12
Ben More (Argyll and Bute) 65 B14
Ben More (Stirling) 67 G14
Ben More Assynt 84 F9
Ben Nevis 72 E13
Ben Starav 66 E14
Ben Vorlich 67 H14
Ben Wyvis 79 G10
Benbecula 76 X11
Benbuie 60 H18
Benderloch (Argyll and Bute) 65 D14
Benderloch (Mountain) 65 E14
Bendronaig Lodge 78 E11
Benenden 12 V30
Benfleet 22 V29
Benington 37 U25
Benllech 40 H23

Benmore 67 G14
Benmore Lodge 84 F9
Benson 20 Q29
Bentley (Doncaster) ...44 Q23
Bentley (East Hampshire) ..20 R30
Bentpath 54 K18
Bentworth 10 Q30
Benwick 29 T26
Beoraid (Loch) 72 D13
Bere Alston 3 H32
Bere Ferrers 3 H32
Bere Regis 9 N31
Berkeley 18 M28
Berkhamsted 21 S28
Berneray (near Barra) ..70 X13
Berneray (near North Uist) ..76 Y10
Bernice 66 E15
Bernisdale 77 B11
Berriew 34 K26
Berrington Hall 26 L27
Berrow 18 K30
Berry Head 4 J32
Berry Hill 18 M28
Berry Pomeroy 4 J32
Berrynarbor 17 H30
Bervie Bay 75 N13
Berwick-St. John 9 N31
Berwick-upon-Tweed ...63 O16
Berwyn 33 J25
Bessacarr 44 Q23
Bethel 33 H24
Bethersden 12 W30
Bethesda 33 H24
Betley 35 M24
Bettisfield 34 L25
Bettws Cedewain 34 K26
Bettws Evan 15 G27
Bettws Gwerfil Goch ..33 J24
Bettyhill 85 H8
Betws-y-Coed 33 I24
Betws yn Rhos 41 J23
Beulah (near Cardigan) ..15 G27
Beulah (near Llandrindod-Wells) 25 J27
Beverley 45 S22
Beverstone 19 N29
Bewaldeth 54 K19
Bewcastle 55 L18
Bewdley 27 N26
Bewholme 51 T22
Bexhill 12 V31
Bexley (London Borough) 21 U29
Beyton 30 W27
Bhaid-Luachraich (Loch) ..78 D10
Bhealaich (Loch a') 84 G9
Bhraoin (Loch a') 78 E10
Bhrollum (Loch) 82 A10
Bibury 19 O28
Bicester 28 Q28
Bicker 37 T25
Bickington 4 I32
Bickleigh (Mid Devon) ...7 J31
Bickleigh (South Hams) ...4 H32

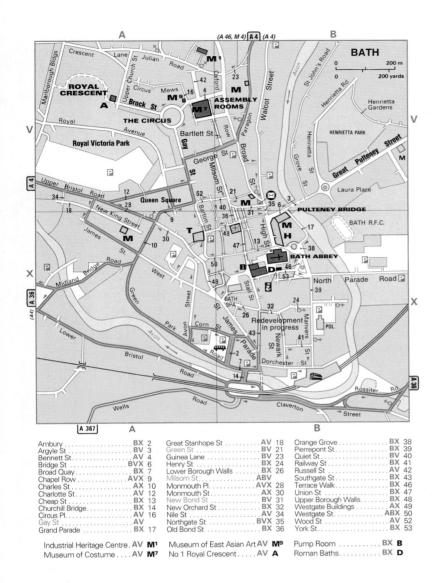

BATH

200 m
200 yards

Ambury . . . . BX 2	Great Stanhope St . . . . AV 18	Orange Grove . . . . BX 38
Argyle St . . . . BV 3	Green St . . . . BV 21	Pierrepont St. . . . . BX 39
Bennett St . . . . AV 4	Guinea Lane . . . . BV 23	Quiet St . . . . BV 40
Bridge St . . . . BVX 6	Henry St . . . . BX 24	Railway St . . . . BX 41
Broad Quay . . . . BX 7	Lower Borough Walls . . . . . BX 26	Russell St . . . . AV 42
Chapel Row . . . . AVX 9	Milsom St. . . . . ABV	Southgate St . . . . BX 43
Charles St . . . . AX 10	Monmouth Pl. . . . . AVX 28	Terrace Walk . . . . BX 46
Charlotte St . . . . AV 12	Monmouth St . . . . AX 30	Union St . . . . BX 47
Cheap St . . . . BX 13	New Bond St . . . . BV 31	Upper Borough Walls . . . . BX 48
Churchill Bridge . . . . BX 14	New Orchard St . . . . BX 32	Westgate Buildings . . . . . . AX 49
Circus Pl. . . . . AV 16	Nile St . . . . AX 34	Westgate St. . . . . ABX 50
Gay St . . . . AV	Northgate St . . . . BVX 35	Wood St . . . . AV 52
Grand Parade . . . . BX 17	Old Bond St . . . . BX 36	York St . . . . BX 53

Industrial Heritage Centre . AV M1	Museum of East Asian Art AV M9	Pump Room . . . . BX B
Museum of Costume . . . . AV M7	No 1 Royal Crescent . . . . . AV A	Roman Baths . . . . BX D

Bicton. 34 L25	Billingborough 37 S25	Birdworld 10 R30
Bicton gardens 5 K31	Billinge 42 L23	Birgham 62 N17
Biddenden 12 V30	Billingham 57 Q20	Birkdale 42 K23
Biddenham 29 S27	Billinghay 37 T24	Birkenhead 42 K23
Biddestone 19 N29	Billingshurst 11 S30	Birkin 44 Q22
Biddulph 35 N24	Billingsley 27 M26	Birling Gap 12 U31
Bidean nam Bian 72 E14	Billington 42 M22	Birmingham 27 O26
Bideford 6 H30	Billockby 39 Y26	Birnam 68 J14
Bidford 27 O27	Billy Row 56 O19	Birsay 86 K6
Bieldside 75 N12	Bilsington 12 W30	Birsemore 75 L12
Bierton 20 R28	Bilsthorpe 36 Q24	Birstall 36 Q25
Big Corlae 60 H18	Bilston 35 N26	Birtley (Gateshead) 56 P19
Bigbury 4 I33	Bilton 45 T22	Birtley (Tynedale) 55 N18
Bigbury-on-Sea 4 I33	Binbrook 45 T23	Birtsmorton Court 27 N27
Biggar (Barrow-in-Furness) . 47 K21	Binfield 20 R29	Bisham 20 R29
Biggar (South Lanarkshire) . 61 J17	Bingham 36 R25	Bishop Auckland 56 P20
Biggin Hill 21 U30	Bingley 43 O22	Bishop Burton 44 S22
Biggleswade 29 T27	Binham 38 W25	Bishop Monkton 50 P21
Bignor 11 S31	Binns (The) 68 J16	Bishop Sutton 18 M29
Bildeston 30 W27	Binsted 10 R30	Bishop Thornton 50 P21
Bildsgreen 27 M26	Birchington 23 X29	Bishop Wilton 50 R22
Bill of Portland 8 M32	Birdham 10 R31	Bishops Cannings 19 O29
Billericay 22 V29	Birdingbury 28 P27	Bishop's Castle 26 L26
Billesdon 36 R26	Birdwell 43 P23	Bishop's Caundle 9 M31

Birdworld 10 R30	Bishop's Cleeve 27 N28	Blaby 36 Q26
	Bishop's Itchington 28 P27	Black Bay 59 D17
	Bishops Lydeard 8 K30	Black Corries 72 F13
	Bishop's Nympton 7 I31	Black Down Hills 8 K31
	Bishop's Palace (near St. David's) . 14 E28	Black Isle 79 G11
	Bishop's Palace (near Tenby) . 16 F28	Black Mount 66 F14
	Bishop's Stortford 30 U28	Black Mountain 25 I28
	Bishop's Tachbrook 28 P27	Black Mountains 26 K28
	Bishop's Tawton 7 H30	Black Notley 30 V28
	Bishop's Waltham 10 Q31	Black Torrington 6 H31
	Bishopsteignton 4 J32	Black Water Valley 78 F11
	Bishopstoke 10 Q31	Blackawton 4 I32
	Bishopston 15 H29	Blackburn (Aberdeenshire) . 75 N12
	Bishopstone (Salisbury) . . .9 O30	Blackburn (Lancs.) 42 M22
	Bishopstone (Swindon) . . 19 P29	Blackburn (West Lothian) . 61 J16
	Bishopthorpe 50 Q22	Blackfield 10 P31
	Bishopton (Darlington) . . 56 P20	Blackford (Cumbria) 54 L19
	Bishopton (Renfrewshire) . 67 G16	Blackford (Perthshire and Kinross) . 67 I15
	Bishton 18 L29	Blackhall 57 Q19
	Bisley 19 N28	Blackhall Rocks 57 Q19
	Bispham 42 K22	Blackhill (Aberdeenshire) . 81 O11
	Bix 20 R29	Blackhill (Highland) 77 A11
	Bixter 87 P3	Blacklunans 74 J13
		Blackmoor Gate 17 I30
		Blackmore 22 U28
		Blackness Castle 68 J15
		Blacko 43 N22
		Blackpool 42 K22
		Blackridge 61 I16
		Blackthorn 28 Q28
		Blacktoft 44 R22
		Blackwater (Hart) 20 R30
		Blackwater (Isle of Wight) . 10 Q31
		Blackwater (River) 22 W28
		Blackwater Reservoir 72 F13
		Blackwaterfoot 59 D17
		Blackwell 50 P20
		Blackwood 18 K29
		Bladnoch 52 G19
		Bladon 20 P28
		Blaenannherch 15 G27
		Blaenau Ffestiniog 33 I25
		Blaenavon 18 K28
		Blaengarw 17 J29
		Blaengrwrach 17 J28
		Blagdon 18 L30
		Blaich 72 E13
		Blaina 18 K28
		Blair Atholl 73 I13
		Blair Castle 73 I13
		Blairgowrie 68 J14
		Blairmore 66 F16
		Blakeney (Glos.) 18 M28
		Blakeney (Norfolk) 38 X25
		Blakesley 28 Q27
		Blamerino 68 K14
		Blandford Forum 9 N31
		Blanefield 67 H16
		Blàr a Chaorainn 72 E13
		Blarmachfoldach 72 E13
		Blarnalearoch 78 E10
		Blawith 48 K21
		Blaxton 44 R23

Blaydon 56 O19	
Bleadon 18 L30	
Bleaklow Hill 43 O23	
Blean 23 X30	
Bleasby 36 R24	
Blenheim Palace 20 P28	
Bletchingdon 20 Q28	
Bletchley 28 R27	
Bletsoe 29 S27	
Blewbury 20 Q29	
Blickling 39 X25	
Blickling Hall 39 X25	
Blidworth 36 Q24	
Blindley Heath 21 T30	
Blisland 3 F32	
Blisworth 28 R27	
Blithe 35 O25	
Blithfield Hall 35 O25	
Blithfield Reservoir 35 O25	
Blockley 27 O27	
Blofield 39 Y26	
Bloxham 28 P27	
Blubberhouses 49 O22	
Blue John Cavern 43 O23	
Bluemull Sound 87 Q1	
Blundellsands 42 K23	
Blundeston 39 Z26	
Blyth (Northumb.) 56 P18	
Blyth (Notts.) 44 Q23	
Blythburgh 31 Y27	
Blythe Bridge 35 N25	
Blyton 44 R23	
Bo' Ness 68 J15	
Boarhills 69 L15	
Boat of Garten 74 I12	
Boathvic 79 G10	
Bocking Churchstreet . . . 30 V28	
Boddam 81 O11	
Bodedern 40 G23	
Bodelwyddan 41 J23	
Bodenham 26 L27	
Bodfari 41 J23	
Bodffordd 40 G23	
Bodham Street 39 X25	
Bodiam Castle 12 V30	
Bodicote 28 Q27	
Bodmin 3 F32	
Bodmin Moor 3 G32	
Bodnant Garden 41 I23	
Bognor Regis 11 R31	
Bogue 53 H18	
Boisdale 70 X12	
Boisdale (Loch) 70 Y12	
Boldon 56 P19	
Bolham 7 J31	
Bollin (River) 42 N23	
Bollington 43 N24	
Bolney 11 T31	
Bolnhurst 29 S27	
Bolsover 44 Q24	
Boltby 50 Q21	
Bolton (Alnwick) 63 O17	
Bolton (Bolton) 42 M23	
Bolton Abbey 49 O22	

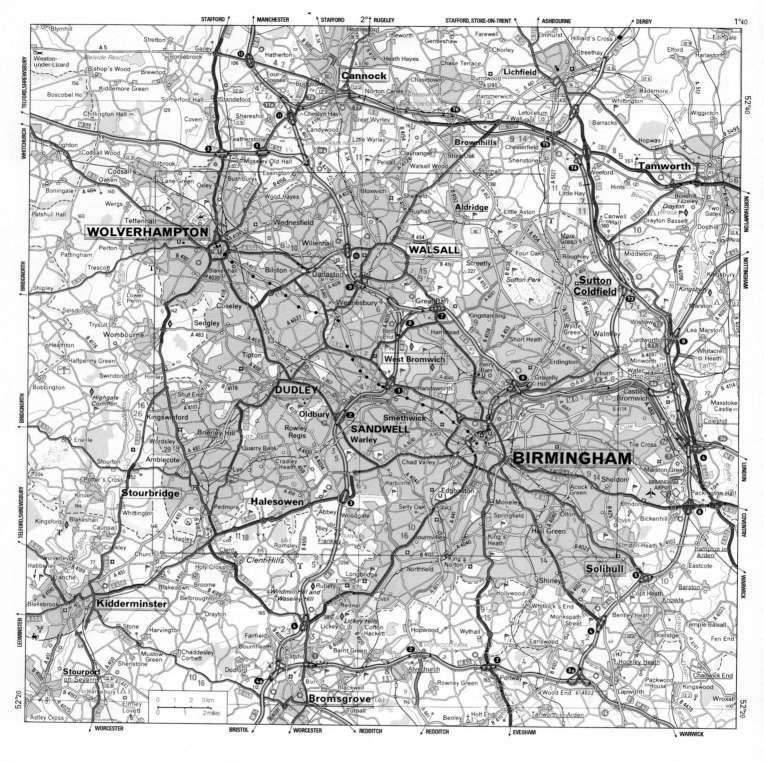

Bolton-by-Bowland	49 N22	Bonnybridge	67 I16	Boreham	22 V28	Borrobol Forest	85 H9	Bosham	10 R31
Bolton-le-Sands	48 L21	Bonnyrigg	61 K16	Boreham Street	12 V31	Borrowash	36 P25	Bosherston	16 F29	Bottesford (Melton)	36 R25
Bolton on Swale	50 P20	Bont-faen / Cowbridge	17 J29	Borehamwood	21 T29	Borth	25 H26	Bosley	35 N24	Bottesford (North Lincolnshire)	44 S23
Bolton-upon-Dearne	44 Q23	Bontgoch Elerch	25 I26	Boreland	54 K18	Borve (Barra Isle)	70 X13	Boston	37 T25	Bottisham	30 U27
Bomere Heath	34 L25	Bontnewydd	32 H24	Borgue (Dumfries and Galloway)	53 H19	Borve (Eilean Siar)	70 X13	Boston Spa	50 P22	Botwnnog	32 G25
Bonar Bridge	79 G10	Boosbeck	50 R20	Borgue (Highland)	85 J9	Borve (Isle of Lewis)	82 A8	Boswinger	3 F33	Boughton	36 Q24
Bonawe Quarries	65 E14	Boot	47 K20	Borness	53 H19	Borve (South Harris)	76 Y10	Botesdale	30 W26	Boughton House	29 R26
Bonby	44 S23	Bootle (Cumbria)	47 J21	Borwick	48 L21	Bothamsall	44 R24	Boughton Street	22 W30
Boncath	15 G27	Bootle (Merseyside)	42 K23	Borough Green	22 U30	Bosbury	26 M27	Bothel	54 K19	Boulmer	63 P17
Bonchester Bridge	62 M17	Border Forest Park (The)	55 M18	Boroughbridge	50 P21	Boscastle	6 F31	Bothwell	60 H16	Boultham	44 S24
Bonhill	66 G16	Bordogan	32 G24	Borreraig	77 Z11	Boscombe	9 O31	Botley	10 Q31	Bourn	29 T27

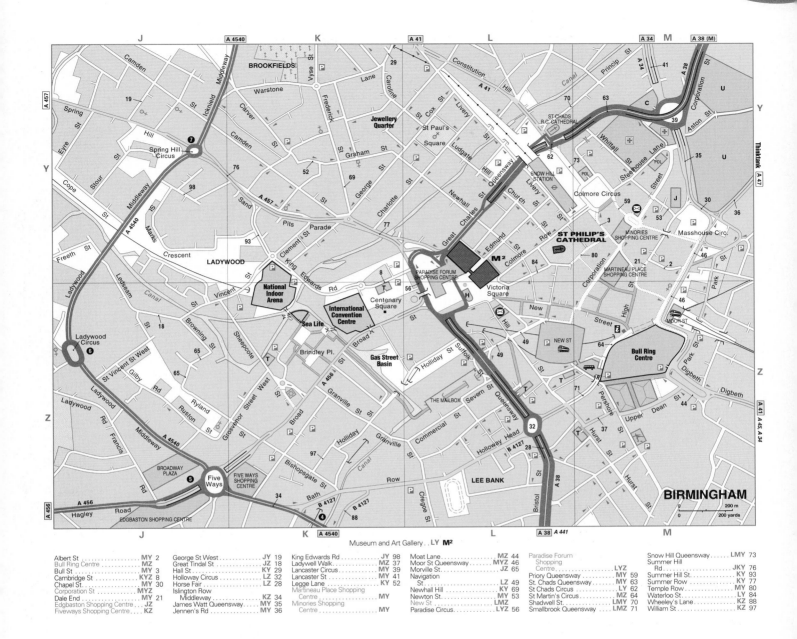

Museum and Art Gallery . . **LY M²**

Albert St . . . . MY 2	George St West . . . . JY 19	King Edwards Rd . . . . JY 98
Bull Ring Centre . . . . MZ	Great Tindal St . . . . JZ 18	Ladywell Walk . . . . MZ 37
Bull St . . . . MY 3	Hall St . . . . KY 29	Lancaster Circus . . . . MY 39
Cambridge St . . . . KYZ 8	Holloway Circus . . . . LZ 32	Lancaster St . . . . MY 41
Chapel St . . . . MY 30	Horse Fair . . . . LZ 28	Legge Lane . . . . KY 52
Corporation St . . . . MYZ	Islington Row	
Dale End . . . . MY 21	Middleway . . . . KZ 34	
Edgbaston Shopping Centre . . JZ	James Watt Queensway . . MY 35	
Fiveways Shopping Centre . . . KZ	Jennen's Rd . . . . MY 36	

Moat Lane . . . . MZ 44	Paradise Forum	Snow Hill Queensway . . . . . LMY 73
Moor St Queensway . . . . MYZ 46	Shopping	Summer Hill
Morville St . . . . JZ 65	Centre . . . . LYZ	Rd . . . . JKY 76
Navigation	Priory Queensway . . . . MY 59	Summer Hill St. . . . . KY 93
St. LZ 49	St. Chads Queensway . . . . . . MY 63	Summer Row . . . . KY 77
Newhall Hill . . . . KY 69	St Chads Circus . . . . LY 62	Temple Row . . . . MY 80
Newhall St . . . . MY 53	St Martin's Circus . . . . MZ 64	Waterloo St . . . . LY 84
New St . . . . LMZ	Shadwell St. . . . . LMY 70	Wheeley's Lane . . . . KZ 88
Paradise Circus . . . . LYZ 56	Smallbrook Queensway . . . LMZ 71	William St . . . . KZ 97

Bourne 37 S25	Bowness 48 L20	Braco 67 I15	Braeantra 79 G10	Bramcote 36 Q25	Brandon (Durham) 56 P19
Bournemouth 9 O31	Bowness-on-Solway 54 K19	Bracora 72 C13	Braedownie 74 K13	Bramfield 31 Y27	Brandon (Suffolk) 30 V26
Bourton (North Dorset) 9 N30	Bowood House 19 N29	Bradan Resr (Loch) 60 G18	Braehead 61 J16	Bramford 31 X27	Brandsby 50 Q21
Bourton (Vale of White	Box 19 N29	Bradfield (Sheffield) 43 P23	Braemar 74 J12	Bramhall 43 N23	Branscombe 5 K31
Horse) 19 P29	Box Hill 21 T30	Bradfield (West Berkshire) . . 20 Q29	Braemore 85 J9	Bramham 43 P22	Bransgore 9 O31
Bourton-on-the-Water 27 O28	Boxford (Babergh) 30 W27	Bradford (Bradford) 43 O22	Braeriach 74 I12	Bramhope 43 P22	Branston 37 S24
Bovey Tracey 4 I32	Boxford (West	Bradford (Taunton	Braeswick 87 L6	Bramley (Basingstoke and	Brant Broughton 37 S24
Bovingdon 21 S28	Berkshire) 20 P29	Deane) 8 K31	Brafferton	Deane) 20 Q30	Brassington 35 P24
Bow 7 I31	Boxley 22 V30	Bradford Abbas 8 M31	Helperby 50 Q21	Bramley (South Yorks.) . . . 44 Q23	Bratton 19 N30
Bow Street 25 H26	Boxworth 29 T27	Bradford-on-Avon 19 N29	Bragar 82 A8	Bramley (Surrey) 21 S30	Bratton Clovelly 6 H31
Bowden 62 L17	Boyton 6 G31	Brading 10 Q31	Braglenbeg 65 D15	Brampton (Cambs.) 29 T27	Bratton Fleming 7 I30
Bower (Highland) 85 K8	Bozeat 29 R27	Bradninch 7 J31	Braich y Pwll 32 F25	Brampton (Cumbria) 55 L19	Braughing 29 U28
Bower (Tynedale) 55 M18	Braaid 46 G21	Bradpole 5 L31	Braidwood 61 I16	Brampton (Eden) 55 M20	Braunston
Bowerchalke 9 O30	Brabourne Lees 12 W30	Bradwell 43 O24	Bràigh Mór 82 Y9	Brampton (Rotherham.) . . . 43 P23	(Daventry) 28 Q27
Bowes 49 N20	Bracadale (Loch) 77 A12	Bradwell-on-Sea 22 W28	Brailes 28 P27	Brampton (Suffolk) 31 Y26	Braunston (Rutland) 36 R26
Bowhill 62 L17	Bracebridge Heath 37 S24	Bradworthy 6 G31	Brailsford 35 P25	Brampton Bryan 26 L26	Braunton 6 H30
Bowland 62 L17	Brackley 28 Q27	Brae 87 P2	Braintree 30 V28	Brancaster 38 V25	Bray-on-Thames 21 R29
Bowland (Forest of) 49 M22	Brackley Hatch 28 Q27	Brae of Achnahaird 83 D9	Braishfield 10 P30	Branderburgh 80 K10	Bray Shop 3 G32
Bowmore 58 B16	Bracknell 20 R29	Brae Roy Lodge 73 F13	Braithwell 44 Q23	Brandesburton 51 T22	Braybrooke 28 R26

BLACKPOOL

Abingdon St. .... AY 2
Adelaide St. .... AY 3
Caunce St. .... AY 7
Church St. .... AY
Clifton St. .... AY 12
Cookson St. .... AY 14
Deansgate .... AY 15
George St. .... AY 17
Grosvenor St. .... AY 21
High St. .... AY 22
Hounds Hill Centre ...... AY
King St. .... AY 23
Lark Hill St. .... AY 24
New Bonny St. .... AY 25
Pleasant St. .... AY 27
South King St. .... AY 35
Talbot Square .... AY 39
Topping St. .... AY 40

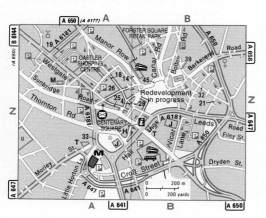

BRADFORD

Bank St. .... AZ 4
Broadway .... BZ 8
Cheapside .... BZ 14
Darley St. .... AZ 18
Drewton Rd .... AZ 19
East Parade .... BZ 21
Forster Square Retail Park .. BZ

Ivegate .... AZ 25
Kirkgate Centre .... AZ 26
Lower Kirkgate .... BZ 45
Market St. .... BZ 28
Oastler Shopping
  Centre .... AZ
Peckover St. .... BZ 32
Prince's Way .... AZ 33
Stott Hill .... BZ 39

Brayford 7 I30
Brayton 44 Q22
Breaclete 82 Z9
Breadalbane 67 G14
Breage 2 D33
Bream 18 M28
Breamore House 9 O31
Brean 18 K30
Breasclete 82 Z9
Breaston 36 Q25
Brechin 75 M13
Breckland 30 V26
Brecon / Aberhonddu 25 J28
Brecon Beacons National
  Park 25 J28
Bredbury 43 N23
Brede 12 V31
Bredenbury 26 M27
Bredgar 22 W30
Bredon 27 N27
Bredwardine 26 L27
Bremhill 19 N29
Brenchley 12 V30
Brendon Hills 7 J30
Brenig Reservoir 33 J24
Brenish 82 Y9
Brent (London Borough) . 21 T29
Brent Knoll 18 L30
Brent Pelham 29 U28
Brentwood 22 U29
Brenzett 12 W30
Brereton 35 O25
Bressay 87 Q3
Bretford 28 P26
Bretherton 42 L22
Brewham 9 M30
Brewlands Bridge 74 K13
Brewood 35 N25
Bride 46 G20
Bridestowe 4 H31
Bridge 23 X30
Bridge of Alford 75 L12

BOURNEMOUTH

Branksome Wood Rd ...... CY 9
Commercial Rd .... CY 13
Durley Rd .... CZ 17
Exeter Rd .... CDZ 20
Fir Vale Rd .... DY 23
Gervis Pl. .... DY 24
Hinton Rd .... DZ 27
Lansdowne Rd .... DY 30

Lansdowne (The) .... DY 28
Madeira Rd .... DY 34
Manor Rd .... EY 35
Meyrick Rd .... EYZ 36
Old Christchurch
  Rd .... DY
Post Office Rd .... CY 43
Priory Rd .... CZ 45
Richmond Hill .... CY 47
Russell Cotes Rd .... DZ 49
St Michael's Rd .... CZ 51

St Paul's Rd .... EY 52
St Peter's Rd .... DY 53
St Stephen's Rd .... CY 55
St Swithuns Rd
  South .... EY 56
Square (The) .... CY 63
Suffolk Rd .... CY 64
Triangle (The) .... CY 67
Upper Hinton Rd .... DZ 68
Westover Rd .... DZ 75
West Cliff Promenade ... CZ 71

Bridge of Allan 67 I15
Bridge of Avon 80 J11
Bridge of Balgie 73 H14
Bridge of Brown 74 J12
Bridge of Buchat 74 L12
Bridge of Craigisla 74 K13
Bridge of Dee 53 I19
Bridge of Don 75 N12
Bridge of Dun 75 M13
Bridge of Dye 75 M13
Bridge of Earn 68 J14
Bridge of Ericht 73 G13
Bridge of Gairn 74 K12
Bridge of Gaur 73 G13
Bridge of Orchy 66 F14
Bridge of Weir 60 G16
Bridge Trafford 42 L24
Bridgemary 10 Q31
Bridgend (Aberdeenshire) 80 L11
Bridgend (Angus) 75 L13
Bridgend (Argyll and Bute) . 65 D15
Bridgend (Islay) 58 B16
Bridgend (Perthshire and
  Kinross) 68 J14
Bridgend / Pen-y-bont .. 17 J29
Bridgend of Lintrathen . 74 K13
Bridgerule 6 G31
Bridgham 30 W26
Bridgnorth 27 M26
Bridgwater 8 L30
Bridlington 51 T21
Bridport 5 L31
Brierfield 43 N22
Brierley 43 P23
Brierley Hill 27 N26
Brigg 44 S23
Brigham 54 J20
Brighouse 43 O22
Brighstone 10 P32

Brighstone Forest 10 P32
Brightling 12 V31
Brightlingsea 22 X28
Brighton 11 T31
Brightwell 20 Q29
Brigstock 29 S26
Brill 20 Q28
Brimfield 26 L27
Brimham Rocks 49 O21
Brimington 43 P24
Brimpsfield 19 N28
Brimpton 20 Q29
Brinkburn Priory 63 O18
Brinkley 30 V27
Brinklow 28 P26
Brinkworth 19 O29
Brinyan 86 L6
Brisley 38 W25
Brislington 18 M29
Bristol 18 M29
Briston 38 X25
Briton Ferry 17 I29
Brittle (Loch) 71 B12
Brittwell Salome 20 Q29
Brixham 4 J32
Brixton 4 H32
Brixworth 28 R27
Brize Norton 20 P28
Broad Bay 83 B9
Broad Blunsdon 19 O29
Broad Chalke 9 O30
Broad Haven 14 E28
Broad Hinton 19 O29
Broad Law 61 J17
Broad Oak 12 V31
Broadbridge
  Heath 11 S30
Broadclyst 7 J31
Broadford 77 C12

Broadlands 10 P31
Broadmayne 9 M31
Broadstairs 23 Y29
Broadstone 9 O31
Broadwas 27 M27
Broadway 27 O27
Broadwell Ho 55 N19
Broadwey 8 M32
Broadwindsor 8 L31
Broadwoodwidger 6 H31
Brochel 77 B11
Brockdish 31 X26
Brockenhurst 10 P31
Brockley 18 L29
Brockworth 19 N28
Brodick 59 E17
Brodick Bay 59 E17
Brodick Castle 59 E17
Brodie Castle 79 I11
Brodsworth 44 Q23
Brodsworth Hall 44 Q23
Brokenborough 19 N29
Brolass 65 B14
Bromborough 42 L24
Brome 31 X26
Bromfield 26 L26
Bromham (Bedford) 29 S27
Bromham (Kennet) 19 N29
Bromley (London Borough) 21 U29
Brompton (Kent) 22 V29
Brompton (near
  Northallerton) 50 P20
Brompton-by-Sawdon 51 S21
Brompton on Swale 49 O20
Brompton Ralph 7 K30
Brompton Regis 7 J30
Bromsgrove 27 N26
Bromyard 26 M27
Bronllys 26 K27

BRIGHTON AND HOVE

Adelaide Crescent . . . . AY 2
Brunswick Pl. . . . . AY 3

Brunswick Square . . . . AYZ 4
Chatham Pl. . . . . BX 6
Churchill Square Shopping
Centre . . . . BYZ
Denmark Rd . . . . BY 7
East St . . . . CZ 8
Gladstone Terrace . . . . CX 12

Gloucester Pl. . . . . CY 13
Gloucester Rd. . . . . CY 14
Goldsmid Rd. . . . . BX 15
Grand Junction Rd . . . . CZ 16
London Rd CX
Marlborough Pl. . . . . CY 21
Montpelier Pl. . . . . BY 22

North St . . . . CZ
Old Steine . . . . CZ 23
Pavillon Parade . . . . CZ 26
Richmond Pl. . . . . CY 27
Richmond Terrace . . . . CX 28
St George's
Pl. CY 30

St Peter's Pl. . . . . CX 31
Terminus Rd . . . . BCX 32
Upper Lewes
Rd . . . . CX 33
Waterloo Pl. . . . . CX 39
Western Rd . . . . ABY
York Pl. . . . . CY 42

Brighton Museum and Art Gallery . CY M   St Bartholomew's . . . . CX B

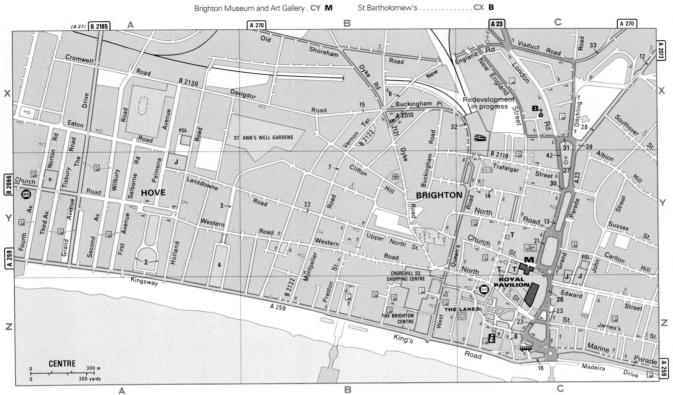

Brook 22 W30
Brooke 39 Y26
Brookmans Park 21 T28
Broom (Loch) 78 E10
Broomfield
(Chelmsford) 22 V28
Broomfield
(Sedgemoor) 8 K30
Broomfleet 44 S22
Broomhaugh 56 O19
Brora 85 I9
Broseley 34 M26
Brotherton 44 Q22
Brotton 57 R20
Brough (East Riding of
Yorkshire) 44 S22
Brough (Eden) 49 N20
Brough (Highland) 86 J8
Brough Head 86 J6
Brough Lodge 87 R2
Brough of Birsay 86 J6
Broughton (Cumbria) 54 J19
Broughton (Flintshire / Sir
y Fflint) 34 L24
Broughton (Hants.) 10 P30
Broughton (Lancs.) 42 L22
Broughton (North Lincs.) . 44 S23
Broughton (Northants.) . . 28 R26
Broughton (Oxon.) 28 P27
Broughton (Scottish
Borders) 61 J17

Broughton-in-Furness . . . 47 K21
Broughton Mills 47 K21
Broughton Moor 54 J19
Broughton Poggs 19 P28
Broughty Ferry 69 L14
Brownhills 35 O26
Brownsea Island 9 O31
Broxbourne 21 T28
Broxburn 68 J16
Bruar Lodge 73 I13
Bruichladdich 58 A16
Brundall 39 Y26
Brushford 7 J30
Bruton 8 M30
Brydekirk 54 K18
Brymbo 34 K24
Bryn-Henllan 24 F27
Brynamman 17 I28
Brynbuga / Usk 18 L28
Bryncethin 17 J29
Bryneglwys 34 K24
Bryngwran 40 G23
Bryngwyn 26 K27
Brynhoffnant 15 G27
Brynmawr 18 K28
Brynsiencyn 32 H24
Brynteg 40 H23
Bualintur 71 B12
Bubwith 44 R22

BRISTOL

Bedminster Parade . . . . CZ 5
Broadmead . . . . DY
Broad Quay . . . . CYZ 13
Broad St . . . . CY 14
Cabot Circus Shopping
Centre . . . . DY
College Green . . . . CZ 30
College St. . . . . CYZ 32
Colston Ave. . . . . CY 33
Fairfax St . . . . CDY 35
Frog Lane . . . . CY 37
Haymarket . . . . DY 38
High St . . . . CDY 39
Horse Fair (The) . . . . DY
Lower Castle St . . . . DY 43
Mall Galleries Shopping Centre
(The) . . . . DY
Marlborough St . . . . CDV 46
Merchant St . . . . DY 47
Narrow Plain . . . . DY 50
Nelson St. . . . . CY 51
New Foundland St . . . . DY 85
North St. . . . . DY 52
Old Market St . . . . DY 54
Park St . . . . CY
Passage St . . . . DY 55
Quay St . . . . CY 58
Queen Charlotte St. . . . . CZ 60
Redcliffe Mead Lane . . . . DZ 61
Rupert St. . . . . CY 65
St Augustine's Parade . . . . . . CY 66
Temple Gate . . . . DZ 75
Trenchard St . . . . CY 77
Wine St . . . . DY 80

Council House . . . . CYZ C
Industrial Museum . . . . CZ M³
Merchant Seamen's
Almshouses . . . . CZ Q
St Stephen's City . . . . . CY S¹
Theatre Royal . . . . CZ T

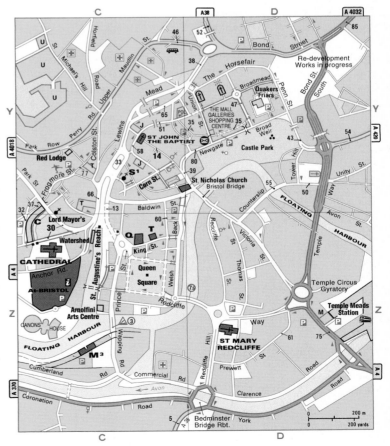

Folkestone Terminal

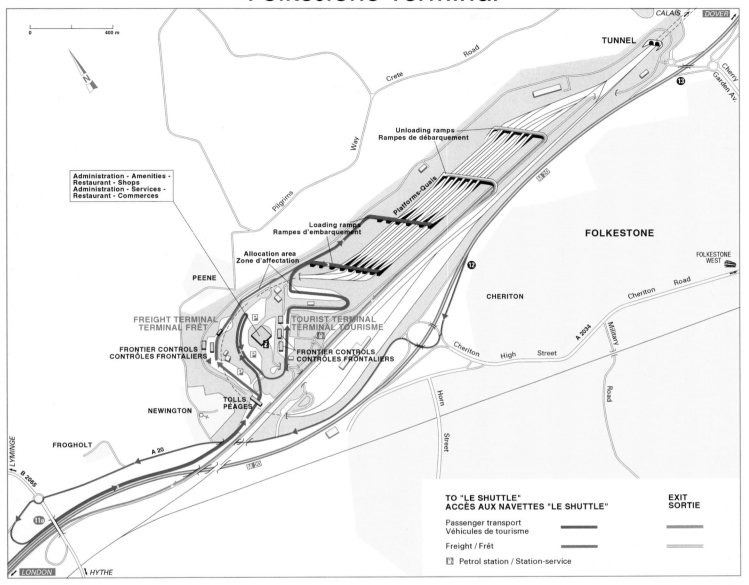

Administration - Amenities - Restaurant - Shops
Administration - Services - Restaurant - Commerces

Unloading ramps
Rampes de débarquement

Loading ramps
Rampes d'embarquement

Allocation area
Zone d'affectation

Platforms-Quais

PEENE

FOLKESTONE

FOLKESTONE WEST

CHERITON

FREIGHT TERMINAL
TERMINAL FRÊT

TOURIST TERMINAL
TERMINAL TOURISME

FRONTIER CONTROLS
CONTRÔLES FRONTALIERS

FRONTIER CONTROLS
CONTRÔLES FRONTALIERS

NEWINGTON

TOLLS
PÉAGES

FROGHOLT

LYMINGE

LONDON   HYTHE

CALAIS   DOVER

TUNNEL

Cherry Garden Av.

Crete Road

Pilgrims Way

Cheriton Road

Cheriton High Street

Horn Street

Military Road

TO "LE SHUTTLE" ACCÈS AUX NAVETTES "LE SHUTTLE"	EXIT SORTIE
Passenger transport Véhicules de tourisme	
Freight / Frêt	

Petrol station / Station-service

Four Marks	10 Q30	Freckenham	30 V27	Fringford	28 Q28	Fuller Street	22 V28
Fovant	9 O30	Freckleton	42 L22	Frinton-on-Sea	31 X28	Fulwood	42 M22
Foveran	81 N12	Freeland	20 P28	Friockheim	75 M14	Funtington	10 R31
Fowey	3 G32	Freethorpe	39 Y26	Frisa (Loch)	71 B14	Funzie	87 R2
Fowlmere	29 U27	Freevater Forest	79 F10	Friskney	37 U24	Furness Abbey	47 K21
Fownhope	26 M27	Freiston	37 U25	Frithville	37 T24	Furness Fells	48 K20
Foxdale	46 G21	Fremington	7 H30	Frittenden	12 V30	Fyfield	22 U28
Foxholes	51 S21	Frensham	10 R30	Fritwell	28 Q28	Fyvie	81 M11
Foxton	28 R26	Freshwater	10 P31	Frizington	47 J20		
Foxup	49 N21	Freshwater Bay	10 P31	Frocester	19 N28		
Foyers	73 G12	Freshwater East	16 F29	Frodsham	42 L24		
Foyle		Freshwater West	14 E29	Froggatt	43 P24	**G**	
Fraddon	3 F32	Fressingfield	31 X26	Frome	19 N30	Gaddesby	36 R25
Framfield	12 U31	Freswick	86 K8	Frosterley	56 O19	Gaick Lodge	73 H13
Framlingham	31 Y27	Freuchie	68 K15	Froxfield	20 P29	Gainford	49 O20
Frampton-on-Severn	19 M28	Freuchie (Loch)	67 I14	Froxholes		Gainsborough	44 R23
Framwellgate Moor	56 P19	Friday Bridge	37 U26	Fuday	70 X12	Gairloch	78 C10
Frant	12 U30	Fridaythorpe	51 S21	Fuiay	70 X13	Gairlochy	72 F13
Fraserburgh	81 O10	Frimley	21 R30	Fulbourn	30 U27	Gairsay	87 L6
Fraserburgh Bay	81 O10			Fulking	11 T31	Gaitsgill	54 L19

Galashiels	62 L17	Garenin	82 Z9
Galgate	48 L22	Garforth	43 P22
Gallan Head	82 Y9	Gargrave	49 N22
Gallanach	65 D14	Gargunnock	67 H15
Galloway Forest Park	52 G18	Garioch	81 M12
Galltair	72 D12	Garlieston	53 G19
Galmisdale	71 B13	Garlogte	75 M12
Galmpton	4 J32	Garmony	65 C14
Galson	82 A8	Garmouth	80 K11
Galston	60 G17	Garrabost	83 B9
Galtrigill	76 Z11	Garragie Lodge	73 G12
Gamblesby	55 M19	Garraron	65 D15
Gamlingay	29 T27	Garreg	33 H25
Gamston	44 R24	Garrigill	55 M19
Ganavan	65 D14	Garrisdale Point	71 A12
Ganton	51 S21	Garros	77 B11
Garboldisham	30 W26	Garrow	67 I14
Gardenstown	81 N10	Garry (Glen) (Highland)	72 E12
Garelochhead	66 F15	Garry (Glen) (Perthshire and Kinross)	73 H13

Garry (Loch)	72 F12	Gayton (Stafford)	35 N25	Gillingham (South Norfolk)	31 Y26	Glasdrum	72 E14	Glenbranter	66 E15	Glenlivet	80 J11
Garsington	20 Q28	Gaywood	38 V25			Glasgow	60 H16	Glenbrittle House	77 B12	Glenluce	52 F19
Garten (Loch)	74 I12	Geary	77 A11	Gills	86 K8	Glasphein	76 Z11	Glenbuchat Castle	74 K12	Glenmassan	66 E15
Garth	25 J27	Geddington	29 R26	Gilmerton	67 I14	Glaspwll	33 I26	Glenbuck	60 I17	Glenmaye	46 F21
Garthorpe	44 R23	Gedney Drove End	37 U25	Gilmorton	28 Q26	Glass (Loch)	79 G10	Glencaple	53 J18	Glenmore	71 C13
Gartmore	67 G15	Gedney Hill	37 T25	Gilston	62 L16	Glassburn	78 F11	Glencarse	68 K14	Glenprosen Village	74 K13
Gartocharn	67 G15	Gelligaer	18 K29	Gilwern	18 K28	Glasserton	52 G19	Glencoe	72 E13	Glenridding	48 L20
Garton-on-The-Wolds	51 S21	Gelston	53 I19	Girthon	53 H19	Glassford	60 H16	Glencoul (Loch)	84 F9	Glenrothes	68 K15
Garvald	69 M16	Georgeham	6 H30	Girton	29 U27	Glasshouses	49 O21	Glendoebeg	73 G12	Glenside	82 A9
Garvamore	73 G12	Georth	86 K6	Girvan	59 F18	Glasson	48 L22	Glendurgan Garden	2 E33	Glenstriven	66 E16
Garve	79 F11	Gerrards Cross	21 S29	Gisburn	49 N22	Glassonby	55 M19	Glenegedale	58 B16	Glentham	44 S23
Garvellachs	65 C15	Gestingthorpe	30 V27	Gisland	55 M19	Glastonbury	8 L30	Glenelg	72 D12	Glentress	61 K17
Garvestone	38 W26	Gifford	62 L16	Gittisham	8 K31	Gleadless	43 P23	Glenelg Bay	72 D12	Glentrool Village	52 G18
Garvock	66 F16	Gigha (Sound of)	58 C17	Gladestry	26 K27	Gleann Beag	78 F10	Glenfarg	68 J15	Glentworth	44 S23
Garway	26 L28	Gigha Island	58 C16	Glaisdale	50 R20	Gleann Mór	79 G10	Glenfeshie Lodge	73 I12	Glenuachdarach	77 B11
Garynahine	82 Z9	Gighay	70 Y12	Glamis	74 K14	Gleaston	48 K21	Glenfiddich Lodge	80 K11	Glenuig	71 C13
Gatehouse of Fleet	53 H19	Gilberdyke	44 R22	Glamis Castle	74 L14	Glecknabae	59 E16	Glenfield	36 Q26	Glespin	61 I17
Gateshead	56 P19	Gilcrux	54 J19	Glanaman	17 I28	Glemsford	30 V27	Glenfinnan	72 D13	Gletness	87 Q3
Gateside	68 K15	Gildersome	43 P22	Glandwr	15 G28	Glen auldyn	46 G21	Glenforsa Airport	65 C14	Glinton	37 T26
Gatley	42 N23	Gilfach Goch	17 J29	Glanton	63 O17	Glen Brittle Forest	77 B12	Glenfyne Lodge	66 F15	Glossop	43 O23
Gatwick Airport	11 T30	Gillamour	50 R21	Glas-allt-Shiel	74 K13	Glen Finglas Reservoir	67 G15	Glengorm	71 B14	Gloucester	27 N28
Gaulden Manor	8 K30	Gilling East	50 Q21	Glas-leac Mór	83 D9	Glen More Forest Park	74 I12	Glengoulandie	73 H14	Gloup	87 Q1
Gavard	64 B15	Gilling West	49 O20	Glas Maol	74 J13	Glen Shee	74 J13	Glengrasco	77 B11	Glusburn	49 O22
Gaydon	28 P27	Gillingham (Dorset)	9 N30	Glasbury	26 K27	Glen Trool Lodge	52 G18	Glenkens (The)	53 H18	Glutt Lodge	85 I9
Gayton (King's Lynn and West Norfolk)	38 V25	Gillingham (Kent)	22 V29	Glascarnoch (Loch)	78 F10	Glenbarr	59 C17	Glenkin die	74 L12	Glympton	28 P28
				Glascwm	26 K27	Glenborrodale	71 C13	Glenkirk	61 J17	Glyn Ceiriog	34 K25

Terminal de Calais

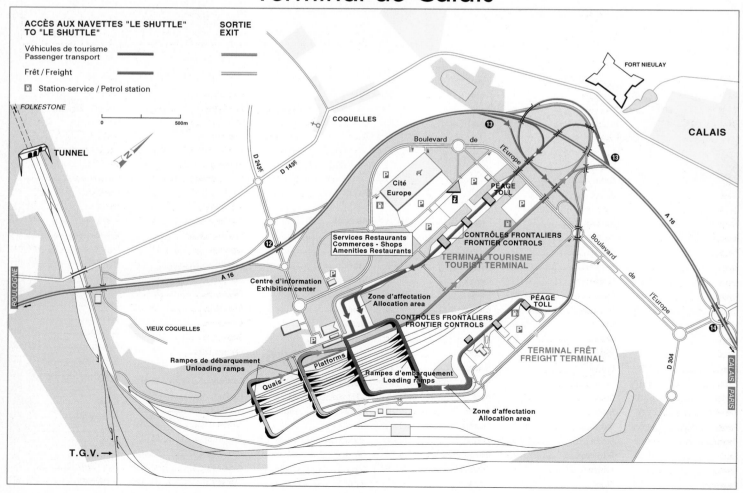

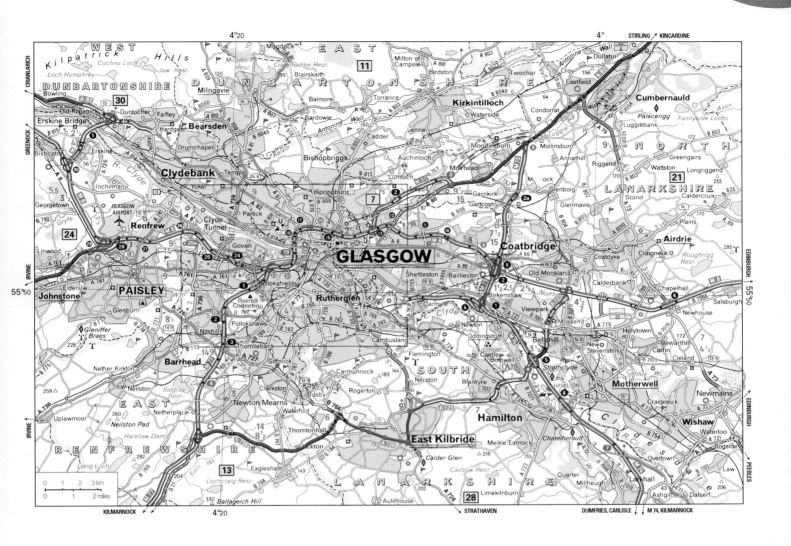

Glyn-Ebwy / Ebbw Vale	18 K28	Goodrington	4 J32	Gowerton	15 H29	Great Altcar	42 K23	Great Coates	45 T23	Great Malvern	27 N27
Glyn-neath	17 J28	Goodwick	24 F27	Goxhill	45 T22	Great Amwell	21 T28	Great-Comberton	27 N27	Great Marton	42 K22
Glyncorrwg	17 J28	Goodwood House	10 R31	Graemsay	86 K7	Great Asby	49 M20	Great Cornard	30 W27	Great Massingham	38 W25
Glynde	11 U31	Goole	44 R22	Grafton		Great Ayton	50 Q20	Great Cubley	35 O25	Great Milton	20 Q28
Glyndebourne	11 U31	Goonhavern	2 E32	Underwood	29 S26	Great Baddow	22 V28	Great Cumbrae Island	59 F16	Great Missenden	21 R28
Glyndyfrdwy	34 K25	Goostrey	42 M24	Grain	22 W29	Great Bardfield	30 V28	Great-Dalby	36 R25	Great Mitton	42 M22
Gnosall	35 N25	Gordon	62 M16	Grainthorpe	45 U23	Great Barford	29 S27	Great Doddington	28 R27	Great Musgrave	49 M20
Goadby	36 R26	Gordonbush	85 I9	Granby	36 R25	Great Barr	35 O26	Great Driffield	51 S21	Great Oakley	31 X28
Goat Fell	59 E17	Gordonstown	80 L11	Grandtully	74 I14	Great Barrow	34 L24	Great-Dunham	38 W25	Great Ormes Head	41 I22
Goathland	50 R20	Gorebridge	61 K16	Grange-over-		Great Barugh	50 R21	Great Dunmow	30 V28	Great Orton	54 K19
Gobowen	34 K25	Goring	20 Q29	Sands	48 L21	Great Bedwyn	19 P29	Great Easton (Essex)	30 U28	Great Ouse (River)	38 V25
Godalming	21 S30	Gorm Loch Mór	84 F9	Grangemouth	67 I15	Great Bentley	31 X28	Great Easton (Leics.)	28 R26	Great Ouseburn	50 Q21
Godmanchester	29 T27	Gorran Haven	3 F33	Grantchester	29 U27	Great Bernera	82 Z9	Great Eccleston	42 L22	Great Ponton	37 S25
Godmanstone	8 M31	Gorseinon	15 H29	Grantham	37 S25	Great Bircham	38 V25	Great Ellingham	38 W26	Great Ryburgh	38 W25
Godshill	10 Q32	Gorsleston-on-Sea	39 Z26	Grantown-on-Spey	80 J12	Great-Bollright	28 P28	Great Finborough	30 W27	Great Salkeld	55 L19
Godstone	21 T30	Gortantaoid	64 B16	Grantshouse	62 N16	Great Bookham	21 S30	Great Glen	36 Q26	Great Sampford	30 V28
Goil (Loch)	66 F15	Gosberton	37 T25	Grasby	45 S23	Great Bourton	28 Q27	Great Gonerby	37 S25	Great Shefford	20 P29
Golborne	42 M23	Gosfield	30 V28	Grasmere	48 K20	Great Bowden	28 R26	Great Gransden	29 T27	Great Shelford	29 U27
Goldcliff	18 L29	Gosforth		Grassington	49 O21	Great Brickhill	29 R28	Great Harrowden	28 R27	Great Smeaton	50 P20
Goldhanger	22 W28	(Cumbria)	47 J20	Grateley	9 P30	Great Bridgeford	35 N25	Great Harwood	42 M22	Great Somerford	19 N29
Goldthorpe	44 Q23	Gosforth (Newcastle upon		Graveley	29 T27	Great Bromley	30 X28	Great Hockham	30 W26	Great Stainton	56 P20
Golspie	85 I10	Tyne)	56 P18	Gravesend	22 V29	Great Broughton	50 Q20	Great Horkesley	30 W28	Great Strickland	55 L20
Gomersal	43 O22	Gosport	10 Q31	Gravir	82 A9	Great-Budworth	42 M24	Great Horwood	28 R28	Great Torrington	6 H31
Gometra	64 B14	Goswick	63 O16	Grayrigg	48 M20	Great Burdon	50 P20	Great Houghton	43 P23	Great Tosson	63 O18
Gomshall	21 S30	Gotham	36 Q25	Grays Thurrock	22 V29	Great Chalfield	19 N29	Great Langton	50 P20	Great Totham	22 W28
Gooderstone	38 V26	Gott Bay	70 Z14	Grayshott	10 R30	Great Chesterford	30 U27	Great-Limber	45 T23	Great Urswick	48 K21
Goodleigh	7 I30	Goudhurst	12 V30	Grayswood	11 R30	Great Chishill	29 U27	Great Livermere	30 W27	Great Wakering	22 W29
Goodrich	26 M28	Gourdon	75 N13	Greasbrough	43 P23	Great Clifton	53 J20	Great Lumley	56 P19	Great Waltham	22 V28
		Gourock	66 F16	Great Addington	29 S26						

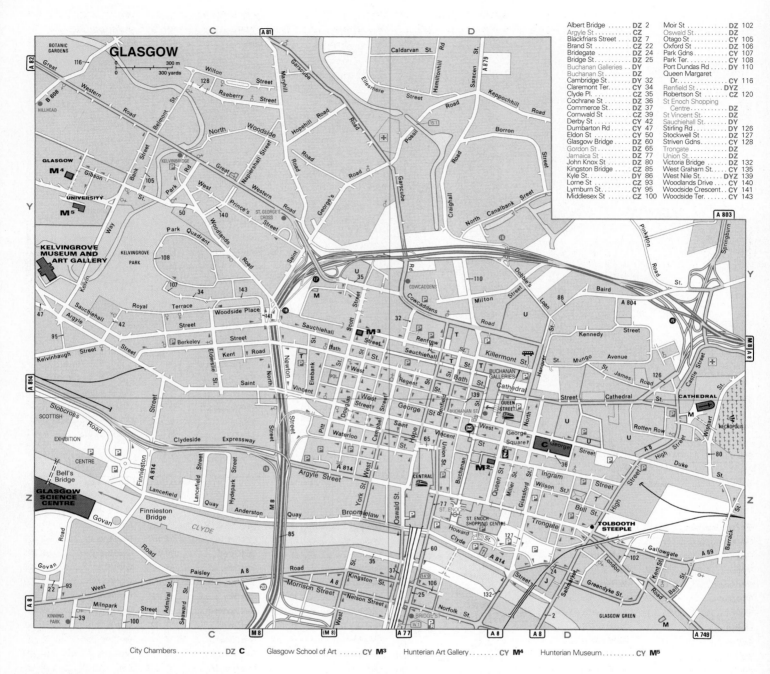

GLASGOW

Albert Bridge	DZ 2	Moir St	DZ 102
Argyle St	CZ	Oswald St	DZ
Blackfriars Street	DZ 7	Otago St	CY 105
Brand St	CZ 22	Oxford St	DZ 106
Bridgate	DZ 24	Park Gdns	CY 107
Bridge St	DZ 25	Park Ter.	CY 108
Buchanan Galleries	DY	Port Dundas Rd	DY 110
Buchanan St	DZ	Queen Margaret	
Cambridge St	DY 32	Dr.	CY 116
Claremont Ter.	CY 34	Renfield St	DYZ
Clyde Pl.	CZ 35	Robertson St	CZ 120
Cochrane St	DZ 36	St Enoch Shopping	
Commerce St	DZ 37	Centre	DZ
Cornwald St	CZ 39	St Vincent St.	DY
Derby St	CY 42	Sauchiehall St.	DY
Dumbarton Rd	CY 47	Stirling Rd.	DY 126
Eldon St	CY 50	Stockwell St	DZ 127
Glasgow Bridge	DZ 60	Striven Gdns	CY 128
Gordon St	DZ 65	Trongate	DZ
Jamaica St	DZ 77	Union St.	DZ
John Knox St	DZ 80	Victoria Bridge	DZ 132
Kingston Bridge	CZ 85	West Graham St.	DY 135
Kyle St	DY 86	West Nile St.	DYZ 139
Lorne St	CZ 93	Woodlands Drive	CY 140
Lymburn St	CY 95	Woodside Crescent	CY 141
Middlesex St	CZ 100	Woodside Ter.	CY 143

City Chambers .... DZ C Glasgow School of Art ...... CY M³ Hunterian Art Gallery .... CY M⁴ Hunterian Museum .... CY M⁵

Great Whernside	49 O21
Great Whittington	56 O18
Great Witley	27 M27
Great Wolford	27 P27
Great Wyrley	35 N26
Great Yarmouth	39 Z26
Great Yeldham	30 V27
Greatford	37 S25
Greatham (Cleveland)	57 Q20
Greatham (Hants.)	10 R30
Greatstone-on-Sea	12 W31
Green Hammerton	50 Q21
Greenfield (Flintshire / Sir y Fflint)	41 K23
Greenfield (Highland)	72 F12
Greenhaugh	55 N18
Greenhead	55 M19
Greenholm	60 H17
Greenhow Hill	49 O21
Greenlaw	62 M16
Greenloaning	67 I15
Greenock	66 F16
Greenodd	48 K21
Greens Norton	28 Q27
Greenside	56 O19
Greenwich (London Borough)	21 U29
Grendon	28 R27
Grendon Underwood	28 Q28
Gresford	34 L24
Greshornish	77 A11
Greshornish (Loch)	77 A11
Gress	83 B9
Gretna	54 K19

GLOUCESTER

Black Dog Way	Y 5
Commercial Rd	Y 6
Eastgate Shopping Centre	Y
Eastgate St	Y 10
Great Western Rd	Y 12
Heathville Rd	Y 13
Lower Westgate St	Y 15
Northgate St	Y 16
Parliament St	Y 18
Pitt St	Y 19
Quay St	Y 20
Royal Oak Rd	Y 21
St Aldate St	Y 22
St Johns Lane	Y 23
Southgate St	Y
Spa Rd	Y 26
Worcester St	Y 31

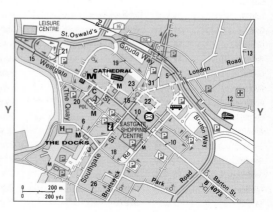

Bishop Hooper's Lodging . Y M

IPSWICH

Argyle St . . . . X 2
Bond St . . . . X 6
Buttermarket Centre . . . . X 9
Carr St . . . . X 10
College St . . . . X 15
Corn Hill . . . . X 16
Dogs Head St . . . . X 18
Falcon St . . . . X 21
Franciscan Way. . . . . X 24
Friars St . . . . X 25
Grey Friars Rd . . . . X 26
Handford Rd . . . . X 30
Lloyds Ave . . . . X 31
Lower Orwell St . . . . X 32
Northgate St . . . . X 33

Orwell Pl. . . . . X 34
Quadling St . . . . X 35
Queen St . . . . X 37
St Helen's St . . . . X 39
St Margarets St . . . . X 40
St Nicholas St . . . . X 41
St Peter's St. . . . . X 42
Salthouse St . . . . X 43
Silent St . . . . X 46
Tavern St . . . . X 47
Tower Ramparts Centre . . . . . X 47
Upper Orwell St . . . . X 49
Waterworks St . . . . X 51
Westgate St . . . . X 52
Wolsey St . . . . X 53

Christchurch Mansion . . . . X B

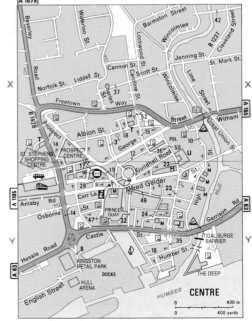

CENTRE

Gretton 37 R26
Greys Court 20 R29
Greysouthen 54 J20
Greystoke 55 L19
Griffithstown 18 K28
Griminish 76 X11
Grimley 27 N27
Grimoldby 45 U23
Grimsay 76 Y11
Grimsby 45 T23
Gringley on the Hill 44 R23
Grinshill 34 L25
Grinton. 49 O20
Gristhorpe 51 T21
Grittleton 19 N29
Groby 36 Q26
Grogport 59 D17
Groombridge 12 U30
Grosebay 76 Z10
Grosmont (Monmouthshire /
    Sir Fynwy). 26 L28
Grosmont
    (Scarborough). 50 R20
Grove 20 P29
Gruinard Bay 78 D10
Gruinard Island 78 D10
Gruinart 58 B16
Gruinart (Loch) 64 B16
Grunavat (Loch) 82 Z9
Grundisburgh 31 X27
Gualachulain 66 E14
Guardbridge 69 L14
Guernsey (Channel I.) 5
Guesting 12 V31
Guildford 21 S30
Guildtown. 68 J14

Guilsborough 28 Q26
Guisborough 50 Q20
Guiseley 43 O22
Guist 38 W25
Gullane 69 L15
Gunna 70 Z14
Gunnerside 49 N20
Gunnerton 55 N18
Gunness 44 R23
Gunnislake 3 H32
Gunthorpe 36 R25
Gurnard. 10 Q31
Gurness Broch 86 K6
Gurnos 17 I28
Gussage All Saints 9 O31
Gutcher 87 Q1
Guthrie. 75 L14
Guyhirn 37 U26
Gwalchmai 40 G23
Gwaun-Cae-Gurwen. 17 I28
Gwbert-on-Sea 15 F27
Gweek 2 E33
Gwennap 2 E33
Gwithian 2 D33
Gwyddelwern 33 J24
Gwyddgrug 15 H28
Gwydir Castle 33 I24
Gwytherin 33 I24

H

Habost 83 B8
Hackney (London
    Borough). 21 T29
Haddenham (Bucks.). 20 R28

Haddenham (Cambs.). 29 U26
Haddington 69 L16
Haddiscoe 39 Y26
Haddo House 81 N11
Haddon Hall 35 P24
Hadfield 43 O23
Hadleigh (Essex) 22 V29
Hadleigh (Suffolk). 30 W27
Hadley 34 M25
Hadlow 22 V30
Hadnall 34 L25
Hadrian's Wall 55 M18
Haggbeck 55 L18
Hagley 27 N26
Hagworthingham 45 U24
Hailsham 12 U31
Hainford 39 X25
Hainton 45 T23
Halam 36 R24
Halberton 7 J31
Hale 42 M23
Hales 39 Y26
Halesowen 27 N26
Halesworth 31 Y26
Halford 27 P27
Halifax 43 O22
Halistra 77 A11
Halkirk 85 J8
Hall. 60 G16
Halland 12 U31
Hallaton 36 R26
Halling 22 V29
Hallington 55 N18
Halloughton 36 R24
Hallow 27 N27
Hallsands. 4 J33
Halsall 42 L23
Halse 8 K30
Halsetown. 2 D33
Halstead. 30 V28
Halstock 8 M31
Haltham 37 T24
Halton (Aylesbury Vale). . .20 R28
Halton (Lancaster) 48 L21
Halton Gill 49 N21
Haltwhistle 55 M19
Halwell 4 I32
Halwill Junction. 6 H31
Hamble 10 Q31
Hambleden 20 R29
Hambledon (Hants.) 10 Q31
Hambledon (Surrey) 11 S30
Hambleton (Lancs.). 42 L22
Hambleton (North Yorks.) . .44 Q22
Hambleton Hills (The). 50 Q21
Hambridge. 8 L31
Hamilton 60 H16
Hammersmith and Fulham
    (London Borough). . . .21 T29
Hamnavoe (near Brae) . . .87 Q2
Hamnavoe (near Scallway). .87 P3
Hampreston. 9 O31
Hampstead Norris 20 Q29
Hampsthwaite 50 P21

Hampton Court. 21 S29
Hampton in Arden 27 O26
Hamstead Marshall 20 P29
Hamsterley 56 O19
Hamstreet 12 W30
Hamworthy 9 N31
Handa Island 84 E8
Handbridge 34 L24
Handbury 27 N27
Handcross 11 T30
Handforth 43 N23
Handley 34 L24
Handsworth 43 P23
Hanham 18 M29
Hanley 35 N24
Hanley Swan 27 N27
Hanningfield 22 V28
Hannington 19 O29
Hanslope 28 R27
Happisburgh 39 Y25
Hapton 42 N22
Harberton 4 I32
Harbertonford 4 I32
Harbledown 23 X30
Harborough Magna 28 Q26
Harbottle 63 N17
Harbury 28 P27
Harby 36 R25
Hardham 11 S31
Hardwick 44 Q24
Hardwick Hall 36 Q24
Hardwicke 19 N28
Hardy Monument 5 M31
Hardy's Cottage 9 M31
Hare Street 29 U28
Haresfield 19 N28
Harewood House 50 P22
Hargrave 29 S27
Hargrave Green 30 V27
Haringey (London
    Borough). 21 T29
Harlaxton 36 R25
Harlech 33 H25
Harleston 31 X26
Harlestone 28 R27
Harley 34 M26
Harlington 29 S28
Harlosh. 77 A11
Harlow 21 U28
Harlow Hill 56 O18
Harmston 37 S24
Haroldswick 87 R1
Harpenden 21 S28
Harpley 38 V25
Harport (Loch) 77 A12
Harray (Loch of) 86 K6
Harrietfield 67 J14
Harrington (Allerdale) 53 J20
Harrington (Kettering) 28 R26
Harringworth 37 S26
Harris (Highland) 71 A13
Harris (Western Isles) 82 Y10
Harris (Sound of) 76 Y10
Harrogate 50 P22

Harrow (London Borough) 21 S29
Harston 29 U27
Hartburn 56 O18
Hartest 30 W27
Hartfield 11 U30
Harthill
    (North Lanarkshire) . . .61 I16
Harthill (Rotherham) 44 Q24
Harting 10 R31
Hartington 35 O24
Hartland 6 G31
Hartland Quay 6 G31
Hartlebury. 27 N26
Hartlepool 57 Q19
Hartley 22 U29
Hartley Wintney 20 R30
Hartpury 27 N28
Hartshill 36 P26
Hartwell 20 R28
Hartwell 28 R27
Harvington 27 O27
Harwell 20 Q29
Harwich 31 X28
Harwood Dale 51 S20
Harworth 44 Q23
Hascosay 87 R2
Haselbury Plucknett. 8 L31
Hasland 43 P24
Haslemere 11 R30
Haslingden 42 N22
Haslingfield 29 U27

Haslington. 35 M24
Hassocks 11 T31
Haster 86 K8
Hastings 12 V31
Hatch Court. 8 L31
Hatfield (County of
    Herefordshire) 26 M27
Hatfield (Herts.) 21 T28
Hatfield (South Yorks.) 44 Q23
Hatfield Broad Oak 22 U28
Hatfield Heath 22 U28
Hatfield Peverel 22 V28
Hatfield Woodhouse 44 R23
Hatherleigh. 7 H31
Hathern 36 Q25
Hathersage 43 P24
Hatton (Aberdeenshire) . . .81 O11
Hatton (Derbs.) 35 O25
Hatton of Fintray 75 N12
Haughton 35 N25
Haunn 71 B14
Havant 10 R31
Havenstreet 10 Q31
Haverfordwest / Hwlffordd . .16 F28
Haverhill 30 V27
Haverigg 47 K21
Havering (London
    Borough). 22 U29
Haverthwaite 48 K21
Hawarden 34 K24

KINGSTON-UPON-HULL

Bond St . . . . X 3
Carr Lane . . . . Y
Commercial Rd . . . . Y 8
Dock Office Row . . . . X 10
Dock St . . . . X 12
Ferensway . . . . XY 14
George St X
Grimston St . . . . X 15
Humber Dock St . . . . X 16
Jameson St . . . . X 17
Jarratt St . . . . X 18
Kingston Retail Park . . . . . Y
King Edward St . . . . X 19

Lowgate . . . . Y 23
Market Pl. . . . . Y 24
Paragon St . . . . Y 29
Princes Quay Shopping
    Centre . . . . Y
Prince's Dock St . . . . Y 32
Prospect Shopping
    Centre X
Prospect St X
Queen St . . . . Y 35
Queen's Dock Ave . . . . . . X 36
Reform St . . . . X 37
Sculcoates Bridge . . . . . . X 42
Waterhouse Lane . . . . X 47
Whitefriargate . . . . Y 49
Wilberforce Drive . . . . X 50
Worship St . . . . X 52

CENTRE

Hawes	49	N21
Hawick	62	L17
Hawkchurch	8	L31
Hawkedon	30	V27
Hawkesbury Upton	19	M29
Hawkhurst	12	V30
Hawkridge	7	J30
Hawkshead	48	L20
Hawkwell	22	V29
Hawley	20	R30
Hawling	27	O28
Haworth	43	O22
Hawsker	51	S20
Haxby	50	Q21
Haxey	44	R23
Hay-on-Wye	26	K27
Haydock	42	M23
Haydon Bridge	55	N19
Haydon Wick	19	O29
Hayfield	43	O23
Hayle	2	D33
Hayling Island	10	R31
Hayscastle	14	E28
Hayton	50	R22
Haywards Heath	11	T31
Hazel Grove	43	N23
Hazelbank	61	I16
Hazelbury Bryan	9	M31
Hazlemere	21	R29
Heacham	38	V25
Headcorn	22	V30
Headington	20	Q28
Headless Cross	27	O27
Headley	10	R30
Heads of Ayr	60	F17
Healey	49	O21
Healing	45	T23
Heanor	36	P24
Heast	71	C12
Heath End	20	Q29
Heath Hayes	35	O25
Heather	36	P25
Heathfield (Renfrewshire)	60	F16
Heathfield (Wealden)	12	U31
Heathrow Airport	21	S29
Hebburn	56	P19
Hebden Bridge	43	N22
Hebrides (Sea of the)	76	Z12
Heckfield	20	R29
Heckington	37	T25
Heddon on the Wall	56	O19
Hedge End	10	Q31
Hednesford	35	O25
Hedon	45	T22
Heighington (Durham)	56	P20
Heighington (Lincs.)	44	S24
Heights of Kinlochewe	78	E11
Helensburgh	66	F15
Helford	2	E33
Hellifield	49	N22
Hellingly	12	U31
Hellisay	70	X12
Hell's Mouth or Porth Neigwl	32	G25

Helmdon	28	Q27
Helmsdale	85	J9
Helmsley	50	Q21
Helpringham	37	T25
Helpston	37	S26
Helsby	42	L24
Helston	2	E33
Helton	55	L20
Helvellyn	48	K20
Hemel Hempstead	21	S28
Hemingbrough	44	R22
Hemingford Grey	29	T27
Hemington	19	M30
Hempnall	39	X26
Hempton	38	W25
Hemsby	39	Z25
Hemswell	44	S23
Hemsworth	43	P23
Hemyock	8	K31
Hendy	15	H28
Henfield	11	T31
Hengoed	18	K29
Henham	30	U28
Henley	27	O27
Henley-on-Thames	20	R29
Henllan	33	J24
Henllys	18	K29
Henlow	29	T27
Hennock	4	J32
Henshaw	55	M19
Henstead	31	Y26
Henstridge	9	M31
Heol Senni	25	J28
Hepple	63	N18
Heptonstall	43	N22
Herbrandston	14	E28
Hereford	26	L27
Heriot	62	L16
Herm (Channel I.)		5
Herma Ness	87	R1
Hermitage	20	Q29
Hermitage Castle	62	L18
Herne Bay	23	X29
Herriard	20	Q30
Herrington	56	P19
Herstmonceux	12	U31
Hertford	21	T28
Hesket Newmarket	54	K19
Hesketh Bank	42	L22
Hesleden	57	Q19
Hessenford	3	G32
Hessle	45	S22
Hest Bank	48	L21
Heswall	42	K24
Hethersgill	55	L19
Hethpool	63	N17
Hetton-le-Hole	56	P19
Heveningham	31	Y27
Hever	21	U30
Heversham	48	L21
Hevingham	39	X25
Hewelsfield	18	M28
Hexham	55	N19

Heybridge	22	W28
Heysham	48	L21
Heyshott	11	R31
Heytesbury	9	N30
Heythrop	28	P28
Heywood	43	N23
Hibaldstow	44	S23
Hickling	36	R25
Hickling Green	39	Y25
Hidcote Manor Garden	27	O27
High Bentham	49	M21
High Bickington	7	I31
High Birkwith	49	N21
High Easter	22	V28
High Ercall	34	M25
High Etherley	56	O20
High Force (The)	55	N20
High Halden	12	W30
High Halstow	22	V29
High Ham	8	L30
High Hesket	55	L19
High Newton (Alnwick)	63	P17
High Newton (South Lakeland)	48	L21
High Offley	35	N25
High Ongar	22	U28
High Peak	43	O23
High Willhays	4	I31
High Wycombe	20	R29
Higham (Kent)	22	V29
Higham (Lancs.)	42	N22
Higham (North East Derbyshire)	36	P24
Higham (Suffolk)	30	V27
Higham Ferrers	29	S27
Higham on the Hill	36	P26
Highbridge	18	L30
Highclere	20	P29
Highcliffe	9	O31
Higher Penwortham	42	L22
Highland Wildlife Park	73	I12
Highley	27	M26
Highmoor Cross	20	R29
Highnam	27	N28
Hightae	54	J18
Hightown (Congleton)	35	N24
Hightown (Sefton)	42	K23
Highworth	19	O29
Hilborough	38	W26
Hildenborough	22	U30
Hilderstone	35	N25
Hilgay	38	V26
Hill	18	M29
Hill of Fearn	79	I10
Hill of Tarvit	69	L15
Hillhead	52	G19
Hillingdon (London Borough)	21	S29
Hillington	38	V25
Hillside	75	M13
Hillswick	87	P2
Hilmarton	19	O29
Hilperton	19	N30
Hilpsford Point	47	K21
Hilton (Aberdeenshire)	81	N11

Hilton (Eden)	55	M20
Hilton (Huntingdonshire)	29	T27
Hilton (North Dorset)	9	N31
Hilton (South Derbyshire)	35	P25
Hilton of Cadboll	79	I10
Himbleton	27	N27
Hinchingbrooke House	29	T27
Hinckley	36	P26
Hinderwell	50	R20
Hindhead	10	R30
Hindley	42	M23
Hindolveston	38	X25
Hindon	9	N30
Hingham	38	W26
Hinstock	34	M25
Hintlesham	31	X27
Hinton-Blewett	18	M30
Hirst Courtney	44	Q22
Hirwaun	17	J28
Histon	29	U27
Hitcham	30	W27
Hitchin	29	T28
Hockering	38	X25
Hockerton	36	R24
Hockley	22	V29
Hockley Heath	27	O26
Hockliffe	29	S28
Hoddesdon	21	T28
Hodnet	34	M25
Hodthorpe	44	Q24
Hogsthorpe	45	U24
Holbeach	37	U25
Holbeach-St. Johns	37	T25
Holbeach-St. Matthew	37	U25
Holbeck	44	Q24
Holbrook	31	X28
Holbury	10	P31
Holcombe	18	M30
Holcombe Rogus	7	J31
Holdenby	28	R27
Holford	8	K30
Holkam Hall	38	W25
Hollandstoun	87	M5
Hollesley	31	Y27
Hollesley Bay	31	Y27
Hollingbourne	22	V30
Hollingworth	43	O23
Hollybush	60	G17
Hollym	45	U22
Holmbridge	43	O23
Holme (Huntingdonshire)	29	T26
Holme (South Lakeland)	48	L21
Holme-next-the-Sea	38	V25
Holme upon Spalding-Moor	44	R22
Holmer Green	21	R29
Holmes Chapel	35	M24
Holmesfield	43	P24
Holmfirth	43	O23
Holmhead	60	H17
Holmpton	45	U22
Holnest	8	M31
Holsworthy	6	G31
Holt (Dorset)	9	O31

Holt (Norfolk)	38	X25
Holt (Wilts.)	19	N29
Holt (Wrexham)	34	L24
Holt Heath	27	N27
Holton (Lincs.)	45	T24
Holton (Norfolk)	31	Y26
Holton (South Somerset)	8	M30
Holton Heath	9	N31
Holton-le-Clay	45	T23
Holwick	55	N20
Holy Island (Anglesey)	40	F23
Holy Island (North Ayrshire)	59	E17
Holy Island (Northumb.)	63	O16
Holybourne	10	R30
Holyhead / Caergybi	40	G23
Holystone	63	N18
Holywell	2	E32
Holywell / Treffynnon	41	K23
Holywell Bay	2	E32
Holywood	53	J18
Honing	39	Y25
Honiton	8	K31
Hoo St. Werburgh	22	V29
Hook (Basingstoke and Deane)	20	R30
Hook (East Riding of Yorkshire)	44	R22
Hook Norton	28	P28
Hooke	8	M31
Hope (Derbs.)	43	O23
Hope (Flintshire)	34	K24
Hope (Highland)	84	G8
Hope (South Shropshire)	34	L26
Hope (Loch)	84	G8
Hope Bowdler	26	L26
Hope under Dinmore	26	L27
Hopeman	80	J10
Hopetoun House	68	J16
Hopton	39	Z26
Horam	12	U31
Horbury	43	P23
Horden	57	Q19
Hordley	34	L25
Horeb	15	G27
Horley	21	T30
Hornby	48	M21
Horncastle	45	T24
Hornchurch	22	U29
Horncliffe	63	N16
Horning	39	Y25
Horninglow	35	P25
Horn's Cross	6	H31
Hornsea	51	T22
Hornton	28	P27
Horrabridge	4	H32
Horseheath	30	V27
Horsehouse	49	O21
Horsell	21	S30
Horsford	39	X25
Horsforth	43	P22
Horsham	11	T30
Horsham St. Faith	39	X25
Horsington (East Lindsey)	37	T24

Horsington (South Somerset)	9	M30
Horsley (Stroud)	19	N28
Horsley (Tynedale)	56	O19
Horsmonden	12	V30
Horstead	39	Y25
Horsted Keynes	11	T30
Horton (Abertawe / Swansea)	15	H29
Horton (East Dorset)	9	O31
Horton (South Somerset)	8	L31
Horton Court	19	M29
Horton-in-Ribblesdale	49	N21
Horwich	42	M23
Hoton	36	Q25
Hott	55	M18
Houghton	10	P30
Houghton Hall	38	V25
Houghton House	29	S27
Houghton-le-Spring	56	P19
Houghton-on-the-Hill	36	R26
Hougton	55	L19
Hounslow (London Borough)	21	S29
Hourn (Loch)	72	D12
Housesteads Fort	55	N18
Houston	60	G16
Houstry	85	J9
Hove	11	T31
Hoveton	39	Y25
Hovingham	50	R21
How Caple	26	M28
Howden	44	R22
Howe of the Mearns	75	M13
Howick	63	P17
Howmore	76	X12
Hownam	62	M17
Howwood	60	G16
Hoxa (Sound of)	86	K7
Hoxne	31	X26
Hoy	86	J7
Hoylake	41	K22
Hoyland Nether	43	P23
Huby	50	Q21
Hucknall	36	Q24
Huddersfield	43	O23
Huggate	51	S22
Hugh Town (I. of Scilly)		2
Hughenden	20	R29
Hughley	34	M26
Huish Champflower	7	J30
Huish Episcopi	8	L30
Hull (River)	45	S22
Hulland	35	P24
Hullavington	19	N29
Hullbridge	22	V29
Humber (River)	45	T23
Humber Bridge	44	S22
Humberston	45	T23
Humbleton	45	T22
Hume Castle	62	M17
Humshaugh	55	N18
Hundleton	16	F28
Hundred House	26	K27

Hungerford 20 P29
Hunmanby 51 T21
Hunstanton 38 V25
Hunter's Inn 17 I30
Hunter's Quay 66 F16
Huntingdon 29 T26
Huntington 50 Q22
Huntingtower Castle 68 J14
Huntly 80 L11
Hunton 49 O21
Huntspill 18 L30
Hunwick 56 O19
Hurlford 60 G17
Hurn 9 O31
Hursley 10 P30
Hurst Green 12 V30
Hurstbourne Priors 20 P30
Hurstbourne Tarrant 20 P30
Hurstpierpoint 11 T31
Hurworth-on-Tees 50 P20
Hury 55 N20
Husbands Bosworth 28 Q26
Huthwaite 36 Q24
Huttoft 45 U24
Hutton (Scottish Borders) 63 N16
Hutton (South Ribble) 42 L22
Hutton Cranswick 51 S22
Hutton Rudby 50 Q20
Huxley 34 L24
Huyton 42 L23
Hwlffordd / Haverfordwest 16 F28
Hyde 43 N23
Hynish 64 Z14
Hynish Bay 64 Z14
Hythe (Hants.) 10 P31
Hythe (Kent) 13 X30

I

Ibsley 9 O31
Ibstock 36 P25
Ickleford 29 T28
Icklingham 30 V27
Ickworth House 30 V27
Iddesleigh 7 H31
Ideford 4 J32
Iden 12 W31
Iden Green 12 V30
Idmiston 9 O30
Idrigill Point 77 A12
Ightham 22 U30
Ightham Mote 22 U30
Ilchester 8 L30
Ilderton 63 O17
Ilfracombe 17 H30
Ilkeston 36 Q25
Ilkley 49 O22
Illogan 2 E33
Ilmington 27 O27
Ilminster 8 L31
Ilsington 4 I32
Ilton 8 L31
Immingham 45 T23

Immingham Dock 45 T23
Ince Blundell 42 K23
Ince-in-Makerfield 42 M23
Inch Kenneth 64 B14
Inchard (Loch) 84 E8
Inchbare 75 M13
Inchgrundle 74 L13
Inchkeith 68 K15
Inchlaggan 72 E12
Inchmarnock 59 E16
Inchnadamph 84 F9
Inchture 68 K14
Indaal (Loch) 58 A16
Inerval 58 B17
Ingatestone 22 V28
Ingbirchworth 43 P23
Ingham 30 W27
Ingleby Barwick 50 Q20
Ingleton (Durham) 56 O20
Ingleton (North Yorks.) 49 M21
Inglewhite 42 L22
Inglewood Forest 55 L19
Ingliston 68 J16
Ingoldmells 38 V24
Ingoldsby 37 S25
Ingram 63 O17
Ings 48 L20
Inkpen 20 P29
Innellan 59 F16
Inner Hebrides 70 Y14
Inner Sound 77 C11
Innerleithen 61 K17
Innerpeffray 67 I14
Innerwick 69 M16
Insch 81 M11
Insh 73 I12
Inshore 84 F8
Instow 6 H30
Inver (Highland) 79 I10
Inver (Perth and Kinross) 68 J14
Inver (Loch) 84 E9
Inver Bay 79 I10
Inver Mallie 72 E13
Inver Valley 84 E9
Inveralligin 78 D11
Inverallochy 81 O10
Inveran 84 G10
Inveraray 66 E15
Inverarity 69 L14
Inverarnan 66 F15
Inverbeg 66 G15
Inverbervie 75 N13
Invercassley 84 G10
Invercauld House 74 J12
Inverchapel 66 F15
Invercreran 72 E14
Inverdruie 73 I12
Inverewe Gardens 78 C10
Inverey 74 J13
Inverfarigaig 79 G12
Invergarry 72 F12
Invergeldie 67 H14
Invergordon 79 H10

Invergowrie 68 K14
Inverie 72 C12
Inverinan 65 E15
Inverinate 78 D12
Inverkeithing 68 J15
Inverkeithny 81 M11
Inverkip 66 F16
Inverkirkaig 84 E9
Inverliever Forest 65 D15
Inverlochlarig 67 G15
Invermoriston 73 G12
Inverness 79 H11
Inversanda 72 D13
Inversnaid Hotel 66 F15
Inveruglas 66 F15
Inverurie 81 M12
Invervar 73 H14
Inwardleigh 7 H31
Iona 64 A15
Ipplepen 4 J32
Ipstones 35 O24
Ipswich 31 X27
Irby (East Lindsey) 37 U24
Irby (Wirral) 42 K23
Irchester 29 S27
Ireby 54 K19
Ireleth 47 K21
Irlam 42 M23
Iron Acton 18 M29
Iron-Bridge 34 M26
Irthington 55 L19
Irthlingborough 29 S27
Irvine 60 F17
Irwell (River) 42 N23
Isbyty Ystwyth 25 I27
Isla (Glen) 74 K13
Islay (Sound of) 64 B16
Isle of Whithorn 53 G19
Isleham 30 V26
Isleornsay 71 C12
Isleworth 21 S29
Islington (London Borough) .. 21 T29
Islip 20 Q28
Islivig 82 Y9
Itchingfield 11 S30
Ithon (River) 25 K27
Itteringham 39 X25
Iver 21 S29
Iver Heath 21 S29
Ivinghoe 21 S28
Ivybridge 4 I32
Ivychurch 12 W30
Iwade 22 W29
Iwerne Minster 9 N31
Ixworth 30 W27

J

Jacobstow 6 G31
Jacobstowe 7 H31
Jameston 15 F29
Jamestown (Dumfries and Galloway) ... 61 K18

Jamestown (West Dunbartonshire) ... 66 G16
Janetstown 85 J9
Jarrow 56 P19
Jaywick 23 X28
Jedburgh 62 M17
Jedburgh Abbey 62 M17
Jeffreyston 15 F28
Jemimaville 79 H11
Jersey (Channel I.) 5
Jevington 12 U31
John Muir 69 M15
John o' Groats 86 K8
Johnshaven 75 N13
Johnston 16 F28
Johnstone 60 G16
Johnstonebridge 54 J18
Jura (Isle of) 58 B16
Jura (Sound of) 65 C16
Jura Forest 65 B16
Jura Ho. 58 B16
Jurby West 46 G20

K

Kainakill 77 C11
Kames 65 E16
Katrine (Loch) 67 G15
Kea 2 E33
Keal 37 U24
Keal (Loch na) 65 B14
Kearsley 42 M23
Keasden 49 M21
Kebock Head 82 A9
Kedington 30 V27
Kedleston Hall 36 P25
Keelby 45 T23
Keevil 19 N30
Kegworth 36 Q25
Keig 75 M12
Keighley 43 O22
Keillmore 65 C16
Keinton Mandeville 8 M30
Keir Mill 53 I18
Keiss 86 K8
Keith 80 L11
Keld 49 N20
Kellas (Angus) 69 L14
Kellas (Moray) 80 J11
Kelleth 49 M20
Kellie Castle 69 L15
Kellington 44 Q22
Kelloe 56 P19
Kelly Bray 3 H32
Kelmarsh 28 R26
Kelsall 34 L24
Kelso 62 M17
Kelston 19 M29
Keltneyburn 73 H14
Kelty 68 J15
Kelvedon 30 W28
Kelvedon Hatch 22 U29
Kemble 19 N28
Kemnay 75 M12

Kempley 26 M28
Kempsey 27 N27
Kempsford 19 O28
Kempston 29 S27
Kemsing 22 U30
Kendal 48 L21
Kenfig 17 I29
Kenilworth 27 P26
Kenknock 67 G14
Kenmore (Highland) 77 C11
Kenmore (Perthshire and Kinross) ... 67 I14
Kenn 18 L29
Kennet (River) 19 O29
Kennethmont 80 L11
Kenninghall 30 X26
Kennington (Kent) 22 W30
Kennington (Oxon.) 20 Q28
Kennoway 68 K15
Kenovay 70 Z14
Kensaleyre 77 B11
Kentallen 72 E13
Kentford 30 V27
Kentisbeare 7 K31
Kentmere 48 L20
Kenton 4 J32
Kents Bank 48 L21
Keoldale 84 F8
Keresley 28 P26
Kerrera 65 D14
Kerry 26 K26
Kersey 30 W27
Kershader 82 A9
Kershopefoot 55 L18
Kesgrave 31 X27
Kessingland 31 Z26
Keswick 54 K20
Kettering 28 R26
Kettleness 50 R20
Kettleshulme 43 N24
Kettletoft 87 M6
Kettlewell 49 N21
Ketton 37 S26
Kew 21 T29
Kewstoke 18 L29
Kexbrough 43 P23
Kexby 44 R23
Keyingham 45 T22
Keymer 11 T31
Keynsham 18 M29
Keyworth 36 Q25
Kibworth Harcourt 36 R26
Kidderminster 27 N26
Kidermorie Lodge 79 G10
Kidlington 20 Q28
Kidsgrove 35 N24
Kidstones 49 N21
Kidwelly / Cydweli 15 H28
Kielder 55 M18
Kielder Forest 55 M18
Kielder Reservoir 55 M18
Kiiphedir 85 I9
Kilamarsh 44 Q24
Kilbarchan 60 G16

Kilbirnie 60 F16
Kilbrannan Sound 59 D17
Kilbride 65 D14
Kilburn (Amber Valley) 36 P24
Kilburn (Hambleton) 50 Q21
Kilchattan 59 E16
Kilchenzie 59 C17
Kilcheran 65 D14
Kilchiaran 58 A16
Kilchoan 71 B13
Kilchoman 58 A16
Kilchrenan 65 E14
Kilconquhar 69 L15
Kilcreggan 66 F16
Kildale 50 Q20
Kildary 79 H10
Kildavanan 59 E16
Kildonan 59 E17
Kildonan Lodge 85 I9
Kildrummy 74 L12
Kildrummy Castle 74 L12
Kilfinnan 72 F12
Kilgetti 15 F28
Kilham (Berwick-upon-Tweed) .. 63 N17
Kilham (East Riding of Yorkshire) ... 51 S21
Kilkhampton 6 G31
Killay 15 H29
Killean 59 D17
Killearn 67 G15
Killen 79 H11
Killerton 7 J31
Killiechronan 65 C14
Killilan 78 D12
Killin 67 H14
Killinghall 50 P21
Killundine 71 C14
Kilmacolm 60 G16
Kilmaluag 77 B10
Kilmany 69 L14
Kilmarie 71 B12
Kilmarnock 60 G17
Kilmartin 65 D15
Kilmaurs 60 G17
Kilmelford 65 D15
Kilmersdon 19 M30
Kilmington (East Devon) 8 K31
Kilmington (Salisbury) 9 N30
Kilmorack 79 G11
Kilmore 71 C12
Kilmory (Ardnamurchan) 71 B13
Kilmory (Argyll and Bute) 65 C16
Kilmory (I. Rhum) 71 A12
Kilmory (North Ayrshire) 59 E17
Kilmuir 77 A11
Kilmun 66 F16
Kilncadzow 61 I16
Kilninver 65 D14
Kilnsey 49 N21
Kiloran 64 B15
Kilpeck 26 L28
Kilrenny 69 L15

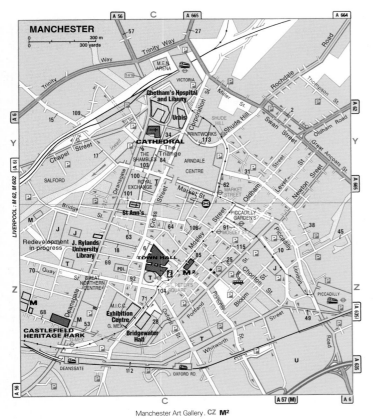

MANCHESTER

Manchester Art Gallery . **CZ M²**

Addington St	CY	2	Fairfield St	CZ	49	Parker St	CZ	91
Albert Square	CZ	6	Great Bridgewater St	CZ	53	Peter St	CZ	92
Aytoun St	CZ	10	Great Ducie St	CY	57	Princess St	CZ	
Blackfriars Rd	CY	15	Great Northern centre			St Ann's Square	CY	100
Blackfriars St	CY	17	High St	CZ	62	St Ann's St	CY	101
Brazennoze St	CZ	18	John Dalton St	CZ	63	St Mary's Gate	CZ	103
Charlotte St	CZ	25	King St	CZ	64	St Peter's Square	CZ	104
Cheetham Hill Rd	CY	27	Liverpool Rd	CZ	68	Shambles Shopping Centre		
Chepstow St	CZ	28	Lloyd St	CZ	69	(The)	CY	
Church St	CY	31	Lower Byrom St	CZ	70	Spring Gardens	CZ	106
Corn Exchange	CY	34	Lower Mosley St	CZ	71	Viaduct St	CY	109
Dale St	CZ	38	Mosley St	CZ		Whitworth St West	CZ	112
Deansgate	CYZ		New Cathedral St	CY	84	Withy Grove	CY	113
Ducie St	CZ	45	Nicholas St	CZ	85	York St	CZ	115

Mitcheldean	26	M28	Monar (Loch)	78	E11	Montrose	75	M13
Mitchell	2	E32	Monar Lodge	78	F11	Monyash	35	O24
Mitford	56	O18	Monaughty Forest	80	J11	Monymusk	75	M12
Mithcham	21	T29	Moneydie	68	J14	Monzie	67	I14
Mithian	2	E33	Moniaive	53	I18	Moonen Bay	76	Z11
Moaness	86	K7	Monifieth	69	L14	Moor Monkton	50	Q21
Mochdre	41	I23	Monikie	69	L14	Moorends	44	R23
Mochrum	52	G19	Monk Fryston	44	Q22	Moorfoot Hills	61	K16
Modbury	4	I32	Monkland	26	L27	Moors (The)	52	F19
Moelfre	40	H22	Monkokehampton	7	H31	Moortown	45	S23
Moffat	61	J17	Monks Eleigh	30	W27	Morar	71	C13
Moidart	72	C13	Monksilver	7	K30	Moray Firth	79	H11
Moira	36	P25	Monkton	60	G17	Morchard Bishop	7	I31
Mol-Chlach	71	B12	Monmouth / Trefynwy	18	L28	Morcott	37	S26
Mold / Yr Wyddgrug	34	K24	Monreith	52	G19	Morden	9	N31
Molland	7	I30	Montacute	8	L31	Mordiford	26	M27
Monach Islands	76	W11	Montgarrie	75	L12	More (Glen)	65	C14
Monadhliath Mountains	73	H12	Montgomery / Trefaldwyn	34	K26	More (Loch) (near Kinloch)	84	F9

Middleton on the Wolds	51	S22	Millmeece	35	N25	Miltonduff	80	J11
Middleton St. George	50	P20	Millom	47	K21	Miltown of Edinvillie	80	K11
Middleton Tyas	49	P20	Millport	59	F16	Milverton	8	K30
Middletown (Powys)	34	K25	Milltown (Dumfries and Galloway)	54	K18	Milwich	35	N25
Middlewich	35	M24	Milltown (Highland)	78	F11	Minard	65	E15
Midgeholme	55	M19	Milltown (Moray)	80	L11	Minch (The)	83	C9
Midhurst	10	R31	Milnathort	68	J15	Minehead	17	J30
Midlem	62	L17	Milngavie	67	H16	Minety	19	O29
Midsomer Norton	18	M30	Milnrow	43	N23	Mingary	76	X12
Midtown	78	C10	Milnthorpe	48	L21	Minginish	77	B12
Miefield	53	H19	Milovaig	76	Z11	Mingulay	70	X13
Migdale (Loch)	79	H10	Milton	79	H10	Minnigaff	52	G19
Milborne Port	8	M31	Milton (Cambs.)	29	U27	Minster (near Sheerness)	22	W29
Milborne St. Andrew	9	N31	Milton (Carlisle)	55	L19	Minster (near Ramsgate)	23	X29
Milbourne	56	O18	Milton (Dumfries)	53	I18	Minsterley	34	L26
Milburn	55	M20	Milton (Highland)	79	G11	Minsterworth	19	N28
Mildenhall (Forest Heath)	30	V26	Milton (Stranraer)	52	F19	Minterne Magna	8	M31
Mildenhall (Kennet)	19	O29	Milton Abbas	9	N31	Minting	45	T24
Mile End	30	W28	Milton Abbot	3	H32	Mintlaw	81	O11
Milfield	63	N17	Milton Bryan	29	S28	Minto	62	L17
Milford	11	S30	Milton Ernest	29	S27	Mirfield	43	O22
Milford Haven / Aberdaugleddau	14	E28	Milton Keynes	28	R27	Miserden	19	N28
Milford-on-Sea	9	P31	Milton Libourne	19	O29	Misson	44	R23
Milland	10	R30	Milton of Campsie	67	H16	Misterton (Notts.)	44	R23
Millbrook	3	H32	Milton of Cushnie	75	L12	Misterton (Somerset)	8	L31
Millhouse	59	E16	Milton-on-Stour	9	N30	Mistley	31	X28

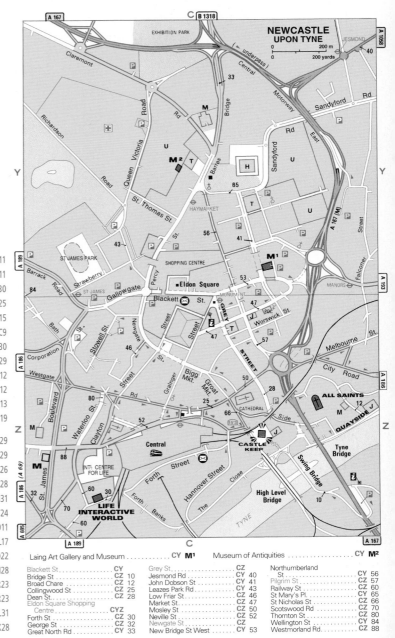

NEWCASTLE UPON TYNE

Laing Art Gallery and Museum . . . . **CY M¹**   Museum of Antiquities . . . . **CY M²**

Blackett St		CY	Grey St		CZ	Northumberland		
Bridge St	CZ	10	Jesmond Rd	CY	40	St	CY	56
Broad Chare	CZ	12	John Dobson St	CY	41	Pilgrim St	CZ	57
Collingwood St	CZ	25	Leazes Park Rd	CY	43	Railway St	CZ	60
Dean St	CZ	28	Low Friar St	CZ	46	St Mary's Pl.	CY	65
Eldon Square Shopping			Market St	CZ	47	St Nicholas St	CZ	66
Centre	CYZ		Mosley St	CZ	50	Scotswood Rd	CZ	70
Forth St	CZ	30	Neville St	CZ	52	Thornton St	CZ	80
George St	CZ	32	Newgate St	CZ		Wellington St	CY	84
Great North Rd	CY	33	New Bridge St West	CY	53	Westmorland Rd	CZ	88

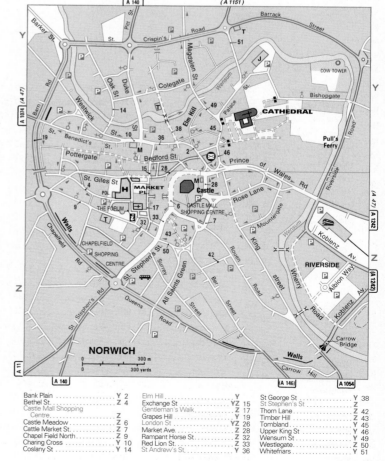

NEWPORT

Allt-yr-yn Ave	AY 2	Commercial St.	AXY 15	Kingsway Centre	AX
Bellevue Lane	BX 5	Dewsland Park Rd	AY 17	Lower Dock	
Blewitt St.	AX 7	Dock St.	AX 19	St.	AXY 35
Caerau Crescent	AXY 9	Godfrey Rd	AX 21	Malpas Rd.	AX 37
Cambrian Centre	AX	Hereford St.	AX 24	Newport Bridge	AX 39
Capel St.	AY 10	High St.	AX 26	Oakfield Rd.	AX 42
Clarence Pl.	AX 12	John Frost Square	AX 27	Queensway	AX 44
Clyffard Crescent	AX 13	Kensington Pl.	AX 30	Summerhill Ave	AX 47
Clytha Park Rd	AX 14	Keynsham Ave	AY 32	Waterloo Rd	AY 50

Muir of Ord	79 G11	Murton (Eden)	55 M20	Nairn	79 I11
Muirdrum	69 L14	Musbury	5 K31	Nant (Loch)	65 E14
Muirhead	60 H16	Musselburgh	68 K16	Nant-y-Moch Reservoir	25 I26
Muirkirk	60 H17	Muston	51 T21	Nant-y-moel	17 J29
Muirshearlich	72 E13	Muthill	67 I15	Nantgwynant Valley	33 H24
Muker	49 N20	Mwnt	15 G27	Nantwich	34 M24
Mulbarton	39 X26	Mybster	85 J8	Nantyglo	18 K28
Mulben	80 K11	Myddfai	25 I28	Napton	28 Q27
Muldoanich	70 X13	Myddle	34 L25	Narberth / Arberth	15 F28
Mull (Isle of)	64 B14	Mydroilyn	15 H27	Narborough (Blaby)	36 Q26
Mull (Sound of)	71 C14	Mynach Falls	25 I26	Narborough (Breckland)	38 V25
Mull of Galloway	52 F20	Mynydd Eppynt	25 J27	Naseby	28 R26
Mull of Oa	58 A17	Mynydd Mawr	32 F25	Nash Point	17 J29
Mullardoch (Loch)	78 E12	Mynydd Preseli	15 F28	Nassington	37 S26
Mullardoch House	78 F11	Myrelandhorn	86 K8	Nateby	49 M20
Mullion	2 E33	Mytchett	21 R30	National Exhibition Centre	27 O26
Mumbles (The)	15 H29	Mytholmroyd	43 O22	National Motor Museum	10 P31
Mumby	45 U24			Naunton	27 O28
Mundesley	39 Y25			Navenby	37 S24
Mundford	30 V26	**N**		Naver (Loch)	84 G9
Mundham	10 R31	Na Cùiltean	58 C16	Nayland	30 W28
Munlochy	79 H11	Naburn	50 Q22	Naze (The)	31 X28
Munlochy Bay	79 H11	Nacton	31 X27	Neap	87 Q3
Munslow	26 L26	Nafferton	51 S21	Neath / Castell-nedd	17 I29
Murlaggan	72 E13	Nailsea	18 L29	Neath (River)	17 I28
Murrayfield	68 K16	Nailstone	36 P26	Nebo	33 I24
Mursley	28 R28	Nailsworth	19 N28	Necton	38 W26
Murton (Easington)	57 P19			Needham Market	31 X27

More (Loch) (near Westerdale)	85 J8	Morton (near Gainsborough)	44 R23	Mount's Bay	2 D33
Morebath	7 J30	Morton (North East Derbyshire)	36 P24	Mountsorrel	36 Q25
Morebattle	62 M17	Morton on Swale	50 P21	Mousa	87 Q4
Morecambe	48 L21	Morval	3 G32	Mousehole	2 D33
Morecambe Bay	48 L21	Morven	85 I9	Mouswald	54 J18
Moresby	53 J20	Morvern	71 C14	Mow Cop	35 N24
Moreton (Epping Forest)	22 U28	Morvich	72 D12	Mowtie	75 N13
Moreton (Purbeck)	9 N31	Morville	34 M26	Moy	79 H11
Moreton-in-Marsh	27 O28	Morwelham	3 H32	Muasdale	59 C17
Moreton-on-lugg	26 L27	Morwenstow	6 G31	Much Dewchurch	26 L28
Moreton Say	34 M25	Mosborough	43 P24	Much Hadham	29 U28
Moretonhampstead	4 I32	Moss Bank	42 L23	Much Hoole	42 L22
Morfa Nefyn	32 G25	Mossdale	53 H18	Much Marcle	26 M28
Moricambe Bay	54 K19	Mossend	60 H16	Much Wenlock	34 M26
Morie (Loch)	79 G10	Mossley	43 N23	Muchalls	75 N12
Moriston (Glen)	72 F12	Mosstodloch	80 K11	Muchelney	8 L30
Morland	55 M20	Mostyn	41 K23	Muchrachd	78 F11
Morley	43 P22	Motherwell	61 I16	Muck	71 B13
Morlich (Loch)	74 I12	Moulin	74 I13	Muckle Roe	87 P2
Morpeth	56 O18	Moulton (Forest Heath)	30 V27	Mucklestone	35 M25
Morriston	17 I29	Moulton (Lincs.)	37 T25	Muddiford	7 H30
Morte Bay	6 H30	Moulton (Northants.)	28 R27	Mudford	8 M31
Mortehoe	16 H30	Moulton Chapel	37 T25	Mugeary	77 B11
Mortimer	20 Q29	Mount Pleasant	9 P31	Muick (Loch)	74 K13
Morton (near Bourne)	37 S25	Mountain Ash / Aberpennar	17 J28	Muie	85 H9
		Muir of Fowlis	75 L12		

NORWICH

Bank Plain	Y 2	Elm Hill	Y	St George St	Y 38
Bethel St.	Z 4	Exchange St	YZ 15	St Stephen's St	Z
Castle Mall Shopping Centre	Z	Gentleman's Walk	Z 17	Thorn Lane	Z 42
Castle Meadow	Z	Grapes Hill	Y 19	Timber Hill	Z 43
Cattle Market St.	Z 7	London St	YZ 26	Tombland	Y 45
Chapel Field North	Z	Market Ave.	Z 28	Upper King St	Y 46
Charing Cross	Y 10	Rampant Horse St	Z 32	Wensum St	Y 49
Coslany St	Y 14	Red Lion St	Z 33	Westlegate	Z 50
		St Andrew's St	Y 36	Whitefriars	Y 51

Needingworth 29 T27
Needles (The) 10 P32
Nefyn 32 G25
Neidpath Castle 61 K17
Neilston 60 G16
Neist Point 76 Z11
Nelson (Caerffili /
   Caerphilly) 18 K29
Nelson (Pendle) 43 N22
Nene (River) 37 T26
Nenthead 55 M19
Nercwys 34 K24
Nereabolls 58 A16
Ness 83 B8
Ness (Loch) 73 G12
Nesscliffe 34 L25
Nestley Marsh 10 P31
Neston 42 K24
Nether Broughton 36 R25
Nether Kellet 48 L21
Nether Langwith 44 Q24
Nether Stowey 8 K30
Nether Wasdale 47 J20
Nether Whitecleuch 61 I17
Netheravon 19 O30
Netherbrae 81 M11
Netherbury 8 L31
Netherend 18 M28
Netherhampton 9 O30
Nethermill 54 J18
Netherthong 43 O23
Netherton 63 N17
Nethertown 86 K7
Netherwitton 56 O18
Nethy Bridge 74 J12
Netley 10 P31
Nettlebed 20 R29
Nettleham 44 S24
Nettleton 45 T23
Nevern 15 F27
Nevis (Glen) 72 E13
Nevis (Loch) 72 C12
New Abbey 53 J19
New Aberdour 81 N11
New Alresford 10 Q30
New Buckenham 31 X26
New Byth 81 N11
New Clipstone 36 Q24
New Cumnock 60 H17
New Deer 81 N11
New Edlington 44 Q23
New Forest National Park ...9 P31
New Galloway 53 H18
New Holland 45 S22
New Hythe 22 V30
New Leeds 81 N11
New Luce 52 F19
New Marske 57 Q20
New Mills 43 O23
New Mills (Powys) 33 K26
New Milton 9 P31
New Pitsligo 81 N11
New Quay / Ceinewydd 24 G27
New Rackheath 39 Y26

New Radnor 26 K27
New Romney 12 W31
New Rossington 44 Q23
New Sauchie 67 I15
New Scone 68 J14
New Silksworth 57 P19
New Tredegar 18 K28
New Waltham 45 T23
Newark-on-Trent 36 R24
Newbiggin (Eden) 55 L19
Newbiggin (Teesdale) 55 N20
Newbiggin-by-the-Sea 56 P18
Newbigging (Angus) 69 L14
Newbigging (South
   Lanarkshire) 61 J16
Newbold Verdon 36 P26
Newborough (East
   Staffordshire) 35 O25
Newborough (Isle of
   Anglesey) 32 G24
Newbridge (Caerffili /
   Caerphilly) 18 K29
Newbridge (Isle of Wight) .10 P31
Newbridge-on-Wye 25 J27
Newbrough 55 N18
Newburgh
   (Aberdeenshire) 81 N12
Newburgh (Fife) 68 K14
Newburgh (Lancashire) 42 L23
Newburn 56 O19
Newbury 20 Q29
Newby Bridge 48 L21
Newby Hall 50 P21
Newcastle (Monmouthshire
   / Sir Fynwy) 18 L28
Newcastle (South
   Shropshire) 26 K26
Newcastle Emlyn / Castell
   Newydd Emlyn 15 G27
Newcastle-under-Lyme 35 N24
Newcastle-upon-Tyne 56 P19
Newcastle-upon-Tyne
   Airport 56 O18
Newcastleton 55 L18
Newchapel 15 G27
Newchurch
   (Carmarthenshire / Sir
   Gaerfyrddin) 15 G28
Newchurch (Isle of Wight) .10 Q32
Newchurch (Powys) 26 K27
Newchurch (Shepway) 12 W30
Newdigate 11 T30
Newent 27 M28
Newgale 14 E28
Newhall 34 M24
Newham (Isle of Wight) 63 O17
Newham (London
   Borough) 21 U29
Newhaven 11 U31
Newick 11 U31
Newington 22 V29
Newland 18 M28
Newlyn 2 D33
Newmachar 75 N12
Newmains 61 I16
Newmarket (Isle of Lewis) .82 A9
Newmarket (Suffolk) 30 V27
Newmill (Moray) 80 L11
Newmill (Scottish Borders) .62 L17

Newmilns 60 G17
Newnham (Daventry) 28 Q27
Newnham (Glos.) 18 M28
Newnham (Kent) 22 W30
Newnham Bridge 26 M27
Newport (Essex) 30 U28
Newport (I.O.W.) 10 Q31
Newport (Pembrokes) 15 F27
Newport (Stroud) 19 M28
Newport (Telford and
   Wrekin) 35 M25
Newport / Casnewydd
   (Newport) 18 L29
Newport-on-Tay 69 L14
Newport Pagnell 28 R27
Newquay 2 E32
Newsham 49 O20
Newstead 36 Q24
Newstead Abbey 36 Q24
Newton (Aberdeenshire) ...81 O11
Newton (Argyll and Bute) ..65 E15
Newton (Babergh) 30 W27
Newton (Moray) 80 J11
Newton (Ribble Valley) 49 M22
Newton (Rushcliffe) 36 R25
Newton Abbot 4 J32
Newton Arlosh 54 K19
Newton-Aycliffe 56 P20
Newton Ferrers 4 H33
Newton Flotman 39 X26
Newton-le-Willows 42 M23
Newton Longville 28 R28
Newton Mearns 60 H16
Newton-on-Rawcliffe 50 R21
Newton-on-Trent 44 R24
Newton Poppleford 5 K31
Newton Reigny 55 L19
Newton St. Cyres 7 J31
Newton Stewart 52 G19
Newton Tracey 7 H30
Newton Wamphray 54 J18
Newtongrange 61 K16
Newtonhill 75 N12
Newtonmore 73 H12
Newtown
   (Cheshire) 43 N23
Newtown (Heref.) 26 M27
Newtown
   (Highland) 73 F12
Newtown (Isle of Man) 46 G21
Newtown / Drenewydd
   (Powys) 26 K26
Newtown Linford 36 Q25
Newtown St. Boswells 62 L17
Newtyle 68 K14
Neyland 16 F28
Nicholaston 15 H29
Nigg 79 H10
Nigg Bay 79 H10
Nine Ladies 35 P24
Ninebanks 55 M19
Ninfield 12 V31
Nisbet 62 M17
Nith (River) 53 J19
Niths 61 I18
Niton 10 Q32

Nocton 37 S24
Nolton 14 E28
Nordelph 38 U26
Norfolk Broads 39 Y25
Norham 63 N16
Normanby 50 R21
Normandy 21 S30
Normanton 43 P22
Normanton-on-the-
   Wolds 36 Q25
North Baddesley 10 P31
North Ballachulish 72 E13
North Berwick 69 L15
North Bovey 4 I32
North Bradley 19 N30
North Brentor 4 H32
North Cadbury 8 M30
North Cave 44 S22
North-Cerney 19 O28
North-Charlton 63 O17
North Cliffe 44 R22
North Cowton 50 P20
North Crawley 29 S27

North Creake 38 W25
North Curry 8 L30
North Dalton 51 S22
North Deighton 50 P22
North Erradale 77 C10
North Esk (Riv.) 75 L13
North Fearns 77 B11
North Foreland 23 Y29
North Frodingham 51 T22
North Grimston 51 R21
North Harris 82 Z10
North Hill 3 G32
North Hinksey 20 Q28
North
   Holmwood 21 T30
North Hykeham 37 S24
North Kelsey 45 S23
North Kessock 79 H11
North Kyme 37 T24
North Leigh 20 P28
North-Molton 7 I30
North Morar 72 C13
North Newbald 44 S22

North Nibley 19 M29
North Otterington 50 P21
North Petherton 8 K30
North Petherwin 6 G31
North Rigton 50 P22
North Ronaldsay 87 M5
North-Scarle 36 R24
North-Shian 65 D14
North Shields 56 P18
North Shore 42 K22
North Somercotes 45 U23
North Sound
   (The) 87 L6
North Stainley 50 P21
North Stainmore 49 N20
North Sunderland 63 P17
North Tamerton 6 G31
North-Tawton 7 I31
North Thoresby 45 T23
North Tidworth 19 P30
North Uist 76 X11
North Walsham 39 Y25
North Warnborough 20 R30

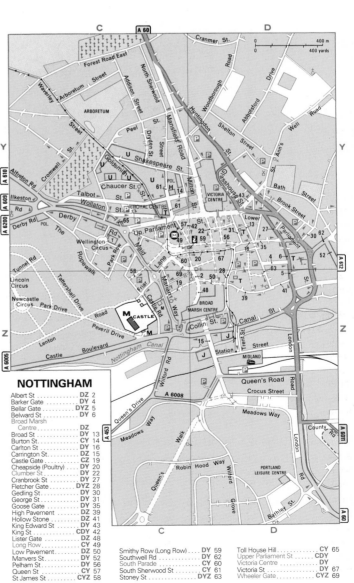

NOTTINGHAM

Albert St .... DZ 2
Barker Gate .... DY 4
Bellar Gate .... DYZ 5
Belward St .... DY 6
Broad Marsh
   Centre .... DZ
Broad St .... DY 13
Burton St .... CY 14
Carlton St .... DY 16
Carrington St .... CZ 19
Castle Gate .... DY 20
Cheapside (Poultry) . DY 22
Clumber St .... DY 27
Cranbrook St .... DY
Fletcher Gate .... DYZ 28
Gedling St .... DY 30
George St .... DY 31
Goose Gate .... DY 35
High Pavement ...... DZ 39
Hollow Stone .... DZ 41
King Edward St ..... DY 43
King St .... CDY 42
Lister Gate .... DZ 48
Long Row .... CY 49
Low Pavement ...... DY 50
Manvers St .... DY 52
Pelham St .... DY 56
Queen St .... DY 57
St James St .... CYZ 58

Smithy Row (Long Row) .... DY 59
Southwell Rd .... DY 62
South Parade .... CY 60
South Sherwood St .... CY 61
Stoney St .... DYZ 63

Toll House Hill .... CY 65
Upper Parliament St ...... CDY
Victoria Centre .... DY
Victoria St .... DY 67
Wheeler Gate .... CYZ 69

OXFORD

Blue Boar St	BY 2
Broad St	BZ 3
Castle St	BZ 5
Clarendon Shopping Centre	BZ
Cornmarket St	BZ 6
George St	BZ 9
High St	BZ
Hythe Bridge St	BZ 12

Little Clarendon St	BY 13
Logic Lane	BZ 14
Magdalen St	BYZ 16
Magpie Lane	BZ 17
New Inn Hall St	BZ 20
Norfolk St	BZ 21
Old Greyfriars St	BZ 23
Oriel Square	BZ 24
Park End St	BZ 30

Pembroke St	BZ 31
Queen St	BZ 32
Queen's Lane	BZ 33
Radcliffe Square	BZ 35
St Michael St	BZ 40
Turl St	BZ 41
Walton Crescent	BY 42
Westgate Shopping Centre	BZ
Worcester St	BZ 47

COLLEGES

All Souls	BZ A
Balliol	BY
Brasenose	BZ B
Christ Church	BZ
Corpus Christi	BZ D
Exeter	BZ
Hertford	BZ E
Jesus	BZ

Keble	BY
Linacre	BY N
Lincoln	BZ
Magdalen	BZ
Merton	BZ
New	BZ
Nuffield	BZ P
Oriel	BZ F
Pembroke	BZ Q
Queen's	BZ

St Catherine's	BY
St Cross	BY R
St Edmund Hall	BZ V
St Hilda's	BZ K
St John's	BY W
Sommerville	BY
Trinity	BZ Y
University	BZ L
Wadham	BY Z
Worcester	BY

OXFORD

200 m
200 yards

Ashmolean Museum	BY M1
Bodleian Library	BZ A1
Pitt Rivers Museum	BY M3
Radcliffe Camera	BZ P1

St Peter's	BZ X
Sheldonian Theatre	BYZ T
University Museum of Natural History	BY M4

North Water Bridge	75	M13
North Weald Bassett	22	U28
North Wootton	38	V25
North York Moors National Park	50	R20
Northallerton	50	P20
Northam	6	H30
Northampton	28	R27
Northaw	21	T28
Northchapel	11	S30
Northchurch	21	S28
Northfleet	22	V29
Northiam	12	V31
Northleach	19	O28
Northleigh	5	K31
Northlew	7	H31
Northop	34	K24
Northrepps	39	Y25
Northton	76	Y10

Northumberland National Park	63	N18
Northwich	42	M24
Northwold	38	V26
Northwood	34	L25
Norton (Daventry)	28	Q27
Norton (Doncaster)	44	Q23
Norton (Ryedale)	50	R21
Norton (Tewkesbury)	27	N28
Norton Disney	36	R24
Norton Fitzwarren	8	K30
Norton in Hales	35	M25
Norton St. Philip	19	N30
Norwich	39	X26
Norwick	87	R1
Noss (Isle of)	87	Q3
Noss Head	86	K8
Nottingham	36	Q25
Nuffield	20	Q29

Nunburnholme	51	R22
Nuneaton	28	P26
Nuneham Courtenay	20	Q28
Nunney	19	M30
Nunthorpe	50	Q20
Nunton	76	X11
Nutley	11	U30
Nympsfield	19	N28

O

Oa (The)	58	B17
Oadby	36	Q26
Oakamoor	35	O24
Oakdale	18	K28
Oakengates	35	M25
Oakford	7	J31
Oakham	36	R25

Oakhill	18	M30
Oakington	29	U27
Oakley (Aylesbury Vale)	20	Q28
Oakley (Bedfordshire)	29	S27
Oakley (Fife)	68	J15
Oaksey	19	N29
Oakworth	43	O22
Oare (Kennet)	19	O29
Oare (Swale)	22	W30
Oare (West Somerset)	17	I30
Oathlaw	74	L13
Oban	65	D14
Occold	31	X27
Ochil Hills	68	I15
Ochiltree	60	G17
Ockbrook	36	P25
Ockle	71	C13
Ockley	11	S30
Odiham	20	R30
Odland	18	M29
Odstock	9	O30
Offa's Dyke Path	26	K26
Offord Cluny	29	T27
Ogbourne St. Andrew	19	O29
Ogbourne St. George	19	O29
Ogil	74	L13
Ogle	56	O18
Ogmore-by-Sea	17	J29
Ogmore Vale	17	J29
Oich (Loch)	73	F12
Oidhche (Loch na h-)	78	D11
Oigh-Sgeir	71	Z13
Okeford Fitzpaine	9	N31
Okehampton	4	H31
Old Alresford	10	Q30
Old Bolingbroke	37	U24
Old Burghclere	20	Q30
Old Castleton	55	L18
Old Colwyn	41	I23
Old Dailly	59	F18
Old Deer	81	N11
Old Fletton	37	T26
Old Harry Rocks	9	O32
Old Head	87	L7
Old Hurst	29	T26
Old Hutton	48	L21
Old Kilpatrick	67	G16
Old Knebworth	29	T28
Old Leake	37	U24
Old Man of Hoy	86	J7
Old Man of Storr	77	B11
Old Radnor	26	K27
Old Rayne	81	M11
Old' Sarum	9	O30
Old Sodbury	19	M29
Old Somerby	37	S25
Old Warden	29	S27
Old Windsor	21	S29
Oldany Island	84	E9
Oldbury	27	N26
Oldbury on Severn	18	M29
Oldcotes	44	Q23
Oldham	43	N23

Oldhamstocks	69	M16
Oldmeldrum	81	N11
Oldshoremore	84	E8
Olgrinmore	85	J8
Ollaberry	87	P2
Ollach	77	B11
Ollay (Loch)	76	X12
Ollerton (Macclesfield)	42	M24
Ollerton (Newark and Sherwood)	36	Q24
Olney	28	R27
Olveston	18	M29
Ombersley	27	N27
Once Brewed	55	M19
Onchan	46	G21
Onecote	35	O24
Onich	72	E13
Onllwyn	17	I28
Opinan	83	D10
Orchy (Glen)	66	F14
Ord	71	C12
Ordie	74	L12
Orford	31	Y27
Orford Ness	31	Y27
Orkney Islands	87	
Orleton	26	L27
Ormesby	50	Q20
Ormesby St. Margaret	39	Z25
Ormiston	62	L16
Ormskirk	42	L23
Oronsay	64	B15
Orosay (near Fuday)	70	X12
Orosay (near Lochboisdale)	70	X12
Orphir	86	K7
Orrin (Glen)	78	F11
Orrin Reservoir	78	F11
Orsay	58	A16
Orsett	22	V29
Orston	36	R25
Orton	48	M20
Orwell	29	T27
Orwell (River)	31	X28
Osborne House	10	Q31
Osdale	77	A11
Osgaig (Loch)	83	E9
Osgodby	45	S23
Oskaig	77	B11
Osmington	9	M32
Ossett	43	P22
Ossington	36	R24
Oswaldtwistle	42	M22
Oswestry	34	K25
Otford	22	U30
Othery	8	L30
Otley (Suffolk)	31	X27
Otley (West Yorks.)	49	O22
Otterbourne	10	P30
Otterburn	55	N18
Otternish	76	Y10
Otterswick	87	Q2
Otterton	5	K32
Ottery St. Mary	5	K31
Ottringham	45	T22

Oulton Broad	39	Z26
Oulton Park Circuit	34	M24
Oundle	29	S26
Ouse (River) (English Channel)	11	T30
Ouse (River) (North Sea)	50	Q21
Out-Rawcliffe	42	L22
Out Skerries	87	R2
Outer Hebrides	82	Y9
Outhgill	49	M20
Outwell	38	U26
Over	29	U27
Over Compton	8	M31
Overseal	35	P25
Overstrand	39	Y25
Overton (Hants.)	20	Q30
Overton (Lancs.)	48	L21
Overton (Wrexham)	34	L25
Overtown	61	I16
Ower	10	P31
Owermoigne	9	N32
Owlswick	20	R28
Owslebury	10	Q30
Owston	36	R26
Owston Ferry	44	R23
Oxburgh Hall	38	V26
Oxen Park	48	K21
Oxenhope	43	O22
Oxford	20	Q28
Oxnam	62	M17
Oxted	21	T30
Oxton (Newark and Sherwood)	36	Q24
Oxton (Scottish Borders)	62	L16
Oxwich	15	H29
Oxwich Bay	15	H29
Oykel (Glen)	84	F9
Oykel Bridge	84	F10
Oyne	81	M12

P

Pabay	77	C12
Pabbay (near Harris)	76	Y10
Pabbay (near Mingulay)	70	X13
Pabbay (Sound of)	76	Y10
Packington	36	P25
Padbury	28	R28
Paddock Wood	22	V30
Paddockhole	54	K18
Padiham	42	N22
Padstow	3	F32
Pagham	10	R31
Paignton	4	J32
Pailton	28	Q26
Painscastle	26	K27
Painswick	19	N28
Paisley	60	G16
Pakefield	31	Z26
Palnackie	53	I19
Pamber End	20	Q30
Pandy (Monmouthshire / Sir Fynwy)	26	L28
Pandy (Powys)	33	J26

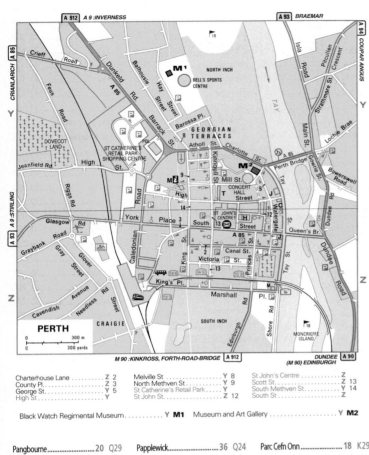

PERTH

Charterhouse Lane . . . . Z 2
County Pl. . . . . Z 3
George St. . . . . Y 5
High St . . . . Y
Melville St . . . . Y 8
North Methven St. . . . . Y 9
St Catherine's Retail Park . . . Y
St John St . . . . Z 12
Scott St. . . . . Z 13
South Methven St. . . . . Y 14
South St . . . . Z

Black Watch Regimental Museum . . . . Y M1   Museum and Art Gallery . . . . Y M2

Pangbourne 20 Q29
Pant 34 K25
Pantymenyn 15 F28
Papa Stour 87 O3
Papa Westray 87 L5
Papplewick 36 Q24
Paps of Jura 65 B16
Papworth Everard 29 T27
Parbh (The) 84 F8
Parbold 42 L23
Parc Cefn Onn 18 K29
Parham House 11 S31
Park Gate 10 Q31
Park of Pairc 82 A9
Parkeston 31 X28

Parkgate 53 J18
Parkhurst 10 Q31
Parnham House 8 L31
Parracombe 17 I30
Parrett (River) 8 K30
Parson Drove 37 U26
Partney 37 U24
Parton (Copeland) 54 J20
Parton (Dumfries and
Galloway) 53 H18
Partridge Green 11 T31
Parwich 35 O24
Patchway 18 M29
Pateley Bridge 49 O21
Path of Condie 68 J15
Pathhead 62 L16
Patna 60 G17
Patrick 46 F21
Patrington 45 T22
Patrixbourne 23 X30
Patterdale 48 L20
Pattingham 35 N26
Pattishall 28 Q27
Paulerspury 28 R27
Paull 45 T22
Paulton 18 M30
Paxton 63 N16
Peacehaven 11 T31
Peak District
National Park 43 O23
Pearsie 74 K13
Peasedown St. John 19 M30
Peasemore 20 P29
Peasenhall 31 Y27
Peaslake 21 S30
Peasmarsh 12 W31
Peat Inn 69 L15

Peatknowe 81 M11
Pebmarsh 30 W28
Pebworth 27 O27
Peebles 61 K17
Peel 46 F21
Peel Fell 62 M18
Pegswood 56 P18
Pegwell Bay 23 Y30
Peinchorran 77 B12
Peldon 22 W28
Pelton 56 P19
Pelynt 3 G32
Pembrey 15 H28
Pembridge 26 L27
Pembroke / Penfro 16 F28
Pembroke Dock / Doc
Penfro 16 F28
Pembrokeshire Coast
National Park 15 F29
Pembury 12 V30
Pen-y-bont / Bridgend . . . 17 J29
Pen-y-groes 32 H24
Penalun 15 F29
Penarth 18 K29
Pencader 15 H27
Pencaitland 62 L16
Pencarrow 3 F32
Penclawdd 15 H29
Pencombe 26 M27
Penderyn 17 J28
Pendine 15 G28
Pendine Sands 15 G28
Pendlebury 42 N23
Pendoylan 17 J29
Penelewey 2 E33
Penfro / Pembroke 16 F28
Pengethley 26 M28

Penhow 18 L29
Penicuik 61 K16
Penifiler 77 B11
Peninver 59 D17
Penistone 43 P23
Penketh 42 L23
Penkridge 35 N25
Penley 34 L25
Penmaen 15 H29
Penmaenmawr 41 I23
Penmaenpool 33 I25
Penmark 17 J29
Penmon 40 H23
Pennal 33 I26
Pennant 33 J26
Pennerley 34 L26
Pennines (The) 49 N20
Pennyghael 65 B14
Penpont 53 I18
Penrhiwpal 15 G27
Penrhyn 40 H23
Penrhyn Bay 41 I23
Penrhyndeudraeth 33 H25
Penrith 55 L19
Penruddock 55 L20
Penryn 2 E33
Pensarn 41 I23
Penshaw 56 P19
Penshurst 22 U30
Pensilva 3 G32
Pentewan 3 F33
Pentire Point 3 F32
Pentland Firth 86 K7
Pentland Hills 61 J16
Pentland Skerries 87 L7
Pentraeth 40 H23
Pentre-Berw 40 H23
Pentre-
Celyn 34 K24
Pentrebeirdd 34 K25
Penwith 2 D33
Penybont 26 K27
Penysarn 40 H22
Penzance 2 D33
Pernrhyncoch 25 I26
Perranaworthal 2 E33
Perranporth 2 E32
Perranzabuloe 2 E33
Pershore 27 N27
Pertenhall 29 S27
Perth 68 J14
Peterborough 37 T26
Peterculter 75 N12
Peterhead 81 O11
Peterlee 57 P19
Petersfield 10 R30
Peterstone Wentlooge . . 18 K29
Peterstow 26 M28
Petham 23 X30
Petrockstowe 7 H31
Pett 12 V31
Pettaugh 31 X27
Petworth 11 S31
Pevensey Bay 12 V31

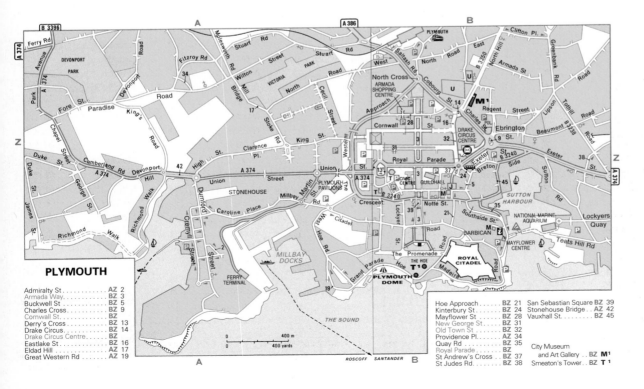

PLYMOUTH

Admiralty St . . . . AZ 2
Armada Way . . . . BZ 3
Buckwell St . . . . BZ 5
Charles Cross . . . . BZ 9
Cornwall St. . . . . BZ
Derry's Cross . . . . BZ 13
Drake Circus . . . . BZ 14
Drake Circus Centre . . . BZ
Eastlake St . . . . BZ 16
Eldad Hill . . . . AZ 17
Great Western Rd . . . . . AZ 19
Hoe Approach . . . . . . BZ 21
Kinterbury St . . . . . . BZ 24
Mayflower St . . . . . BZ 28
New George St . . . . BZ 31
Old Town St . . . . . BZ 32
Providence Pl. . . . . AZ 34
Quay Rd . . . . BZ 35
Royal Parade . . . . . BZ
St Andrew's Cross . . BZ 37
St Judes Rd . . . . . . BZ 38
San Sebastian Square BZ 39
Stonehouse Bridge . . AZ 42
Vauxhall St . . . . . BZ 45

City Museum
and Art Gallery . . BZ M1
Smeaton's Tower . . BZ T1

PORTSMOUTH AND SOUTHSEA

Alec Rose Lane	CY	2
Arundel St	CY	5
Bellevue Terrace	CZ	6
Cambridge Junction	BY	7
Cascade Centre	CY	
Commercial Rd.	CY	
Eldon St	CY	10
Great Southsea St	CZ	15
Guildhall Walk	CY	17
Gunwharf Quay Shopping Centre	BY	
Hampshire Terrace	CY	18
Hard (The)	BY	20
High St	BYZ	21
Isambard Brunel Rd	CY	22
Kings Road Roundabout	CY	23
Landport Terrace	CY	25
Lombard St	BYZ	29
Main Rd.	BY	31
Norfolk St	CYZ	32
Ordnance Row	BY	34
Palmerston Rd	CZ	
Paradise St	CY	35
Penny St	BZ	36
Pier Road Roundabout	CY	37
St George's Square	BY	39
St Michael's Rd.	CY	41
Southsea Terrace	CZ	43
Spring St	CY	45
Stanhope Rd	CY	48
Unicorn Rd	CY	49
Warblington St	BY	53
White Hart Rd	BYZ	57
Wiltshire St	CY	59

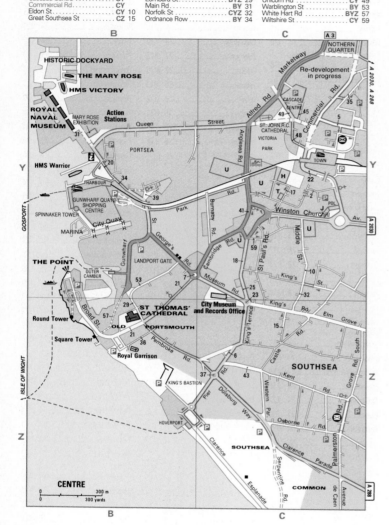

Pewsey	19	O29	
Pickering	50	R21	
Picklescott	34	L26	
Picton Castle	16	F28	
Piddlehinton	9	M31	
Piddletrenthide	9	M31	
Piercebridge	49	O20	
Pierowall	86	L6	
Pilgrims Hatch	22	U29	
Pillerton Hersey	28	P27	
Pillerton Priors	27	P27	
Pilley	43	P23	
Pilling	48	L22	
Pilning	18	M29	
Pilton	8	M30	
Pinchbeck	37	T25	
Pinchbeck-West	37	T25	
Pinhoe	4	J31	
Pinmore Mains	52	F18	
Pinner	21	S29	
Pinvin	27	N27	
Pinwherry	52	F18	
Pinxton	36	Q24	
Pirbright	21	S30	
Pirnmill	59	D17	
Pirton	29	T28	
Pishill	20	R29	
Pitcaple	81	M12	
Pitcombe	8	M30	
Pitcur	68	K14	
Pitlochry	74	I13	
Pitmedden	81	N11	
Pitminster	8	K31	
Pitscottie	69	L15	
Pitsford	28	R27	
Pittentrail	85	H10	
Pittenween	69	L15	
Pladda	59	E17	
Plaistow	11	S30	
Plas Newydd (Anglesey)	33	H24	
Plas Newydd (Denbighshire)	34	K25	
Plean	67	I15	
Pleasington	42	M22	
Pleasley	36	Q24	
Plenmeller	55	M19	
Plockton	78	D11	
Pluckley	22	W30	
Plumbland	54	K19	
Plumpton	11	T31	
Plympton	4	H32	
Plymouth	4	H32	
Plymstock	4	H32	
Plymtree	7	J31	
Plynlimon (Pumlumon Fawr)	25	I26	
Pocklington	50	R22	
Point Lynas	40	H22	
Point of Ayr (Flintshire)	41	K22	
Point of Ayre (Isle of Man)	46	G20	
Polbain	83	D9	
Pole of Itlaw (The)	81	M11	
Polebrook	29	S26	
Polegate	12	U31	
Polesden Lacey	21	S30	
Polesworth	35	P26	
Polkerris	3	F32	
Polloch	72	D13	
Pollock House	60	H16	
Polmont	67	I16	
Polperro	3	G33	
Polruan	3	G33	
Polwarth	62	M16	
Pondersbridge	29	T26	
Pont-ar-Gothi	15	H28	
Pontardawe	17	I28	
Pontarddulais	15	H28	
Pontarfynach / Devil's Bridge	25	I26	
Pontargothi	15	H28	
Pontarsais	15	H28	
Pontefract	44	Q22	
Ponteland	56	O18	
Ponterwyd	25	I26	
Pontesbury	34	L26	
Pontlottyn	18	K28	
Pontlyfni	32	G24	
Pontneddfechan	17	J28	
Pontrhydfendigaid	25	I27	
Pontrhydygroes	25	I26	
Pontrilas	26	L28	
Pontsticill	17	J28	
Pontyates	15	H28	
Pontyberem	15	H28	
Pontyclun	17	J29	
Pontycymer	17	J29	
Pontypool / Pontypŵl	18	K28	
Pontypridd	17	J29	
Pontypŵl / Pontypool	18	K28	
Poole	9	O31	
Poole Bay	9	O31	
Poolewe	78	D10	
Pooley Bridge	55	L20	
Pooltiel (Loch)	76	Z11	
Porlock	17	J30	
Port Appin	65	D14	
Port Askaig	58	B16	
Port Bannatyne	59	E16	
Port Carlisle	54	K19	
Port Charlotte	58	A16	
Port Driseach	65	E16	
Port Ellen	58	B17	
Port Erin	46	F21	
Port-Eynon	15	H29	
Port-Eynon Point	15	H29	
Port Gaverne	3	F32	
Port Glasgow	66	F16	
Port Henderson	77	C10	
Port Isaac	3	F32	
Port Lamont	59	E16	
Port Logan	52	F19	
Port Mór	71	B13	
Port of Menteith	67	H15	
Port of Ness	83	B8	
Port Ramsay	65	D14	
Port St. Mary	46	F21	
Port Talbot	17	I29	
Port William	52	G19	
Portavadie	59	E16	
Portchester	10	Q31	
Portencross	59	F16	
Portesham	5	M31	
Portgordon	80	K11	
Portgower	85	I9	
Porth	17	J29	
Porth Neigwl or Hell's Mouth	32	G25	
Porth Tywyn / Burry Port	15	H28	
Porthaethwy / Menai Bridge	40	H23	
Porthcawl	17	I29	
Porthcothan	2	E32	
Porthcurno	2	D33	
Porthgwarra	2	C33	
Porthkerry	17	K29	
Porthleven	2	E33	
Porthmadog	33	H25	
Porthtowan	2	E33	
Porthyrhyd	15	H28	
Portinnisherrich	65	E15	
Portishead	18	L29	
Portknockie	80	L10	
Portland (Isle of)	8	M32	
Portlethen	75	N12	
Portmahomack	79	I10	
Portmeirion	33	H25	
Portnacroish	72	D14	
Portnaguran	83	B9	
Portnahaven	58	A16	
Portnalong	77	A12	
Portobello	68	K16	
Portreath	2	E33	
Portree	77	B11	
Portscatho	3	F33	
Portskerra	85	I8	
Portskewett	18	L29	
Portslade	11	T31	
Portslogan	52	E19	
Portsmouth	10	Q31	
Portsoy	81	L10	
Portuairk	71	B13	
Postbridge	4	I32	
Potten End	21	S28	
Potter Heigham	39	Y25	
Potter Street	21	U28	
Potterhanworth	37	S24	
Potterne	19	N30	
Potters Bar	21	T28	
Potton	29	T27	
Poughill	6	G31	
Poulshot	19	N29	
Poulton	19	O28	
Poulton-le-Fylde	42	L22	
Poundstock	6	G31	
Powburn	63	O17	
Powerstock	8	L31	
Powick	27	N27	
Powis	34	K26	
Powmill	68	J15	
Poynings	11	T31	
Poynton	43	N23	
Praa Sands	2	D33	
Prawle Point	4	I33	
Praze-an-Beeble	2	E33	
Prees	34	M25	
Preesall	48	L22	
Prendwick	63	O17	
Prescot	42	L23	
Prestatyn	41	J22	
Prestbury (Cheltenham)	27	N28	
Prestbury (Macclesfield)	43	N24	
Presteigne	26	K27	
Preston (East Riding of Yorks.)	45	T22	
Preston (Kent)	23	X30	
Preston (Lancs.)	42	L22	
Preston (Rutland)	36	R26	
Preston (West Sussex)	11	S31	
Preston Candover	10	Q30	
Preston Capes	28	Q27	
Prestonpans	69	L16	
Prestwich	42	N23	
Prestwick	60	G17	
Prestwood	20	R28	
Prickwillow	30	V26	
Priest Island	83	D10	
Priest Weston	34	K26	
Princes Risborough	20	R28	
Princethorpe	28	P26	
Princetown	4	I32	
Priors Marston	28	Q27	
Probus	3	F33	
Prosen (Glen)	74	K13	
Prudhoe	56	O19	
Puckeridge	29	U28	
Pucklechurch	19	M29	
Pucks Gutter	23	X30	
Puddletown	9	M31	
Pudsey	43	P22	
Pulborough	11	S31	
Pulford	34	L24	
Pulham	9	M31	
Pulham Market	31	X26	
Punchardon	7	H30	
Puncheston	24	F28	
Purbeck (Isle of)	9	N32	
Purbrook	10	Q31	
Puriton	8	L30	
Purleigh	22	V28	
Purley	20	Q29	
Purse Caundle Manor	9	M31	
Purston Jaglin	43	P22	
Purton	19	O29	
Putsborough	6	H30	
Pwllheli	32	G25	
Pyecombe	11	T31	
Pyle	17	I29	
Pylle	8	M30	

Q

Quainton	28	R28	
Quantock Hills	8	K30	
Quarff	87	Q3	
Quarr	10	Q31	

Quatt.................................27 M26
Quedgeley.........................19 N28
Queen Camel.......................8 M30
Queen Elizabeth Forest
  Park..............................67 G15
Queenborough...................22 W29
Queensbury.......................43 O22
Queensferry......................34 K24
Quendon...........................30 U28
Quenington........................19 O28
Quinag..............................84 E9
Quines's Hill.....................46 G21
Quinish Point.....................71 B14
Quiraing...........................77 B11
Quoich (Loch)....................72 E12
Quorndon..........................36 Q25
Quothquan........................61 J17

R

Raasay (Island of)..............77 B11
Raasay (Sound of)..............77 B11
Raasay Ho.........................77 B11
Rachub.............................33 H24
Rackenford.........................7 J31
Rackwick...........................86 J7
Radcliffe...........................42 N23
Radcliffe-on-Trent..............36 Q25
Radlett.............................21 T28
Radley..............................20 Q28
Radnor Forest....................26 K27
Radstock...........................18 M30
Radyr...............................18 K29
Rafford.............................80 J11
Raglan..............................18 L28
Ragley Hall........................27 O27
Rainford............................42 L23

Rainham............................22 V29
Rainworth.........................36 Q24
Rait.................................68 K14
Ramasaig...........................76 Z11
Rampisham..........................8 M31
Rampside...........................47 K21
Rampton............................44 R24
Ramsbottom........................42 N23
Ramsbury...........................19 P29
Ramsey (Cambs.).................29 T26
Ramsey (Isle of Man)...........46 G21
Ramsey Bay........................46 G21
Ramsey Island.....................14 D28
Ramsey St. Mary's...............29 T26
Ramsgate...........................23 Y29
Ramsgill-in-Nidderdale........49 O21
Ranby...............................44 Q24
Ranfurly............................60 G16
Rangeworthy......................18 M29
Ranish.............................82 A9
Rankinston........................60 G17
Rannoch (Loch)..................73 H13
Rannoch Moor.....................73 F14
Rannoch Sta......................73 G13
Ranskill............................44 Q23
Ranton..............................35 N25
Ranworth...........................39 Y25
Rapness............................87 L6
Rappach............................84 F10
Ratby...............................36 Q26
Rathen..............................81 O11
Rathmell...........................49 N21
Ratho...............................68 J16
Ratlinghope.......................34 L26
Rattlesden.........................30 W27
Rattray.............................68 K14
Rattray Head......................81 O11

Raunds.............................29 S26
Ravenglass........................47 J20
Ravenscar..........................51 S20
Ravensthorpe.....................28 Q27
Ravenstone........................36 P25
Ravenstonedale...................49 M20
Ravensworth.......................49 O20
Rawcliffe...........................44 R22
Rawmarsh..........................44 P23
Rawtenstall........................42 N22
Rayleigh............................22 V29
Rayne...............................30 V28
Read................................42 M22
Reading.............................20 R29
Rearsby............................36 Q25
Reay...............................85 I8
Reay Forest.......................84 F9
Reculver............................23 X29
Red Wharf Bay....................40 H23
Redbourn..........................21 S28
Redbourne.........................44 S23
Redbridge (London
  Borough)........................21 U29
Redcar.............................57 Q20
Redcliff Bay......................18 L29
Reddding...........................67 I16
Redditch...........................27 O27
Redesmouth........................55 N18
Redford.............................69 L14
Redhill (North
  Somerset).......................18 L29
Redhill (Reigate and
  Banstead).......................21 T30
Redisham...........................31 Y26
Redmarley
  d'Abitot........................27 M28
Redmarshall.......................57 P20
Redmire............................49 O21
Redpoint...........................77 C11

Redruth.............................2 E33
Redwick............................18 L29
Reedham............................39 Y26
Reekie Linn........................74 K13
Reepham............................45 S24
Reeth...............................49 O20
Regarby............................46 G20
Reiff...............................83 D9
Reigate.............................21 T30
Reighton............................51 T21
Reiss...............................86 K8
Relubbus............................2 D33
Rempstone.........................36 Q25
Rendcomb..........................19 O28
Rendham............................31 Y27
Renfrew.............................60 G16
Renish Point......................76 Z10
Renishaw............................44 P24
Rennington........................63 O17
Renton..............................66 G16
Renwick............................55 M19
Repps...............................36 P25
Repton.............................36 P25
Rescobie............................75 L14
Resipole............................72 C13
Resolven............................17 I28
Resort (Loch)......................82 Z9
Restalrig............................68 K16
Reston..............................63 N16
Restormel Castle...................3 G32
Retford..............................44 R24
Rettendon..........................22 V29
Reynoldston.......................15 H29
Rhaeadr / Rhayader...............25 J27
Rhaeadr Ddu.......................33 I25
Rhandirmwyn.......................25 I27
Rhayader / Rhaeadr...............25 J27
Rheidol (Vale of).................25 I26
Rhenigidale........................82 Z10
Rhian...............................84 G9
Rhiconich..........................84 F8
Rhigos..............................17 J28
Rhilochan..........................85 H9
Rhinns of Galloway
  (The)............................52 E19
Rhinns of Kells...................53 G18
Rhondda............................17 J29
Rhoose..............................17 J29
Rhos...............................17 I28
Rhoscolyn..........................40 G23
Rhoscrowther......................14 E28
Rhosllanerchrugog................34 K24
Rhosmaen..........................25 I28
Rhosneigr..........................40 G23
Rhossili............................15 H29
Rhostyllen.........................34 K24
Rhosybol............................40 G22
Rhu.................................66 F15
Rhuddlan...........................41 J23
Rhum...............................71 A13
Rhuthun / Ruthin.................34 K24
Rhyd-Ddu...........................33 H24
Rhydaman / Ammanford..........15 I28
Rhydcymerau......................15 H27
Rhydd...............................27 N27

Rhyddhywel........................25 J26
Rhydowen..........................15 H27
Rhyl.................................41 J23
Rhymmi /
  Rhymney.........................18 K28
Rhymney /
  Rhymmi..........................18 K28
Rhynie..............................80 L12
Ribble (River)....................49 N22
Ribblesdale........................49 N21
Ribchester.........................42 M22
Riber Castle.......................36 P24
Riccall..............................44 Q22
Riccarton..........................60 G17
Richards Castle...................26 L27
Richborough.......................23 X30
Richmond...........................49 O20
Richmond-upon-Thames
  (London Borough)..............21 T29
Rickarton..........................75 N13
Rickmansworth...................21 S29
Ridgeway Cross....................27 M27
Ridgeway Path (The)............20 P29
Ridsdale............................55 N18
Rievaulx Abbey...................50 Q21
Rigg.................................77 B11
Rigside.............................61 I17
Rillington..........................51 R21
Rimington..........................49 N22
Rimsdale (Loch)...................85 H9
Ringford............................53 H19
Ringmer............................11 U31
Ringshall..........................30 W27
Ringstead (East
  Northamptonshire)............29 S26
Ringstead (King's Lynn and
  West Norfolk)..................38 V25
Ringwood............................9 O31
Ringwould..........................23 Y30
Rinnes (Glen).....................80 K11
Rinns of Islay.....................58 A16
Rinns Point.......................58 A16
Ripe.................................12 U31
Ripley (Derbs.)...................36 P24
Ripley (North Yorks.)...........50 P21
Ripley (Surrey)...................21 S30
Riplingham.........................44 S22
Ripon...............................50 P21
Rippingale.........................37 S25
Ripponden.........................43 O22
Risabus.............................58 B17
Risby...............................30 V27
Risca...............................18 K29
Risegate............................37 T25
Riseley.............................29 S27
Rishton.............................42 M22
Risplith............................50 P21
Ristol (Isle)......................83 D9
Roadside of Kinneff..............75 N13
Roag................................77 A11
Roag (Loch)........................82 Z9
Roan of Graigoch..................60 F18
Roberton (Dumfries and
  Galloway)........................61 I17
Roberton (Scottish
  Borders).........................62 L17
Robertsbridge....................12 V31

Robin Hood's Bay.................51 S20
Roby...............................42 L23
Rocester............................35 O25
Rochdale............................43 N23
Roche...............................3 F32
Rochester..........................22 V29
Rochester
  (Northumberland).............63 N18
Rochford...........................22 W29
Rock................................3 F32
Rockcliffe (Cumbria)............54 K19
Rockcliffe (Dumfries and
  Galloway).......................53 I19
Rockfield...........................18 L28
Rockingham........................28 R26
Rode................................19 N30
Rode Heath........................35 N24
Rodel...............................76 Z10
Rodmell............................11 U31
Rodney Stoke.....................18 L30
Rogart..............................85 H9
Rogerstone........................18 K29
Rogiet..............................18 L29
Rokeby Hall.......................49 O20
Rolleston (Notts.)...............36 R24
Rolleston-on-Dove
  (Staffs.)........................35 P25
Rolvenden.........................12 V30
Romannobridge....................61 J16
Romiley............................43 N23
Romney Marsh.....................12 W30
Romsey.............................10 P31
Romsley............................27 N26
Rona (Island of)..................77 C11
Ronaldsway........................46 G21
Ronas Voe.........................87 P2
Ronay..............................76 Y11
Rookhope..........................55 N19
Roos...............................45 T22
Rootpark...........................61 I16
Ropley.............................10 Q30
Ropsley............................37 S25
Rora...............................81 O11
Rora Head.........................86 J7
Rosedale Abbey...................50 R20
Rosehearty........................81 N10
Rosemarket........................16 F28
Rosemarkie........................79 H11
Rosewell...........................61 K16
Rosgill.............................48 L20
Roshven...........................71 C13
Rosley..............................54 K19
Roslin...............................61 K16
Rosliston...........................35 P25
Rosneath...........................66 F15
Ross
  (Berwick-upon-Tweed).......63 O17
Ross (Dumfries and
  Galloway).......................53 H19
Ross of Mull.......................64 B15
Ross-on-Wye.......................26 M28
Rossall Point.....................48 K22
Rossett.............................34 L24
Rossudgeon..........................2 D33
Rosyth..............................68 J15
Rothbury............................63 O18

READING

Blagrave St . . . . Y 3
Bridge St . . . . Z 4
Broad St . . . . Y
Broad St Mall Shopping
  Centre . . . . Z
Castle St . . . . Z 6
Chain St . . . . Z 7

Crown St . . . . Z 13
Duke St . . . . Z 15
Greyfriars Rd . . . . Y 17
Gun St . . . . Z 18
King St . . . . Z 20
Mill Lane . . . . Z 21
Minster St . . . . Z 22
Mount Pleasant . . . . Z 23
Oracle Shopping
  Centre . . . . Z

Queen Victoria
  St . . . . Y 28
St Mary's Butts . . . . Z 29
Station Hill . . . . Y 30
Station Rd . . . . Y 31
Tilehurst Rd . . . . Z 33
Tudor Rd . . . . Y 34
Valpy St . . . . Y 37
Watlington St . . . . Z 40
West St . . . . Y 41

Rothbury Forest	63	O18
Rotherfield	12	U30
Rotherham	43	P23
Rothersthorpe	28	R27
Rothes	80	K11
Rothesay	59	E16
Rothienorman	81	M11
Rothiesholm	87	M6
Rothwell (Leeds.)	43	P22
Rothwell (Northamp.)	28	R26
Rotterspury	28	R27
Rottingdean	11	T31
Roughburn	73	F13
Roughsike	55	L18
Roughton	39	X25
Rounton	50	P20
Rousay	86	K6
Rousdon	5	L31
Routh	45	S22
Rowardennan Lodge	66	G15
Rowington	27	O27
Rowland's Castle	10	R31
Rowland's Gill	56	O19
Rownhams	10	P31
Rowsley	35	P24
Roxburgh	62	M17
Roxwell	22	V28
Roy (Glen)	72	F13
Royal Leamington Spa	28	P27
Royal Military Academy	20	R29
Royal Tunbridge Wells	12	U30
Roybridge	72	F13
Roydon (Essex)	21	U28
Roydon (Norfolk)	31	X26
Royston (Herts.)	29	T27
Royston (South Yorks.)	43	P23
Royton	43	N23
Ruabon	34	K25
Ruan High Lanes	3	F33
Ruan Minor	2	E34
Ruardean	18	M28
Rubbha na Faing	58	A16
Rubha a' Mhail	64	B16
Rubha Còigeach	83	D9
Rubha Dubh	70	Z14
Rubha Hunish	77	A10
Rubha na h-Easgainne	71	B12
Rubha Réidh	77	C10
Rubha Suisnish	71	B12
Rubh'an Dùnain	71	A12
Rudbaxton	24	F28
Ruddington	36	Q25
Rudgeway	18	M29
Rudgwick	11	S30
Rudha Ban	70	Y12
Rudston	51	T21
Rufford Old Hall	42	L23
Rufforth	50	Q22
Rugby	28	Q26
Rugeley	35	O25
Rumburgh	31	Y26
Rumney	18	K29
Runcorn	42	L23
Runswick Bay	50	R20
Runtaleave	74	K13
Runwell	22	V29
Rushall	19	O30
Rushden	29	S27
Ruskington	37	S24
Rusland	48	K21
Rusper	11	T30
Ruspidge	18	M28
Rustington	11	S31
Ruswarp	51	S20
Rutherglen	60	H16
Ruthin / Rhuthun	34	K24
Ruthven (Aberdeenshire)	80	L11
Ruthven (Angus)	74	K14
Ruthven (Highland)	79	I11
Ruthven (Loch)	79	H12
Ruthven Barracks	73	H12
Ruthwell	54	J19
Rutland Water	37	S26
Ruyton of the Eleven Towns	34	L25
Ryal	56	O18
Ryan (Loch)	52	E19
Rycote	20	Q28
Rydal	48	L20
Ryde	10	Q31
Rye	12	W31
Ryhall	37	S25
Ryhill	43	P23
Ryhope	57	P19
Ryton	56	O19

S

Sabden	42	M22
Sacriston	56	P19
Sadberge	50	P20
Saddell	59	D17
Saddell Bay	59	D17
Sadgill	48	L20
Saffron Walden	30	U27
Saham Toney	38	W26
St. Abbs	63	N16
St. Abb's Head	63	N16
St. Agnes	2	E33
St. Albans	21	T28
St. Aldhelm's Head	9	N32
St. Andrews	69	L14
St. Ann's	54	J18
St. Ann's Head	14	E28
St. Arvans	18	L29
St. Asaph	41	J23
St. Athan	17	J29
St. Austell	3	F32
St. Bees	47	J20
St. Bees Head	47	J20
St. Blazey	3	F32
St. Boswells	62	M17
St. Breock	3	F32
St. Breward	3	F32
St. Briavels	18	M28
St. Brides	14	E28
St. Bride's Bay	14	E28
St. Brides Major	17	J29
St. Brides-Super-Ely	17	K29
St. Bridge-Wentlooge	18	K29
St. Buryan	2	D33
St. Catherine's Point	10	Q32
St. Clears / Sanclêr	15	G28
St. Cleer	3	G32
St. Columb Major	3	F32
St. Combs	81	O11
St. Cyrus	75	M13
St. David's / Tyddewi	14	E28
St. David's Head	14	D28
St. Day	2	E33
St. Dennis	3	F32
St. Dogmaels	15	F27
St. Dominick	3	H32
St. Donats	17	J29
St. Endellion	3	F32
St. Erth	2	D33
St. Ewe	3	F33
St. Fagans	18	K29
St. Fergus	81	O11
St. Fillans	67	H14
St. Florence	15	F28
St. Gennys	6	G31
St. Germans	3	H32
St. Giles	7	H31
St. Giles-on-the-Heath	6	H31
St. Govan's Head	16	F29
St. Harmon	25	J26
St. Helen Auckland	56	O20
St. Helens (I.O.W.)	10	Q31
St. Helens (Merseyside)	42	L23
St. Helier (Jersey)	5	
St. Ishmael's	14	E28
St. Issey	3	F32
St. Ive	3	G32
St. Ives (Cambs.)	29	T27
St. Ives (Cornwall)	2	D33
St. John's	46	G21
St. John's Chapel	55	N19
St. John's Loch	86	J8
St. Jude	46	G20
St. Just	2	C33
St. Just in Roseland	2	F33
St. Keverne	2	E33
St. Kew	3	F32
St. Leonards (Dorset)	9	O31
St. Leonards (East Sussex)	12	V31
St. Mabyn	3	F32
St. Magnus Bay	87	P2
St. Margaret's at Cliffe	23	Y30
St. Margaret's Bay	23	Y30
St. Margaret's Hope	87	L7
St. Mark's	46	G21
St. Martin's	34	K25
St. Mary in the Marsh	12	W30
St. Mary's (Orkney Islands)	86	L7
St. Mary's (Perth and Kinross)	73	I14
St. Mary's-Bay	13	W30
St. Mary's-Hoo	22	V29
St. Mary's Loch	61	K17
St. Mawes	2	E33
St. Mawgan	3	F32
St. Mellion	3	H32
St. Mellons	18	K29
St. Merryn	3	F32
St. Michael Penkivel	2	E33
St. Michael's Mount	2	D33
St. Michaels-on-Wyre	42	L22
St. Minver	3	F32
St. Monans	69	L15
St. Neot	3	G32
St. Neots	29	T27
St. Nicholas (Pembrokes)	14	E28
St. Nicholas (Vale of Glamorgan)	17	K29
St. Nicholas-at-Wade	23	X29
St. Ninian's Isle	87	P4
St. Osyth	23	X28
St. Patrick's Isle	46	F21
St. Paul's Walden	29	T28
St. Peter Port (Guernsey)	5	
St. Peter's	23	Y29
St. Pool	4	I33
St. Stephen	3	F32
St. Teath	3	F32
St. Tudwal's Islands	32	G25
St. Tudy	3	F32
St. Vigeans	69	M14
St. Wenn	3	F32
St. Weonards	26	L28
Salcombe	4	I33
Salcombe Regis	5	K31
Sale	42	N23
Salehurst	12	V31
Salen (Argyll and Bute)	65	C14
Salen (Highland)	71	C13
Salford	42	N23
Salfords	21	T30
Salhouse	39	Y25
Saline	68	J15
Salisbury	9	O30
Salisbury Plain	19	O30
Sallachy (Ben More Assybt)	84	G9
Sallachy (near Kyle of Lochalsh)	78	D12
Saltash	3	H32
Saltburn	79	H10
Saltburn-by-the-Sea	57	R20
Saltcoats	59	F17
Salter	48	M21
Saltfleet	45	U23
Saltford	18	M29
Salthouse	38	X25
Saltney	34	L24
Salton	50	R21
Samala	76	X11
Samlesbury Old Hall	42	M22
Sampford Courtenay	7	I31
Sampford Peverell	7	J31
Sanaigmore	58	A16
Sanclêr / St. Clears	15	G28
Sancreed	2	D33
Sancton	44	S22
Sand Side	47	K21
Sanda Island	59	D18
Sanday (Highland)	71	A12
Sanday (Orkney Islands)	87	M6
Sandbach	35	M24
Sandbank	66	F16
Sandbanks	9	O31
Sandend	80	L10
Sandford (Eden)	49	M20
Sandford (Mid Devon)	7	J31
Sandford (North Somerset)	18	L30
Sandford (South Lanarkshire)	60	H17
Sandford Orcas	8	M31
Sandgate	13	X30
Sandgreen	53	H19
Sandhaven	81	N10
Sandhead	52	F19
Sandhurst (Berks.)	20	R29
Sandhurst (Kent)	12	V30
Sandleigh	20	Q28
Sandlins	31	Y27
Sandness	87	P3
Sandon (North Hertfordshire)	29	T28
Sandon (Stafford)	35	N25
Sandown	10	Q32
Sandray	70	X13
Sandridge	21	T28
Sandringham House	38	V25
Sandsend	51	R20
Sandwell	27	O26
Sandwich	23	Y30
Sandwick (Eden)	48	L20
Sandwick (Eilean Siar)	76	Y11
Sandwick (Shetland Islands)	87	Q4
Sandwood Loch	84	E8
Sandy	29	T27
Sandygate	46	G20
Sandyhills	53	I19
Sanna	71	B13
Sanquhar	61	I17
Santon Downham	30	W26
Santon Head	46	G21
Sapperton	19	N28
Saracen's Head	37	T25
Sarclet	86	K8
Sarisbury	10	Q31
Sark (Channel I.)	5	
Sarn Meyllteyrn	32	G25
Sarre	23	X29
Satley	56	O19
Satterthwaite	48	K21
Sauchen	75	M12
Saughall	42	L24
Saughtree	62	L18
Saundersfoot	15	F28
Saunderton	20	R28
Sawbridgeworth	21	U28
Sawrey	48	L20
Sawston	29	U27
Sawtry	29	T26
Saxby	36	R25
Saxilby	44	S24
Saxlingham Nethergate	39	X26
Saxmundham	31	Y27
Saxtead Green	31	X27
Scadavay (Loch)	76	Y11
Scaddle (Glen)	72	D13
Scafell Pikes	47	K20
Scagglethorpe	50	R21
Scalasaig	64	B15
Scalby	51	S21
Scaleby	55	L19
Scalford	36	R25
Scalloway	87	Q3
Scalpay (Highland)	77	C12
Scalpay (Western Isles)	77	A10
Scamblesby	45	T24
Scampton	44	S24
Scaniport	79	H11
Scapa Flow	86	K7
Scarba	65	C15
Scarborough	51	S21
Scarcliffe	44	Q24
Scardroy	78	F11
Scarfskerry	86	K8
Scarisbrick	42	L23
Scarista	76	Y10
Scarp	82	Y9
Scavaig (Loch)	71	B12
Scawby	44	S23
Schiehallion	73	H13
Scilly (Isles of)	2	B34
Scone Palace	68	J14
Scopwick	37	S24
Scoraig	83	D10
Scorton	50	P20
Scotby	55	L19
Scotch-Corner	49	P20
Scothern	45	S24
Scotlandwell	68	K15
Scotney	12	V30
Scotstown	72	D13
Scotter	44	S23
Scotton (Harrogate)	50	P21
Scotton (Richmondshire)	49	O20
Scottow	39	Y25
Scourie	84	E8
Scousburgh	87	Q4
Scrabster	85	J8
Scraptoft	36	Q26
Scredington	37	S25
Scridain (Loch)	64	B14
Scruton	50	P21
Sculthorpe	38	W25
Scunthorpe	44	S23
Sea Palling	39	Y25
Seaford	12	U31
Seaforth (Loch)	82	Z10
Seaforth Head	82	A9
Seagrave	36	Q25
Seaham	57	P19
Seale	21	R30
Sealga (Loch na)	78	D10
Seamer (Hambleton)	50	Q20
Seamer (Scarborough)	51	S21
Seamill	59	F16
Seasalter	23	X29
Seascale	47	J20

WINDSOR

Bexley St	Z 2	
Castle Hill	Z 4	
Charles St	Z 5	
Claremont Rd	Z 6	
Clarence Crescent	Z 7	

Clewer Crescent Rd	Z 8	
Datchet Rd	Z 9	
Goswell Rd	Z 10	
Grove Rd	Z 12	
High St	Z 13	
Keats Lane	Z 17	
King Edward Court Centre	Z	

Peascod St	Z 19	
River St	Z 21	
Stovell Rd	Z 23	
Thames Ave	Z 24	
Thames St	Z 25	
Trinity Pl	Z 27	
Windsor Bridge	Z 28	

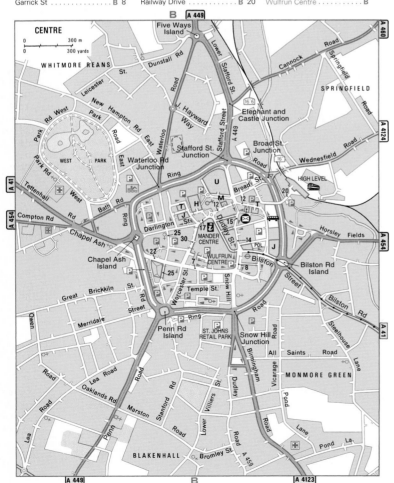

Wysall	36	Q25
Wyvis Lodge	79	G10

Y

Y-Fenni / Abergavenny	18	L28
Y Ffor	32	G25
Y Llethr	33	I25
Y Rhiw	32	G25
Yafforth	50	P20
Yalding	22	V30
Yapton	11	S31
Yardley Gobion	28	R27
Yardley Hastings	28	R27
Yare (River)	38	W26
Yarm	50	P20
Yarmouth	10	P31
Yarnton	20	Q28
Yarrow	62	K17
Yate	19	M29
Yateley	20	R29
Yatton	18	L29
Yatton Keynell	19	N29

Yaxham	38	W26
Yaxley	29	T26
Yeadon	43	O22
Yealand Conyers	48	L21
Yealmpton	4	I32
Yedingham	51	S21
Yelden	29	S27
Yell	87	Q1
Yelvertoft	28	Q26
Yelverton	4	H32
Yeolmbridge	6	G32
Yeovil	8	M31
Yeovilton	8	M30
Yesnaby	86	J6
Yetminster	8	M31
Yetts o' Muckhart	68	J15
Yielden	29	S27
Ynys / Lochtyn	15	G27
Ynysddu	18	K29
Ynyslas	25	H26
Ynysybwl	17	J29
Yockenthwaite	49	N21
Yockleton	34	L25

York	50	Q22
Yorkletts	23	X30
Yorkley	18	M28
Yorkshire Dales National Park	49	N21
Yorkshire Wolds	51	S21
Youlgreave	35	O24
Yoxall	35	O25
Yoxford	31	Y27
Yr Wyddfa / Snowdon	33	H24
Yr Wyddgrug / Mold	34	K24
Ysbyty Ifan	33	I24
Ystalyfera	17	I28
Ystrad-Aeron	25	H27
Ystrad Mynach	18	K29
Ystradfellte	17	J28
Ystradgynlais	17	I28
Ystradowen	17	J29
Ystwyth (River)	25	H26

Z

Zennor	2	D33

WOLVERHAMPTON

Cleveland St	B 7	
Darlington St	B	
Garrick St	B 8	

Lichfield St	B 12	
Mander Centre	B	
Market St	B 14	
Princess St	B 15	
Queen Square	B 17	
Railway Drive	B 20	

St Johns Retail Park	B	
Salop St	B 22	
School St	B 25	
Victoria St	B 30	
Wulfrun Centre	B	

YORK

Bishopgate St	CZ	3
Bishophill Senior	CZ	4
Blake St	CY	5
Church St	DY	8
Clifford St	DY	10
Colliergate	CZ	12
Coney St	CY	13
Cromwell Rd	CZ	15
Davygate	CY	16
Deangate	DY	18
Duncombe Pl	CY	20
Fawcett St	DZ	21

Fetter Lane	CY	22
Goodramgate	DY	25
High Ousegate	DY	26
High Petergate	DY	28
Leeman Rd	CY	30
Lendal	CY	32
Lord Mayor's Walk	DX	33
Low Petergate	DY	35
Museum St	CY	39
Parliament St	DY	42
Pavement	DY	43
Peasholme Green	DY	45
Penley's Grove St	DX	46
Queen St	CZ	49

St Leonard's Pl	CY	52
St Maurice's Rd	DXY	53
Shambles (The)	DY	54
Station Rd	CY	55
Stonebow (The)	DY	56
Stonegate	DY	58
Tower St	DZ	59

Castle Museum	DZ	M2
Fairfax House	DY	A
Jorvik Viking Centre	DY	M1

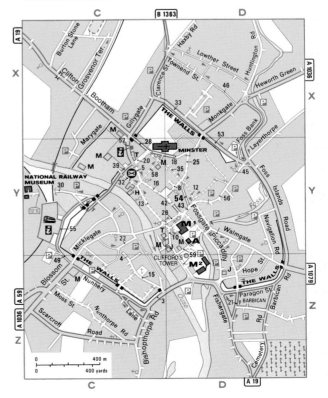

IRELAND

A

Aasleagh 105 D7
Abbert 106 F7
Abbey 100 G8
Abbeydorney 93 C10
Abbeyfeale 93 E10
Abbeylara 107 J6
Abbeyleix /
  Mainistir Laoise 101 J9
Abbeyshrule 107 J7
Abington 94 G10
Achill 104 C6
Achill Head 110 B6
Achill Island 104 B6
Achill Sound 104 C6
Achillbeg Island 104 C6
Achonry 112 G5
Aclare 112 F5
Acoose (Lough) 89 C11
Adamstown 96 L10
Adare 94 F10
Adrigole 89 C12
Aghaboe 101 J9
Aghabullogue 90 F12
Aghada 90 H12
Aghadiffin 106 F6
Aghadoe 89 D11
Aghadoon 110 B5
Aghadowey 118 M2
Aghagallon 114 N4
Aghagower 105 D6
Aghalane 113 J5
Aghalee 114 N4
Aghamore (Leitrim) 107 I6
Aghamore (Mayo) 105 F6
Aghamuck 106 H6
Aghavannagh 103 M9
Aghavas 107 I6
Aghaville 89 D13
Aghinlig 114 M4
Aghla Mountain 116 H3
Aghleam 110 B5
Aghnablaney 113 I4
Aghnacliff 107 J6
Aghnamullen 108 L5
Aghowle 96 M9
Agivey 118 M2
Aglish (Tipperary) 100 H8
Aglish (Waterford) 91 I11
Agnew's Hill 115 O3
Ahakista 89 D13
Ahalia (Loughs) 105 D7
Ahascragh 106 G7
Ahenny 95 J10
Aherla 90 F12
Aherlow 94 H10
Aherlow (Glen of) 95 H10
Ahoghill 118 M3
Aillwee Cave 99 E8
Ailt an Chorráin /
  Burtonport 116 G3
Aird Mhór / Ardmore 91 I12
Akeragh Lough 93 C10
Aldergrove 115 N4
Allaghaun 93 E10
Allen 102 L8
Allen
  (Bog of) 102 K8
Allen (Lough) 112 H5
Allenwood 102 L8
Allihies 88 B13
Allistragh 114 L4
Alloon Lower 106 G7
Allow 94 F11

Allua (Lough) 89 E12
Altagowlan 112 H5
Altan Lough 117 H2
Altnamackan 114 M5
Altnapaste 117 I3
An Blascaod Mór / Blasket
  Islands 92 A11
An Bun Beag / Bunbeg ..116 H2
An Caisleán Nua /
  Newcastle West 93 E10
An Caisleán Riabhach /
  Castlerea 106 G6
An Chathair / Caher 95 I10
An Cheathrú Rua /
  Carraroe 98 D8
An Chloich Mhóir /
  Cloghmore 104 C6
An Clochán / Clifden 104 B7
An Clochán / Cloghan
  (Donegal) 117 I3
An Clochán Liath /
  Dunglow 116 G3
An Cloigeann / Cleegan ..104 B7
An Cóbh / Cobh 90 H12
An Coimín / Commeen ..117 I3
An Coireán / Waterville ..88 B12
An Corrán / Currane 104 C6
An Creagán / Mount
  Bellew 106 G7
An Daingean / Dingle 92 B11
An Dúchoraidh /
  Doocharry 116 H3
An Fál Carrach / Falcarragh ..117 H2
An Fhairche / Clonbur ..105 D7
An Geata Mór 110 B5
An Gleann Garbh /
  Glengarriff 89 D12
An Gort / Gort 99 F8
An Gort Mór / Gortmore ..105 D7
An Leacht / Lahinch 98 D9
An Longfort / Longford ..107 I6
An Mám / Maam Cross ..105 D7
An Mhala Raithní /
  Mulrany 104 C6
An Móta / Moate 101 I7
An Muileann gCearr /
  Mullingar 107 J7
An Nás / Naas 102 M8
An Ráth / Charleville 94 F10
An Ros / Rush 109 N7
An Sciobairín / Skibbereen ..89 E13
An Seanchaisleán /
  Oldcastle 108 K6
An Spidéal / Spiddal 99 E8
An tAonach / Nenagh ...100 H9
An Teampall Mór /
  Templemore 101 I9
An Tearmann / Termon ..117 I2
An tInbhear Mór / Arklow ..97 N9
An Tulach / Tullow 102 L9
An Uaimh / Navan 108 L7
Anascaul 92 B11
Anayalla 114 L5
Anglesborough 94 H10
Anglesey Bridge 95 H9
Annacarriga 99 G9
Annacarty 95 H10
Annaclone 115 N5
Annacloy 115 O4
Annacotty 94 G9
Annadorn 115 O5
Annagary 116 H2
Annagassan 109 M6
Annageeragh (River) 98 D9
Annagh Head 110 B5
Annagh Island 110 C6
Annaghdown 105 E7

Annaghmore Lough 106 H6
Annahilt 115 N4
Annalee 107 J5
Annalong 109 O5
Annamoe 103 N8
Annes Grove Gardens ..94 G11
Annestown 91 K11
Annfield 95 I9
Annie Brady Bridge 111 C5
Annsborough 115 O5
Antrim 115 N3
Antrim (Glens of) 119 N2
Antrim Coast 119 O2
Antrim Mountains 119 N2
Anure (Lough) 116 H3
Araglin 95 H11
Árainn Mhór / Aran or
  Aranmore Island 116 G2
Aran Islands / Oileáin
  Árainn 98 C8
Archdale (Castle) 113 I4
Archerstown 108 K7
Ard 104 C8
Ardagh (Donegal) 117 J3
Ardagh (Limerick) 93 E10
Ardan 101 J8
Ardanairy 103 N9
Ardanew 108 L7
Ardara 116 G3
Ardattin 96 L9
Ardboe 114 M4
Ardcath 109 M7
Ardcloon 105 F7
Ardcrony 100 H9
Ardea 89 C12
Arderin 101 J8
Ardfert 93 C11
Ardfield 89 F13
Ardfinnan 95 I11
Ardgehane 90 F13
Ardglass 115 P5
Ardglass 90 H11
Ardgroom 88 C12
Ardgroom Harbour 88 C12
Ardkeen 115 P4
Ardlea 101 J9
Ardlougher 107 J5
Ardmillan 115 O4
Ardmoney 113 J5
Ardmore (Derry) 117 K3
Ardmore (Galway) 104 C8
Ardmore Point (Antrim) ..114 N4
Ardmore Point
  (Craigavon) 114 M4
Ardmore Point
  (Dunganstown East) ..103 N9
Ardmorney 101 J7
Ardmoy 106 G6
Ardnagreevagh 104 B7
Ardnasodan 105 F7
Ardpatrick 94 G10
Ardrahan 99 F8
Ardreagh 118 M2
Ardress House 114 M4
Ards Forest Park 117 I2
Ards Peninsula 115 P4
Ardscull 102 L8
Ardshankill 113 I4
Ardstraw 113 J3
Argideen 89 F13
Argory (The) 114 M4
Arigna 112 H5
Arinagh 112 F5
Arless 102 K9
Armagh 114 M4
Armaghbrague 114 M5

Armoy 118 N2
Arney 113 I5
Arra Mountains 100 G9
Arrow (Lough) 106 H5
Arryheernabin 117 J2
Artane 103 N7
Arthurstown 96 L11
Articlave 118 L2
Artigarvan 117 J3
Arvagh 107 J6
Asdee 93 D10
Ashbourne 109 M7
Ashford (Glenealy) 103 N8
Ashford (Limerick) 93 E10
Ashford Castle 105 E7
Ashleam Bay 104 B6
Ashton 90 F12
Askamore 97 M9
Askanagap 103 M9
Askeaton 94 F10
Askill 112 H4
Atedaun (Lough) 99 E9
Áth Cinn / Headford 105 E7
Athassel Abbey 95 I10
Athboy 108 L7
Athea 93 E10
Athgarvan 102 L8
Athlacca 94 G10
Athleague 106 H7
Athnid 95 I9
Athy / Baile Átha Í 102 L9
Atlantic Drive (The) 104 C6
Atorick (Lough) 99 G8
Attanagh 101 J9
Attavally 111 C5
Attical 109 N5
Attymass 111 E5
Attymon 99 G8
Aucloggen 105 F7
Audley's Castle 115 P4
Aughacasla 92 C11
Aughagault 117 I3
Aughamullan 114 M4
Augher 114 K4
Aughils 92 C11
Aughinish 99 E8
Aughinish Island 93 E10
Aughkeely 117 I3
Aughnacleagh 118 M3
Aughnacloy 114 L4
Aughnanure Castle 105 E7
Aughnasheelan 107 I5
Aughrim (Galway) 100 H8
Aughrim (Wicklow) 103 N9
Aughris 101 F5
Aughris Head 112 F5
Aughrus More 104 B7
Avoca 103 N9
Avoca (River) 103 N9
Avoca (Valle of) 103 N9
Avonbeg 103 M9
Avondale Forest Park ...103 N9
Avonmore (River) 103 N9
Awbeg 94 G11

B

Baginbun Head 96 L11
Baile an Fheirtéaraigh /
  Ballyferriter 92 A11
Baile an Mhóta /
  Ballymote 112 G5
Baile an Róba / Ballinrobe ..105 E7
Baile an Sceilg /
  Ballinskelligs 88 B12

Baile Átha an Rí / Athenry ..99 F8
Baile Átha Cliath / Dublin ..103 N8
Baile Átha Fhirdhia / Ardee ..108 M6
Baile Átha Luain / Athlone ..107 I7
Baile Átha Troim / Trim ..108 L7
Baile Brigín / Balbriggan ..109 N7
Baile Chláir / Claregalway ..99 F7
Baile Locha Riach /
  Loughrea 99 G8
Baile Mhic Andáin /
  Thomastown 96 K10
Baile Mhistéala /
  Mitchelstown 94 H11
Baile na Finne / Fintown ..117 H3
Baile na Lorgan /
  Castleblayney 108 L5
Baile Uí Fhiacháin /
  Newport 105 D6
Baile Uí Mhatháin /
  Ballymahon 107 I7
Baileysmill 115 O4
Baldoyle 103 N7
Balla 105 E6
Ballaba 99 F8
Ballagan Point 109 N5
Ballagh (Fermanagh) 113 J5
Ballagh (Galway) 106 F7
Ballagh (Limerick) 93 E10
Ballagh (near Curraghroe) ..107 H6
Ballagh (near Nahara) ..106 H7
Ballagh (Tipperary) 95 I10
Ballagh (Neck of the) 112 G3
Ballaghaderreen / Bealach
  an Doirín 106 G6
Ballaghbeama Gap 89 C12
Ballaghbehy 93 E10
Ballaghisheen Pass 88 C12
Ballaghkeen 97 M10
Ballaghmore 101 I9
Ballaghnatrillick 112 G4
Ballard 97 M9
Ballardiggan 99 F8
Balleen 101 J9
Ballickmoyler 102 K9
Balligan 115 P4
Ballina 99 G9
Ballina / Béal an Átha ...111 E5
Ballinaboy 104 B7
Ballinabrackey 102 K7
Ballinabranagh 102 L9
Ballinaclash 103 N9
Ballinacor 103 N9
Ballinadee 90 G12
Ballinafad (Aghanagh) ..106 G5
Ballinafad (Galway) 104 C7
Ballinagar 101 J8
Ballinagleragh 113 H5
Ballinakill 101 K9
Ballinalack 107 J7
Ballinalea 103 N8
Ballinalee 107 J6
Ballinamallard 113 J4
Ballinamara 95 J9
Ballinameen 106 H6
Ballinamore Bridge 106 G7
Ballinamuck 107 I6
Ballinascarty 90 F12
Ballinaspick 91 I11
Ballinclashet 90 G12
Ballinclea 103 M9
Ballincloher 93 C10
Ballincollig 90 G12
Ballincrea 96 K11
Ballincurrig 90 H12
Ballindaggan 96 L10
Ballindarragh 113 J5
Ballinderreen 99 F8

Ballinderry (Cookstown) ..114 M4
Ballinderry (Terryglass) ..100 H8
Ballinderry (Wicklow) ...103 N9
Ballinderry Bridge 114 M4
Ballindine 105 F6
Ballindrait 117 J3
Ballineanig 92 A11
Ballineen 89 F12
Ballingarrane 94 F10
Ballingarry (Galway) 100 H8
Ballingarry (Limerick) ...94 F10
Ballingarry (Tipperary) ..95 J10
Ballingeary / Béal Átha an
  Ghaorthaidh 89 E12
Ballingurteen 89 E12
Ballinhassig 90 G12
Ballinkillin 96 L10
Ballinlea 118 M2
Ballinleeny 94 F10
Ballinloghig 92 B11
Ballinlough (Meath) 108 K6
Ballinlough (Roscommon) ..106 G6
Ballinluska 90 H12
Ballinruan 99 F9
Ballinskelligs Bay 88 B12
Ballinspittle 90 G12
Ballintober 106 G6
Ballintogher 112 G5
Ballintotty 100 H9
Ballintoy 118 M2
Ballintra (Donegal) 112 H4
Ballintra (near
  Leabgarrow) 116 G3
Ballintubber 105 E6
Ballinunty 95 I10
Ballinure 95 I10
Ballinure (River) 100 H8
Ballinvarry 96 L10
Ballitore 102 L8
Ballivor 108 L7
Ballon 96 L9
Balloo Cross
  Roads 115 O4
Balloor 112 G4
Balloughter 97 M10
Ballure 112 H4
Ballvengland 94 F10
Ballyagran 94 F10
Ballyallinan 94 F10
Ballyalton 115 P5
Ballyard 113 J4
Ballybannon 102 L9
Ballybay (near
  Carrickmacross) 108 L5
Ballybay (near
  Castelblayney) 108 L5
Ballybeg 95 I11
Ballyboghil 109 N7
Ballybogy 118 M2
Ballyboley Forest 115 O3
Ballyboy 101 I8
Ballybrack (Dublin) 103 N8
Ballybrack (Kerry) 88 B12
Ballybrittas 101 K8
Ballybrommel 96 L9
Ballybrood 94 G10
Ballybrophy 101 J9
Ballybryan 101 K7
Ballybunnion 93 D10
Ballycahill 95 I9
Ballycallan 95 J10
Ballycanew 97 N10
Ballycarney 97 M10
Ballycarry 115 O3
Ballycastle (Mayo) 111 D5
Ballycastle (Moyle) 119 N2
Ballycastle Bay 119 N2

Ballyclare (Newtonabbey)	115	N3	Ballyhean	105	E6	Ballylanders	94	G10	Ballymagorry	117	J3	Ballynaclogh	100	H9	Ballynare	103	M7

Ballyclare (Newtonabbey) ... 115 N3
Ballyclare (Roscommon) ... 107 I6
Ballyclerahan ... 95 I10
Ballyclery ... 99 I8
Ballyclogh ... 94 F11
Ballycolla ... 101 J9
Ballycommon ... 100 H9
Ballyconneely ... 104 B7
Ballyconneely Bay ... 104 B7
Ballyconnell (Cavan) ... 113 J5
Ballyconnell (Sligo) ... 112 G4
Ballycorick ... 99 E9
Ballycotton ... 91 H12
Ballycotton Bay ... 91 H12
Ballycrossaun ... 100 H8
Ballycrovane Harbour ... 88 C12
Ballycroy ... 110 C5
Ballycuirke Lough ... 99 E8
Ballycullane ... 96 L11
Ballycullen ... 103 N8
Ballycumber ... 101 I8
Ballydangan ... 100 H7
Ballydavid (Galway) ... 100 G8
Ballydavid (Kilmalkedar) ... 92 A11
Ballydavid Head ... 92 A11
Ballydavis ... 101 K8
Ballydehob ... 89 D13
Ballydesmond ... 93 E11
Ballydonegan ... 88 B13
Ballydonegan Bay ... 88 B13
Ballyduff (Dingle) ... 92 B11
Ballyduff (Kerry) ... 93 D10
Ballyduff (Waterford) ... 91 H11
Ballyduff (Wexford) ... 97 M10
Ballyeaston ... 115 O3
Ballyeighter Loughs ... 99 F9
Ballyfad ... 97 N9
Ballyfair ... 102 L8
Ballyfarnagh ... 105 F6
Ballyfarnan ... 106 H5
Ballyfasy ... 96 K10
Ballyfeard ... 90 G12
Ballyferis Point ... 115 P4
Ballyfin ... 101 J8
Ballyfinboy ... 100 H8
Ballyforan ... 106 H7
Ballyfore ... 102 K8
Ballyfoyle ... 96 K9
Ballygalley ... 119 O3
Ballygalley Head ... 119 O3
Ballygar ... 106 H7
Ballygarrett ... 97 N10
Ballygarries ... 105 E6
Ballygarvan ... 90 G12
Ballygawley (Dungannon) ... 114 K4
Ballygawley (Sligo) ... 112 G5
Ballyglass (near Cornanagh) ... 105 E6
Ballyglass (near Kilmovee) ... 106 G6
Ballygorman ... 117 K1
Ballygowan (Ards) ... 115 O4
Ballygowan (Newry-Mourne) ... 109 N5
Ballygriffin ... 95 I10
Ballyhack ... 96 L11
Ballyhacket ... 102 L9
Ballyhaght ... 94 G10
Ballyhahill ... 93 E10
Ballyhaise ... 107 K5
Ballyhalbert ... 115 P4
Ballyhale (Galway) ... 105 E7
Ballyhale (Kilkenny) ... 96 K10
Ballyhar ... 93 D11
Ballyhaunis / Béal Átha hAmhnais ... 106 F6

Ballyhear ... 105 E7
Ballyheelan ... 107 J6
Ballyheerin ... 117 I2
Ballyheige ... 93 C10
Ballyheige Bay ... 93 C10
Ballyhillin ... 117 J1
Ballyhoe Bridge ... 118 N2
Ballyhoe Lough ... 108 L6
Ballyhoge ... 96 M10
Ballyhooly ... 94 G11
Ballyhornan ... 115 P5
Ballyhoura Mountains ... 94 G11
Ballyhuppahane ... 101 J8
Ballyjamesduff ... 107 K6
Ballykean ... 101 K8
Ballykeefe ... 95 J10
Ballykeel ... 115 N4
Ballykeeran ... 107 I7
Ballykelly ... 118 K2
Ballykilleen ... 102 K8
Ballykinler ... 115 O5
Ballyknockan ... 103 M8
Ballylacy ... 97 N9
Ballylaghnan ... 99 G9

Ballylaneen ... 91 J11
Ballylesson ... 115 O4
Ballylickey ... 89 D12
Ballyliffin ... 117 J2
Ballyline ... 95 J10
Ballylintagh ... 118 L2
Ballylongford ... 93 D10
Ballylongford Bay ... 93 D10
Ballylooby ... 95 I11
Ballyloughbeg ... 118 M2
Ballylynan ... 102 K9
Ballymacarbry ... 95 I11
Ballymacaw ... 96 K11
Ballymachugh ... 107 K6
Ballymack ... 96 K10
Ballymackey ... 100 H9
Ballymackilroy ... 114 K4
Ballymacoda ... 91 I12
Ballymacreven ... 115 N4
Ballymacurly ... 106 H6
Ballymacward ... 106 G7
Ballymadog ... 91 I12
Ballymagan ... 117 J2
Ballymagaraghy ... 118 K2

Ballymagorry ... 117 J3
Ballymakeagh ... 91 I12
Ballymakeery / Baile Mhic Íre ... 89 E12
Ballymakenny ... 109 M6
Ballymartin ... 109 O5
Ballymartle ... 90 G12
Ballymena ... 119 N3
Ballymoe ... 106 G6
Ballymoney (Ballymoney) ... 118 M2
Ballymoney (Limavady) ... 118 K3
Ballymore (Donegal) ... 117 I2
Ballymore (Westmeath) ... 107 I7
Ballymore Eustace ... 103 M8
Ballymore Lough ... 111 E5
Ballymurphy ... 96 L10
Ballymurragh ... 93 E10
Ballymurray ... 106 H7
Ballynabola ... 96 L10
Ballynacallagh ... 88 B13
Ballynacally ... 99 E9
Ballynacarrick ... 116 H3
Ballynacarriga ... 89 E12
Ballynacarrigy ... 107 J7
Ballynacarrow ... 112 G5

Ballynaclogh ... 100 H9
Ballynacorra ... 90 H12
Ballynacourty ... 91 J11
Ballynadrumny ... 102 L7
Ballynafid ... 107 J7
Ballynagaul ... 91 J11
Ballynagoraher ... 105 D6
Ballynagore ... 101 J7
Ballynagree ... 90 F12
Ballynaguilkee ... 95 I11
Ballynahinch ... 115 O4
Ballynahinch Lake ... 104 C7
Ballynahow ... 88 A12
Ballynahown (Kilcummin) ... 98 D8
Ballynahown (Westmeath) ... 101 I7
Ballynakill (Carlow) ... 96 L9
Ballynakill (Offaly) ... 101 K8
Ballynakill (Westmeath) ... 107 I7
Ballynakill Harbour ... 104 B7
Ballynakilla ... 88 B7
Ballynakilly Upper ... 88 C11
Ballynamallaght ... 117 K3
Ballynamona ... 90 G11
Ballynamult ... 95 I11
Ballynana ... 92 A11

Ballynare ... 103 M7
Ballynashannagh ... 117 J2
Ballynaskeagh ... 114 N5
Ballynaskreena ... 93 C10
Ballynastangford ... 105 E6
Ballynastraw ... 97 M10
Ballynchatty ... 113 K4
Ballyneaner ... 118 K3
Ballyneety ... 94 G10
Ballyneill ... 95 J10
Ballynoe (Cork) ... 90 H11
Ballynoe (Down) ... 115 O5
Ballynure ... 115 O3
Ballyorgan ... 94 G11
Ballypatrick ... 95 J10
Ballypatrick Forest ... 119 N2
Ballyporeen ... 95 H11
Ballyquin ... 92 B11
Ballyquintin Point ... 115 P5
Ballyragget ... 101 J9
Ballyrashane ... 118 M2
Ballyreagh (Dungannon) ... 114 L4
Ballyreagh (Fermanagh) ... 113 J4
Ballyroan ... 101 K9
Ballyroddy ... 106 H6

Ballyroebuck	97	M10
Ballyronan	114	M3
Ballyroney	115	N5
Ballyroon	88	C13
Ballysadare	112	G5
Ballysadare Bay	112	G5
Ballyshannon (Donegal)	112	H4
Ballyshannon (Kildare)	102	L8
Ballysloe	95	J10
Ballysteen	94	F10
Ballyteige Bay	96	L11
Ballytoohy	104	C6
Ballyvaughan	99	E8
Ballyvaughan Bay	99	E8
Ballyvester	115	P4
Ballyvoge / Baile Uí Bhuaigh	89	E12
Ballyvoneen	106	G7
Ballyvourney / Baile Bhuirne	89	E12
Ballyvoy	119	N2
Ballyvoyle Head	91	J11
Ballywalter	115	P4
Ballyward	115	N5
Ballywilliam	96	L10
Balnamore	118	M2
Balrath	108	M7
Balrothery	109	N7
Balscaddan	109	N7
Baltimore	89	D13
Baltray	109	N6
Banada	106	F5
Banagher	101	I8
Banagher Forest	118	L3
Banbridge	114	N4
Bandon River	89	F12
Bangor (Mayo)	111	C5
Bangor (North-Down)	115	O4
Bangor Trail	111	C5
Bann (River) (Lough Neagh)	115	N5
Bann (River) (River Slaney)	97	M10
Banna	93	C10
Banna Strand	93	C11
Bannow	96	L11
Bannow Bay	96	L11
Bansha	95	H10
Banteer	94	F11
Bantry / Beanntraí	89	D12
Bantry Bay	89	C13
Barefield	99	F9
Barley Cove	88	C13
Barna (Limerick)	94	H10
Barna (Offaly)	101	I9
Barnacahoge	105	F6
Barnaderg	106	F7
Barnesmore	113	H3
Barnesmore Gap	113	I3
Barnmeen	115	N5
Barnycarroll	105	F6
Baronscourt Forest	113	J3
Barr na Trá / Barnatra	110	C5
Barra (Lough)	117	H3
Barrack Village	101	K9
Barraduff	89	D11
Barrigone	93	E10
Barringtonsbridge	94	G10
Barrow (River)	102	K8
Barrow Harbour	93	C11
Barry	107	I7
Barry's Point	90	F13
Batterstown	108	M7
Baunskeha	96	K10
Bauntlieve	99	E9
Baurtregaum	93	C11

Bawn Cross Roads	94	F11
Bawnboy	113	I5
Beagh (Galway)	105	F7
Beagh (Roscommon)	112	H5
Beagh (Lough)	117	I2
Beagh (Slieve)	113	K4
Beal	93	D10
Béal an Átha / Ballina	111	E5
Béal an Átha Mhóir / Ballinamore	107	I5
Béal an Mhuirthead / Belmullet	110	C5
Béal Átha an Ghaorthaidh / Ballingeary	89	E12
Béal Átha na Muice / Swinford	105	F6
Béal Átha na Sluaighe / Ballinasloe	100	H8
Béal Átha Seanaidh / Ballyshannon	112	H4
Béal Deirg / Belderrig	111	D5
Béal Tairbirt / Belturbet	107	J5
Bealach Conglais / Baltinglass	102	L9
Bealach Féich / Ballybofey	117	I3
Bealaclugga / New Quay	99	E8
Bealad Cross Roads	89	F13
Bealadangan	105	D8
Bealaha	98	D9
Bealalaw Bridge	88	C12
Bealanabrack	104	C7
Bealin	107	I7
Bealnablath	90	F12
Beara	89	C12
Bearna / Barna	99	E8
Beaufort	89	D11
Bective	108	L7
Beehive Huts	92	A11
Beenmore	88	B11
Beennaskehy	90	G11
Beenoskee	92	B11
Beg (Lough) (Antrim)	114	N4
Beg (Lough) (River Bann)	114	M3
Beginish Island	88	B12
Behy	88	C11
Bekan	105	F6
Belcarra	105	E6
Belclare	105	F7
Belcoo	113	I5
Belderg Harbour	111	D5
Belfarsad	104	C6
Belfast	115	O4
Belfast Lough	115	O3
Belgooly	90	G12
Belhavel Lough	112	H5
Bellacorick	111	D5
Belladrihid	112	G5
Bellagarvaun	110	C6
Bellaghy	114	M3
Bellahy	106	F6
Bellameeny	106	H7
Bellamont Forest	108	K5
Bellanaboy Bridge	111	C5
Bellanacargy	107	K5
Bellanagare	106	G6
Bellanagraugh Bridge	112	F5
Bellanaleck	113	J5
Bellanamore	117	H3
Bellanamullia	107	H7
Bellananagh	107	J6
Bellanode	114	K5
Bellarena	118	L2
Bellavary	105	E6
Belleek	114	M5
Belleek	113	H4
Bellewstown	109	M7

Belmont	101	I8
Belmore Mountain	113	I5
Beltra (Croaghmoyle)	105	D6
Beltra (Sligo)	112	G5
Beltra Lough	105	D6
Belvelly	90	H12
Belview Port	96	K11
Belville	111	D5
Ben Gorm	104	C7
Benbane Head	118	M2
Benbaun	104	C7
Benbo	112	H5
Benbrack	113	I5
Benbreen	104	C7
Benbulben	112	G4
Benburb	114	L4
Bencroy or Gubnaveagh	113	I5
Bendooragh	118	M2
Benettsbridge	96	K10
Benmore	111	D5
Benmore or Fair Head	119	N2
Bennacunneen	105	D7
Benwee Head	111	C4
Beragh	114	K4
Bere Haven	88	C13
Bere Island	88	C13
Bernish Rock	114	M5
Berrings	90	F12
Bertraghboy Bay	104	C7
Bessbrook	114	M5
Bettystown	109	N6
Big Dog Forest	113	I4
Big Island	100	H8
Big Trosk	119	N2
Bilboa	102	K9
Bilboa (River)	95	H10
Billis Bridge	108	K6
Bills Rocks	86	B6
Binevenagh	118	L2
Binn Éadair / Howth	103	N7
Biorra / Birr	101	I8
Birdhill	99	G9
Birreencorragh	105	D6
Bishops Court	115	P5
Black (Galway)	105	E7
Black (River) (Longford)	107	I6
Black Ball Head	88	B13
Black Bull	103	M7
Black Gap (The)	113	I4
Black Head (Clare)	99	E8
Black Head (Larne)	115	O3
Black Lion	101	J8
Black Rock	110	B5
Blacklion	113	I5
Blackpool	94	G10
Blackrock (Cork)	90	G12
Blackrock (Louth)	109	M6
Blackrock (Rathdown)	103	N8
Blackskull	114	N4
Blacksod Bay	110	B5

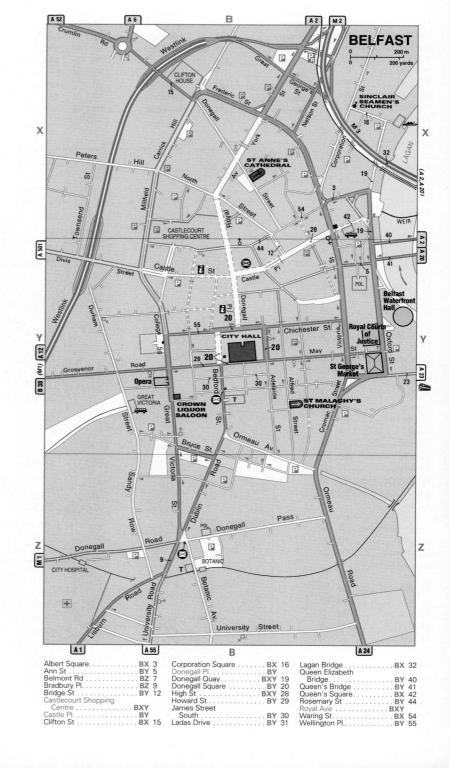

Albert Square	BX 3	Corporation Square	BX 16	Lagan Bridge	BX 32
Ann St	BY 5	Donegall Pl.	BY	Queen Elizabeth Bridge	BY 40
Belmont Rd	BZ 7	Donegall Quay	BXY 19	Queen's Bridge	BY 41
Bradbury Pl.	BZ 9	Donegall Square	BY 20	Queen's Square	BX 42
Bridge St	BY 12	High St	BXY 28	Rosemary St	BX 44
Castlecourt Shopping Centre	BXY	Howard St	BY 29	Royal Ave	BXY
Castle Pl.	BY	James Street South	BY 30	Waring St	BX 54
Clifton St	BX 15	Ladas Drive	BY 31	Wellington Pl.	BY 55

Blacksod Point ... 110 B5
Blackstairs Mountains ... 96 L10
Blackwater ... 97 M10
Blackwater (River) (Cork) ... 89 F11
Blackwater (River) (Lough Neagh) ... 114 L4
Blackwater (River) (River Boyne) ... 108 L6
Blackwater Bridge (Innfield) ... 102 L7
Blackwater Bridge (Tahilla) ... 88 C12
Blackwater Harbour ... 97 N10
Blackwatertown ... 114 L4
Blanchardstown ... 103 M7
Blane Bridge ... 93 E10
Blaney ... 113 I4
Blarney ... 90 G12
Blasket Sound ... 92 A11
Bleach ... 99 G8
Bleach Lake ... 94 F10
Blennerville ... 93 C11
Blessington ... 103 M8
Bloody Foreland ... 116 H2
Blue Ball ... 101 J8
Blue Stack Mountains ... 113 H3
Blueford ... 93 E11
Boa Island ... 113 I4
Boardmills ... 115 O4
Boderg (Lough) ... 107 I6
Bodyke ... 99 G9
Bofeenaun ... 105 E6
Bofin ... 104 B7
Bofin (Lough) (Galway) ... 105 D7
Bofin (Lough) (Roscommon) ... 107 I6
Bogay ... 117 J3
Boggan (Meath) ... 108 L6
Boggan (Tipperary) ... 95 J9
Boggaun ... 101 I9
Boggeragh Mountains ... 89 F11
Bohateh ... 99 G9
Bohaun ... 105 D6
Boheeshil ... 88 C12
Boher ... 94 G10
Boheraphuca ... 101 I8
Boherbue ... 93 E11
Bohereen ... 94 G10
Boherlahan ... 95 I10
Bohermeen ... 108 L7
Boherquill ... 107 J6
Boho ... 113 I4
Bohola ... 105 E6
Bola (Lough) ... 104 C7
Bolea ... 118 L2
Boleran ... 118 L2
Boley ... 102 L8
Bolinglanna ... 104 C6
Boliska Lough ... 99 E8
Bolton's Cross Roads ... 93 D10
Bolus Head ... 88 A12
Bonet ... 112 H5
Boola ... 91 I11
Boolakennedy ... 95 H10
Boolattin ... 95 J11
Boolteens ... 93 C11
Boolyduff ... 99 E8
Boolyglass ... 96 K10
Borris ... 96 L10
Borris in Ossory ... 101 J9
Borrisoleigh ... 100 I9
Boston ... 99 F8
Bottlehill ... 90 G11
Bouladuff ... 95 I9
Boviel ... 118 L3
Bow ... 99 G9
Boyerstown ... 108 L7
Boyle (River) ... 106 H6

Boyne (River) ... 102 K7
Brackagh ... 101 K8
Brackley Lough ... 113 I5
Bracklin ... 108 K7
Brackloon (Mayo) ... 106 F6
Brackloon (Roscommon) ... 106 G6
Bracknagh (Offaly) ... 102 K8
Bracknagh (Roscommon) ... 107 H7
Brackwanshagh ... 111 E5
Brandon Bay ... 92 B11
Brandon Head ... 92 B11
Brandon Hill ... 96 L10
Brannock Islands ... 98 C8
Brannockstown ... 102 L8
Bray Head (Kerry) ... 88 A12
Bray Head (Wicklow) ... 103 N8
Bré / Bray ... 103 N8
Breaghva ... 98 C10
Breaghwy ... 105 E6
Bree ... 96 M10
Breenagh ... 117 I3
Brickeens ... 105 F6
Bricklieve Mountains ... 106 G5
Bride (Cork) ... 89 F12
Bride (River Blackwater) ... 91 I11
Bridebridge ... 90 H11
Brideswell (Ballyellis) ... 97 M9
Brideswell (Ballynamona) ... 106 H7
Bridge End ... 117 J2
Bridgeland ... 103 M9
Bridget Lough ... 99 G9
Bridgetown (Cannock Chase) ... 96 M11
Bridgetown (Clare) ... 99 G9
Bridgetown (Donegal) ... 112 H4
Briensbridge ... 99 G9
Brittas (Limerick) ... 94 G10
Brittas (Saggart) ... 103 M8
Brittas Bay ... 103 N9
Britway ... 90 H11
Broad Haven ... 110 C5
Broad Meadow ... 109 N7
Broadford (Clare) ... 99 G9
Broadford (Limerick) ... 94 F10
Broadway ... 97 M11
Brookeborough ... 113 J5
Broomfield ... 108 L5
Brosna ... 93 E11
Brosna (River) ... 101 I8
Broughal ... 101 I8
Broughane Cross Roads ... 93 D11
Brougher Mount ... 113 J4
Broughshane ... 119 N3
Brow Head ... 88 C13
Brown Flesk ... 93 D11
Brownstown ... 96 K11
Brownstown Head ... 96 K11
Bruckless ... 112 G4
Bruff ... 94 G10
Bruree ... 94 G10
Bryansford ... 115 O5
Buckna ... 119 N3
Buckode ... 112 H4
Buiríos Uí Chéin / Borrisokane ... 100 H9
Bulgaden ... 94 G10
Bull (The) ... 88 B13
Bull Point ... 119 N2
Bullaba ... 117 I3
Bullaun ... 99 G8
Bull's Head ... 92 B11
Bun Cranncha / Buncrana ... 117 J2
Bun Dobhráin / Bundoran ... 112 H4
Bun na hAbhna / Bunnahowen ... 110 C5
Bun na Leaca / Brinlack ... 116 H2

Bunaclugga Bay ... 93 D10
Bunacurry ... 110 C6
Bunatrahir Bay ... 111 D5
Bunaveela Lough ... 111 D5
Bunaw ... 88 C12
Bunbrosna ... 107 J7
Bunclody ... 96 M10
Bunlahy ... 107 J6
Bunmahon ... 91 J11
Bunnafollistran ... 105 E7
Bunnaglass ... 99 F8
Bunnahown ... 104 C7
Bunnanaddan ... 112 G5
Bunny (Lough) ... 99 F8
Bunnyconnellan ... 111 E5
Bunowen ... 105 C6
Bunratty ... 99 F9
Burnchurch ... 96 K10
Burncourt ... 95 H11
Burnfoot (Birdstown) ... 117 J2
Burnfoot (Limavady) ... 118 L3
Burnfort ... 90 G11
Burr Point ... 115 P4
Burren (Clare) ... 99 E8
Burren (Cork) ... 90 F12
Burren (Mayo) ... 105 E6
Burren (The) ... 99 E8
Burren Centre Kifenora ... 99 E8
Burrenfadda ... 99 E9
Burrishoole Abbey ... 105 D6
Burrow ... 97 M11
Burtown ... 102 L9
Bush ... 118 M2
Bush (The) (Dungannon) ... 114 L4
Bush (The) (Rathcor) ... 109 N6
Bushfield ... 100 G9
Bushmills ... 118 M2
Butler's Bridge ... 107 J5
Butlerstown ... 90 F13
Buttevant ... 94 F11
Butts (The) ... 101 K9
Bweeng ... 90 F11

C

Cabragh ... 114 L4
Cadamstown (Kildare) ... 102 L7
Cadamstown (Offaly) ... 101 J8
Caddy ... 114 N3
Caggan ... 105 D7
Caha Mountains ... 89 C12
Caha pass ... 89 D12
Caher (Clare) ... 99 G9
Caher (Mayo) ... 105 E7
Caher Island ... 104 B6
Caher Roe's Den ... 96 L10
Caheradrine ... 99 F8
Caheragh ... 89 E13
Caherbarnagh (Corcaigh / Cork) ... 89 E11
Caherbarnagh (Kerry) ... 88 B12
Caherconlish ... 94 G10
Caherconnel ... 99 E8
Caherconree ... 92 C11
Caherdaniel ... 88 B12
Caherea ... 99 E9
Caherlistrane ... 105 E7
Cahermore (Cork) ... 88 B13
Cahermore (Galway) ... 99 F8
Cahermurphy ... 98 D9
Cahernahallia ... 95 H10
Cahore Point ... 97 N10
Caiseal / Cashel ... 95 I10
Caisleán an Bharraigh / Castlebar ... 105 E6

Caisleán an Chomair / Castlecomer ... 101 K9
Calafort Ros Láir / Rosslare Harbour ... 97 M11
Caledon ... 114 L4
Calf Islands ... 89 D13
Callaghansmills ... 99 F9
Callainn / Callan ... 95 J10
Callow (Galway) ... 104 B7
Callow (Mayo) ... 105 E6
Callow (Roscommon) ... 106 G6
Caltra ... 106 G7
Caltraghlea ... 100 H7
Calverstown ... 102 L8
Cam Forest ... 118 L2
Camlin (River) ... 107 I6
Camlough ... 114 M5
Camoge ... 94 G10
Camolin ... 97 M10
Camowen ... 113 K4
Camp ... 92 C11
Campile ... 96 L11
Campsey ... 118 K2
Camross ... 101 J8
Camus Bay ... 105 D8
Canglass Point ... 88 B12
Canningstown ... 108 K6
Canon Island ... 99 E9
Cappagh (Dungannon) ... 114 L4
Cappagh (Limerick) ... 94 F10
Cappagh (River) ... 100 G8
Cappagh White ... 95 H10
Cappaghmore ... 99 F8
Cappalinnan ... 101 J9
Cappamore ... 94 G10
Cappanacreha ... 105 D7
Cappanrush ... 101 J7
Cappataggle ... 100 G8
Cappeen ... 89 F12
Car (Slieve) ... 111 D5
Caragh (Lough) ... 88 C11
Caragh (River) ... 89 C12
Caragh Bridge ... 92 C11
Caragh Lake ... 92 C11
Carbery's Hundred Isles ... 89 D13
Carbury ... 102 L7
Cardy ... 115 P4
Cargan ... 119 N3
Carhan House ... 88 B12
Cark ... 117 I3
Cark Mountain ... 117 I3
Carland ... 114 L4
Carlanstown ... 108 L6
Carlingford ... 109 N5
Carlingford Lough ... 109 N5
Carn ... 113 I4
Carna ... 104 C8
Carnageer ... 119 O3
Carnaghan ... 117 J2
Carnalbanagh Sheddings ... 119 N3
Carnanelly ... 114 L3
Carnanreagh ... 118 K3
Carnaross ... 108 L6
Carnaween ... 112 H3
Carncastle ... 119 O3
Carndonagh / Carn Domhnach ... 118 K2
Carnduff ... 119 N2
Carne ... 97 M11
Carneatly ... 119 N2
Carnew ... 97 M9
Carney (Sligo) ... 112 G4
Carney (Tipperary) ... 100 H9
Carnlough ... 119 O3
Carnlough Bay ... 119 O3
Carnmore ... 99 F8
Carnoneen ... 105 F7

Carnowen ... 117 J3
Carnsore Point ... 97 M11
Carnteel ... 114 L4
Carntogher ... 118 L3
Carra (Lough) ... 105 E6
Carracastle ... 106 F6
Carragh ... 102 L8
Carraholly ... 105 D6
Carraig Airt / Carrigart ... 117 I2
Carraig Mhachaire Rois / Carrickmacross ... 108 L6
Carraig na Siúire / Carrick-on-Suir ... 95 J10
Carran ... 99 E8
Carrantuohill ... 89 C11
Carrick (Wexford) ... 96 L11
Carrick / An Charraig (Donegal) ... 112 G4
Carrick-a-Rede Rope Bridge ... 118 M2
Carrick-on-Shannon / Cora Droma Rúisc ... 107 H6
Carrickaboy ... 107 K6
Carrickashedoge ... 108 L6
Carrickboy ... 107 I7
Carrickfergus ... 115 O3
Carrickhugh ... 118 K2
Carrickmore ... 114 K4
Carrickroe ... 114 K4
Carrig ... 94 G11
Carrig Island ... 93 D10
Carrigadrohid ... 90 F12
Carrigafoyle Castle ... 93 D10
Carrigagulla ... 90 F11
Carrigaholt ... 93 C10
Carrigaholt Bay ... 93 C10
Carrigahorig ... 100 H8
Carrigaline ... 90 G12
Carrigallen ... 107 J6
Carrigan ... 107 J6
Carrigan Head ... 112 F4
Carriganimmy ... 89 E12
Carrigans ... 117 J3
Carrigatogher ... 100 H9
Carrigfadda ... 89 E13
Carrigglass Manor ... 107 I6
Carriggower ... 103 N8
Carrigkerry ... 93 E10
Carrignavar ... 90 G12
Carrigrohane ... 90 G12
Carrigtohill ... 90 H12
Carrowbehy ... 106 G6
Carrowdore ... 115 P4
Carrowkeel (Donegal) ... 117 J2
Carrowkeel (Galway) ... 99 G8
Carrowkennedy ... 105 D6
Carrowmore (Galway) ... 99 F8
Carrowmore (Kilmacowen) ... 112 G5
Carrowmore (near Cloonacool) ... 112 F5
Carrowmore (near Crossboyne) ... 105 E6
Carrowmore (near Killasser) ... 105 F6
Carrowmore (near Killogeary) ... 111 E5
Carrowmore Lake ... 110 C5
Carrowmore Point ... 98 D9
Carrowmoreknock ... 105 E7
Carrownacon ... 105 E6
Carrowneden ... 112 F5
Carrownisky ... 104 C6
Carrowntanlis ... 117 F7
Carrowreagh (Roscommon) ... 100 H7
Carrowreagh (Sligo) ... 112 F5

Carrowrory ... 107 I7
Carry Bridge ... 113 J5
Carrybeg ... 95 J10
Carryduff ... 115 O4
Casheen bay ... 98 C8
Cashel (Donegal) ... 117 I2
Cashel (Mayo) ... 104 C6
Cashel (near Glennamaddy) ... 106 G7
Cashel / An Caiseal (Galway) ... 104 C7
Cashel (Rock of) ... 95 I10
Cashelgarran ... 112 G4
Cashelmore ... 117 I2
Cashen River ... 93 D10
Cashla ... 99 F8
Cashla Bay ... 98 D8
Cashleen ... 104 B7
Casla / Costelloe ... 98 D8
Casltepollard ... 107 K6
Cassagh ... 96 L10
Castle Carry ... 118 K2
Castle Coole ... 113 J4
Castle Gardens ... 90 F13
Castle Haven ... 89 E13
Castle Island ... 89 D13
Castle Point ... 98 C10
Castlebaldwin ... 112 G5
Castlebar (River) ... 105 E6
Castlebellingham ... 109 M6
Castleblakeney ... 106 G7
Castlebridge ... 97 M10
Castlecaulfield ... 114 L4
Castleconnell ... 99 G9
Castleconor ... 111 E5
Castlecor ... 94 F11
Castlecove ... 88 B12
Castlecuffe ... 101 J8
Castledawson ... 114 M3
Castlederg ... 113 J3
Castledermot ... 102 L9
Castlefinn ... 117 J3
Castlefreke ... 89 F13
Castlegal ... 112 G4
Castlegar ... 99 E8
Castlegregory ... 92 B11
Castlehill (Ballycroy South) ... 110 C6
Castlehill (near Rake Street) ... 111 D5
Castlejordan ... 102 K7
Castleknock ... 103 M7
Castlellis ... 97 M10
Castlelyons ... 90 H11
Castlemaine ... 93 C11
Castlemaine Harbour ... 92 C11
Castlemartyr ... 90 H12
Castleplunket ... 106 G6
Castlequin ... 88 B12
Castlerahan ... 108 K6
Castlerock ... 118 L2
Castleroe ... 118 M2
Castleshane ... 114 L5
Castletown (Clare) ... 99 E8
Castletown (Cork) ... 89 F12
Castletown (Laois) ... 101 J9
Castletown (Limerick) ... 94 F10
Castletown (Meath) ... 108 L6
Castletown (near Finnea) ... 107 K6
Castletown (Westmeath) ... 107 J7
Castletown (Wexford) ... 97 N9
Castletown House ... 103 M7
Castletownbere ... 88 C13
Castletownroche ... 94 G11
Castletownshend ... 89 E13

Castleville	105	E7
Castleward House	115	P4
Castlewarren	96	K9
Castlewellan	115	O5
Castlewellan Forest Park	115	O5
Cathair na Mart / Westport	105	D6
Cathair Saidhbhín / Cahersiveen	88	B12
Cathedral Rocks	104	B6
Causeway	93	C10
Causeway Head	118	M2
Cavan / An Cabhán	107	J6
Cavanagarvan	114	L5
Cavangarden	112	H4
Cé Bhréanainn / Brandon	92	B11
Ceanannas / Ceanannus Mór (Kells)	108	L6
Ceann Toirc / Kanturk	94	F11
Ceapach Choinn / Cappoquin	91	I11
Ceatharlach / Carlow	102	L9
Ceathrú Thaidhg / Carrowteige	111	C5
Cecilstown	94	F11
Celbridge	103	M7
Chanonrock	108	M6
Chapeltown (Down)	115	P5
Chapeltown (near Portmagee)	88	A12
Chapeltown (near Tralee)	93	C11
Charlemont	114	L4
Charlestown (Craigavon)	114	M4
Charlestown (Mayo)	106	F6
Cheekpoint	96	K11
Cherryville	102	L8
Chesney's Corner	114	M3
Church Ballee	115	P5
Church Cross	89	D13
Church Hill (Donegal)	117	I3
Church Hill (Fermanagh)	113	I4
Church Quarter	119	N2
Church Town	117	J3
Church Village	105	E6
Churchstreet	106	G6
Churchtown (Cookstown)	114	L3
Churchtown (Cork)	90	H12
Churchtown (Down)	115	P4
Churchtown (Wexford)	96	L11
Churchtown Point	114	M3
Cill Airne / Killarney	89	D11
Cill Chainnigh / Kilkenny	96	K10
Cill Chaoi / Kilkee	98	D9
Cill Dalua / Killaloe	99	G9
Cill Dara / Kildare	102	L8
Cill Mhantáin / Wicklow	103	N9
Cill Mocheallóg / Kilmallock	94	G10
Cill Orglan / Killorglin	93	C11
Cill Rois / Kilrush	93	D10
Cill Rónáin / Kilronan	98	C8
Cionn tSáile / Kinsale	90	G12
City Walls	96	K11
Clabby	113	J4
Cladagh	113	I5
Claddagh	106	F7
Claddaghduff	104	B7
Clady (Antrim)	115	N4
Clady (Magherafelt)	118	M3
Clady (Strabane)	117	J3
Clady (River)	116	H2
Clady Milltown	114	M5
Claggan (Donegal)	117	J2
Claggan (Mayo)	104	C6
Clamper Cross	93	E11
Clanabogan	113	J4
Clane	102	L8
Clár Chlainne Mhuiris / Claremorris	105	F6

Clara	103	N9
Clara (Valle of)	103	N9
Clarahill	101	J8
Clare (Armagh)	114	M5
Clare (Craigavon)	114	N4
Clare (River)	105	F7
Clare Island	104	B6
Clarecastle	99	F9
Clareen	101	I8
Clarina	94	F10
Clarinbridge	99	F8
Clark's Cross Roads	107	J7
Clash	100	H9
Clash North	93	E10
Clashmore	91	I11
Claudy	118	K3
Clear (Cape)	89	D13
Cleggan / An Cloigeann	104	B7
Cleggan Bay	104	B7
Cléire (Oilean) / Clear Island	89	D13
Cleristown	96	M11
Clew Bay	104	C6
Clifden Bay	104	B7
Cliff	112	H4
Clifferna	108	K6
Cliffony	112	G4
Clogga (Kilkenny)	96	K11
Clogga (Wicklow)	97	N9
Clogh (Ballymena)	119	N3
Clogh (Kilkenny)	101	K9
Clogh (Laois)	101	J9
Clogh (Wexford)	97	M10
Clogh Mills	118	N3
Cloghan (Offaly)	101	I8
Cloghan (Westmeath)	107	K7
Cloghane	92	B11
Cloghaneely	117	H2
Clogharinka	102	K7
Cloghaun	105	F7
Cloghboley	112	G4
Cloghbrack (Cloonbur)	105	D7
Cloghbrack (Meath)	108	K7
Clogheen	95	I11
Clogher (Dungannon)	113	K4
Clogher (Kerry)	93	D11
Clogher (near Carrownacon)	105	E6
Clogher (near Westport)	105	D6
Clogher (Roscommon)	107	H6
Clogher Head (Kerry)	92	A11
Clogher Head (Louth / Lú)	109	N6
Cloghera	99	G9
Clogherhead	109	N6
Cloghjordan	100	H9
Cloghmacoo	108	L6
Cloghoge	109	M5
Cloghroe (Cork)	90	G12
Cloghroe (Donegal)	117	I3
Cloghy	115	P4
Cloghy Bay	115	P4
Clohamon	96	M10
Clohernagh	96	K11
Cloich na Coillte / Clonakilty	89	F13
Clóirtheach / Clara	101	J7
Clomantagh	95	J9
Clonakenny	101	I9
Clonakilty Bay	90	F13
Clonalis House	106	G6
Clonalvy	109	M7
Clonard	108	K7
Clonaslee	101	J8
Clonavoe	101	K8
Clonbern	106	G7
Clonbulloge	102	K8
Cloncagh	94	F10

Clonco Bridge	100	G8
Cloncrave	108	K7
Cloncullen	107	I7
Cloncurry	102	L7
Clondalkin	103	M8
Clondaw	97	M10
Clonderalaw Bay	93	E10
Clondulane	90	H11
Clonea	95	J11
Clonea Bay	91	J11
Clonee	103	M7
Cloneen	95	J10
Clonegall	96	M9
Clonelly	113	I4
Clonevin	97	N10
Clonfert	100	H8
Clonfert Cross Roads	100	H8
Clonkeevy	112	G5
Clonleigh	117	J3
Clonlost	107	K7
Clonmacnoise	101	I8
Clonmany	117	J2
Clonmellon	108	K7
Clonmore (Carlow)	103	M9
Clonmore (Tipperary)	101	I9
Clonmult	90	H12
Clonony	101	I8
Clonoulty	95	I10
Clonroche	96	L10
Clonsilla	103	M7
Clontarf	103	N7
Clontibret	114	L5
Clontubbrid	101	J9
Clonycavan	108	L7

Clonygowan	101	K8
Cloon Lake	88	C12
Cloonacleigha Lake	112	G5
Cloonacool	112	F5
Cloonagh Lough	106	F6
Cloonaghlin Lough	88	C12
Cloonaghmore	111	D5
Cloonboo	105	E7
Cloondaff	105	D6
Cloondara	107	I6
Cloone	107	I6
Cloone Grange	107	I6
Cloone Loughs	89	C12
Clooneen	107	J6
Clooney	116	G3
Cloonfad (Kiltullagh)	106	F6
Cloonfad (near Old Town)	100	H8
Cloonfallagh	105	F6
Cloonfinish	105	F6
Cloonfower	106	G6
Cloonfree Lough	106	H6
Cloonkeen (Kerry)	89	E12
Cloonkeen (Mayo)	105	D6
Cloonkeen (Roscommon)	106	G6
Cloonlara	99	G9
Cloonloogh	106	G6
Cloonlusk	95	H10
Cloonmore	106	F6
Cloonoon	100	H8
Cloonteen	94	H10
Cloontia	106	G6
Cloonusker	99	G9
Cloonymorris	100	G8
Cloonyquin	106	H6

Cloran	108	L7
Clough	115	O5
Cloverhill (Cavan)	107	J5
Cloverhill (Galway)	105	E7
Cloyfin	118	M2
Cloyne	90	H12
Cluain Eois / Clones	113	K5
Cluain Meala / Clonmel	95	I10
Cluainín / Manorhamilton	112	H5
Clydagh	105	E6
Clynacantan	88	A12
Coachford	90	F12
Coagh	114	M4
Coalbrook	95	J10
Coalisland	114	L4
Coan	101	K9
Cod's Head	88	B13
Coill an Chollaigh / Bailieborough	108	L6
Colbinstown	102	L8
Coldwood	99	F8
Colebrooke	113	J5
Colehill	107	I7
Coleraine	118	L2
Colgagh	112	G5
Colgagh Lough	112	G5
Colligan (River)	95	I11
Collin Top	119	N3
Collinstown	107	K7
Collon	109	M6
Collooney	112	G5
Colly	88	C12
Colmanstown	106	G7
Comber	115	O4

Comeragh Mountains	95	J11
Commeen	117	H3
Commons	95	J10
Conay Island	112	G5
Cong / Conga	105	E7
Conlig	115	O4
Conn (Lough)	111	E5
Conna	90	H11
Connagh	100	G9
Connemara	104	C7
Connemara National Park	104	C7
Connolly	99	E9
Connonagh	89	E13
Connor	115	N3
Connor Pass	92	B11
Convoy	117	I3
Coogue	105	F6
Cookstown	114	L4
Coola	112	G5
Coolagarry	106	H7
Coolaney	112	G5
Coolattin	97	M9
Coolbaun	101	K9
Coolbawn	100	H9
Coolboy	97	M9
Coolcull	96	L11
Coolderry	101	I8
Coole (Castle)	113	J4
Coole Abbey	90	H11
Coolea / Cúil Aodha	89	E12
Coolearagh	102	L8
Cooley Point	109	N6
Coolgrange	96	K10
Coolgreany	97	N9

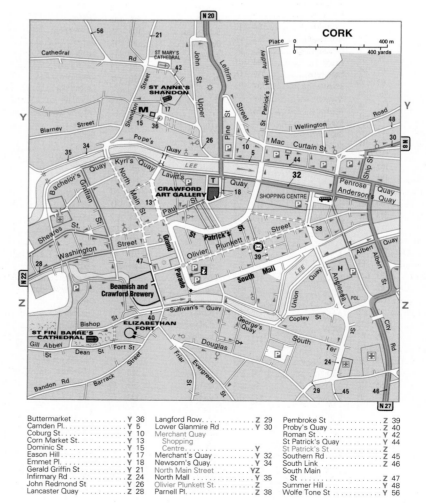

Buttermarket	Y	36	Langford Row	Z	29	Pembroke St	Z	39
Camden Pl.	Y	5	Lower Glanmire Rd	Y	30	Proby's Quay	Z	40
Coburg St.	Y	10	Merchant Quay			Roman St.	Y	42
Corn Market St.	Y	13	Shopping			St Patrick's Quay	Y	44
Dominic St.	Y	15	Centre	Y		St Patrick's St.	Z	
Eason Hill	Y	17	Merchant's Quay	Y	32	Southern Rd	Z	45
Emmet Pl.	Y	18	Newsom's Quay	Y	34	South Link	Z	46
Gerald Griffin St	Y	21	North Main Street	YZ		South Main		
Infirmary Rd	Z	24	North Mall	Y	35	St.	Z	47
John Redmond St	Y	26	Olivier Plunkett St.	Z		Summer Hill	Y	48
Lancaster Quay	Z	28	Parnell Pl.	Z	38	Wolfe Tone St	Y	56

Name	Page	Grid
Coolkeeragh	117	K2
Coolkellure	89	E12
Coolmeen	93	E10
Coolmore	112	H4
Coolnareen	101	J9
Coolrain	101	J9
Coolroebeg	96	K10
Coolshaghtena	107	H6
Coolteige	106	H6
Coomacarrea	88	B12
Coomakesta Pass	88	B12
Coomasaharn Lake	88	C12
Coomhola	89	D12
Coomhola Bridge	89	D12
Coonagh	94	F10
Cooraclare	98	D9
Coorleagh	96	K9
Coornagillagh	89	C12
Cootehall	106	H6
Copany	113	H4
Copeland Island	115	P3
Coppanagh	108	L6
Cora Droma Rúisc / Carrick-on-Shannon	107	H6
Corbally (Castleconor West)	111	E5
Corbally (Clare)	98	D9
Corbally (Kildare)	102	L8
Corbay Upper	107	I6
Corbet Milltown	115	N4
Corcaigh / Cork	90	G12
Corclogh	110	B5
Corcomroe Abbey	99	E8
Cordal	93	D11
Cordarragh	105	D6
Corduff	109	N7
Cork Harbour	90	H12
Corkey	119	N2
Corkscrew Hill	99	E8
Corlea	107	I7
Corlee	105	E5
Corlis Point	93	D10
Corn Hill	107	I6
Cornafulla	101	H7
Cornagillagh	117	I3
Cornamona	105	D7
Cornanagh	105	E6
Corracloona	113	H4
Corrakyle	99	G9
Corraleehan	113	I5
Corran Cross Roads	114	M5
Corrandulla	105	F7
Corranny	113	K5
Corraree	106	H7
Corraun Hill	104	C6
Corraun Peninsula	104	C6
Corraun Point	110	B5
Corrawaleen	107	I5
Correllstown	107	K7
Corrib (Lough)	105	E7
Corries	96	L10
Corriga	101	I6
Corrigeenroe	106	H5
Corrofin	99	E9
Corronoher	94	F10
Corroy	111	E5
Corry	112	H5
Corstown	95	J10
Cortown	108	L6
Corvally	108	L6
Corvoley	111	D5
Cottoners	89	C11
Coulagh Bay	88	B12
Coumfea	95	J11
Courtmacsherry	90	F13
Courtmacsherry Bay	90	G13
Courtown	97	N10
Cousane Gap	89	E12
Craanford	97	M9
Craffield	103	M9
Crag Cave	93	D11
Craggaunowen Megalithic Centre	99	F9
Craig	118	K3
Craigantlet	115	O4
Craigavad	115	O4
Craigavon	114	M4
Craignamaddy	114	K3
Craigs	118	M3
Crana	117	J2
Cranagh	114	K3
Cranfield Point	109	N5
Cranford	117	I2
Crannogeboy	116	G3
Cranny	99	E9
Cratloe	99	F9
Craughwell	99	F8
Crawfordsburn	115	O4
Crazy Corner	107	K7
Creagh	113	J4
Creagh (The)	114	M3
Creaghanroe	114	L5
Crean's Cross Roads	90	F12
Crecora	94	F10
Creegh	98	D9
Creeslough	117	I2
Creevagh	111	D5
Creevagh Head	111	E5
Creeves	93	E10
Creevykeel	112	G4
Cregg (Clare)	99	E8
Cregg (Cork)	89	E13
Cregg (Galway)	105	E7
Cregg (Sligo)	112	G5
Creggan (Armagh)	108	M5
Creggan (Dungannon)	114	K4
Cregganbaun	104	C6
Creggaun	94	F10
Creggs	106	G7
Crilly	114	L4
Crindle	118	L2
Crinkill	101	I8
Croagh (Donegal)	112	G3
Croagh (Limerick)	94	F10
Croagh Patrick	105	C6
Croaghaun	110	B6
Croaghmoyle	105	D6
Croaghnageer	113	I3
Croaghnakeela Island	104	C8
Croaghrimbeg	105	D6
Croan (Lough)	106	H7
Croangar (Lough)	116	H3
Crockaneel	119	N2
Crockets Town	111	E5
Crockmore	113	I4
Crocknasmug	118	L2
Croghan (Offaly)	101	K7
Croghan (Roscommon)	106	H6
Croghan Mountain	103	N9
Crohane	89	D12
Crohy Head	116	G3
Crois Mhaoilíona / Crossmolina	111	E5
Croithlí / Crolly	116	H2
Cromane	92	C11
Cromoge	101	J9
Croob (Slieve)	115	N4
Crookedwood	107	K7
Crookhaven	88	C13
Crookstown (Kildare)	102	L8
Crookstown (Moviddy)	90	F12
Croom	94	F10
Croos	106	H7
Cross (Cong)	105	E7
Cross (Waterford)	91	I11
Cross (River)	105	D7
Cross Barry	90	G12
Cross Keys (Cavan)	107	K6
Cross Keys (Meath)	108	K6
Cross Keys (Meath)	108	M7
Cross Roads	117	I3
Crossabeg	97	M10
Crossakeel	108	K6
Crossboyne	105	E6
Crossconnell	100	H8
Crossdoney	107	J6
Crossea	107	J7
Crosserlough	107	K6
Crossgar	115	O4
Crossgare	118	L2
Crosshaven	90	H12
Crossmaglen	108	M5
Crossna	106	H5
Crossooha	99	F8
Crosspatrick (Kilkenny)	101	J9
Crosspatrick (Wicklow)	97	M9
Crosswell	106	G7
Crove	112	G3
Crow Head	88	B13
Crownarad	112	G4
Cruit Island	116	G2
Crumlin (Antrim)	115	N4
Crumlin (Cong)	105	D7
Crusheen	99	F9
Crutt	101	K9
Cúil an tSúdaire / Portarlington	101	K8
Cuilcagh	113	I5
Cuilkillew	111	E5
Cuilmore	105	F6
Culdaff	118	K2
Culdaff Bay	118	K2
Culfadda	106	G5
Culfin	104	C7
Culky	113	J5
Cullahill	101	J9
Cullane	94	G10
Cullaun	94	H10
Cullaville	108	M5
Culleens	111	F5
Cullen (Cork)	94	H10
Cullen (Tipperary)	93	E11
Cullenagh (River)	99	E9
Cullenstown (near Duncormick)	96	L11
Cullenstown (near Newbawn)	96	L10
Cullin	105	E6
Cullin (Lough)	105	E6
Cullybackey	118	M3
Cullyhanna	108	M5
Culmore	117	K2
Culnady	118	M3
Cummeragh	88	B12
Cunningburn	115	P4
Curlew Mountains	106	G6
Curracloe	97	M10
Curragh	91	I12
Curragh (The)	102	L8
Curragh Camp	102	L8
Curragh West	106	G7
Curragha	109	M7
Curraghbonaun	106	F6
Curraghboy	106	H7
Curraghmore Gardens	95	J11
Curraghroe	107	H6
Curraglass	91	H11
Currahchase Forest Park	94	F10
Curran	114	M3
Currane (Lough)	88	B12
Currans	93	D11
Curraun	105	D7
Curreel (Lough)	104	C7
Curreeny	100	H9
Currow	93	D11
Curry	105	E6
Curryglass	88	C12
Curryskeskin	118	M2
Cushendall	119	N2
Cushendun	119	N2
Cusher	114	M5
Cushina	101	K8
Cut (The)	101	J8
Cutra (Lough)	99	F8

D

Name	Page	Grid
Dahybaun (Lough)	111	D5
Daingean	101	K8
Dalgar	105	F7
Dalkey	103	N8
Damastown	109	N7
Damerstown	101	K9
Damhead	118	M2
Dan (Lough)	103	N8
Danesfort (Kilkenny)	96	K10
Danesfort (Longford)	107	I6
Dangan (Cork)	91	H12
Dangan (Waterford)	96	K11
Darby's Gap	97	M10
Dargle	103	N8
Darkley	114	L5
Darragh	99	E9
Dartry Mountains	112	G4
Davagh Forest Park	114	L3
Davidstown	103	M9
Dawros	104	C7
Dawros Head	116	G3
Dead	94	H10
Dealagh	98	D9
Dee	108	L6
Deel (Limerick)	94	F10
Deel (Mayo)	111	D5
Deel (Westmeath)	108	K7
Deel Bridge	111	D5
Deele (River)	117	I3
Deelish	89	E12
Deenish Island	88	B12
Delamont	115	O4
Delgany	103	N8
Delphi	104	C7
Delvin	108	K7
Delvin (River)	109	N7
Dennet (Burn)	117	J3
Derg	113	J3
Derg (Lough) (near Donegal)	113	I4
Derg (Lough) (near Nenagh)	100	H9
Dergalt	117	J3
Dernagree	93	E11
Derravaragh (Lough)	107	J7
Derreen (near Ballynagoraher)	105	D6
Derreen (near Cloghmore)	104	C6
Derreen (near Formoyle)	99	E8
Derreen (near Lahinch)	98	D9
Derreen Gardens	89	C12
Derreendarragh	89	C12
Derreeny	88	C12
Derreeny Bridge	89	E13
Derriana Lough	88	C12
Derries	101	J8
Derry	112	G5
Derryadd	114	M4
Derryanvil	114	M4
Derrybeg	116	H2
Derryboye	115	O4
Derrybrien	99	G8
Derryclare Lough	104	C7
Derrycooly	101	I8
Derrycraff	105	D6
Derrydruel	116	G3
Derryerglinna	105	D7
Derryfadda	101	J9
Derrygolan	101	J8
Derrygonnelly	113	I4
Derrygoolin	100	G9
Derrygrogan	101	J8
Derrykeevan	114	M4
Derrykeighan	118	M2
Derrylea	104	C7
Derrylin	113	J5
Derrylough	116	G3
Derrymore	93	C11
Derrymore Island	93	C11
Derrynane	88	B12
Derrynane House	88	B12
Derrynasaggart Mountains	89	E11
Derrynawilt	113	K5
Derryneen	104	C7
Derrynoose	114	L5
Derryrush	104	C7
Derrytrasna	114	M4
Derryveagh Mountains	117	H3
Derryvohy	105	E6
Derryvode	106	G6
Dervock	118	M2
Desertmartin	114	L3
Devenish Island	113	J4
Devilsbit	101	I9
Devilsmother	105	D7
Diamond (The) (Antrim)	114	N4
Diamond (The) (Cookstown)	114	M4
Diamond (The) (Omagh)	113	J4
Dingle Bay	92	B11
Dingle Harbour	92	B11
Divis	115	N4
Doagh (Newtownabbey)	115	N3
Doagh (Rosguill)	117	I2
Doagh Beg / Dumhaigh Bhig	117	J2
Doagh Isle	117	J2
Dodder	103	M8
Doe Castle	117	I2
Dolla	100	H9
Dollingstown	114	N4
Domhnach Phádraig / Donaghpatrick	108	L6
Donabate	109	N7
Donacarney	109	N6
Donadea	102	L7
Donagh	113	J5
Donaghadee	115	P4
Donaghaguy	109	N5
Donaghcloney	114	N4
Donaghey	114	L4
Donaghmore	114	L4
Donaghmore (Meath)	109	M7
Donard (Wexford)	96	L10
Donard (Wicklow)	103	M8
Donard (Slieve)	115	O5
Donaskeagh	95	H10
Donegal / Dún na nGall	113	H4
Donegal Airport	116	G2
Donegal Bay	112	G5
Donegal Point	98	D9
Doneraile	94	G11
Donohill	95	H10
Donore	109	M6
Donoughmore	90	F12
Doo (Lough)	99	E9
Doo Lough	104	C7
Doo Lough Pass	104	C7
Dooagh	110	B6
Doobehy	111	D5
Doocastle	106	G5
Dooega Head	104	B6
Dooey Point	116	G3
Doogary	107	J5
Dooghbeg	104	C6
Doogort	110	B5
Doohooma	110	C5
Dooish Mount	117	J3
Doolough Point	110	C5
Doon (Galway)	100	G7
Doon (Limerick)	94	H10
Doon Lough	99	F9
Doona	110	C5
Doonaha	93	D10
Doonbeg	98	D9
Doonloughan	104	B7
Doonmanagh	92	B11
Doorin Point	112	H4
Dooyork	110	C5
Dore	116	H2
Dorrusawillin	107	H5
Dough	88	C13
Douglas	90	G12
Douglas Bridge	113	J3
Doulus Bay	88	A12
Doulus Head	88	A12
Dowdallshill	109	M5
Dowling	96	K10
Downhill	118	L2
Downpatrick	115	O5
Downpatrick Head	111	D5
Downs (The)	107	K7
Dowra	113	H5
Dowth	109	M6
Drains Bay	119	O3
Drangan	95	J10
Draperstown	114	L3
Dreen	118	K3
Dreenagh	92	C10
Drimoleague	89	E13
Drinagh (Cork)	89	E13
Drinagh (Wexford)	97	M11
Drinaghan	111	E5
Dring	107	J6
Dripsey	90	F12
Dripsey (River)	90	F11
Drishaghaun	105	D7
Drishane Bridge	89	D13
Droichead Átha / Drogheda	109	M6
Droichead na Bandan / Bandon	90	F12
Drom	101	J9
Dromahair	112	H5
Dromara	115	N4
Dromcolliher	94	F10
Dromin (Limerick)	94	G10
Dromin (Louth)	109	M6
Dromina	94	F11
Dromineer	100	H9
Dromiskin	109	M6
Dromkeen	94	G10
Drommahane	90	F11
Dromod	107	I6
Dromoland Castle	99	F9
Dromore (Banbridge)	115	N4
Dromore (Omagh)	113	J4

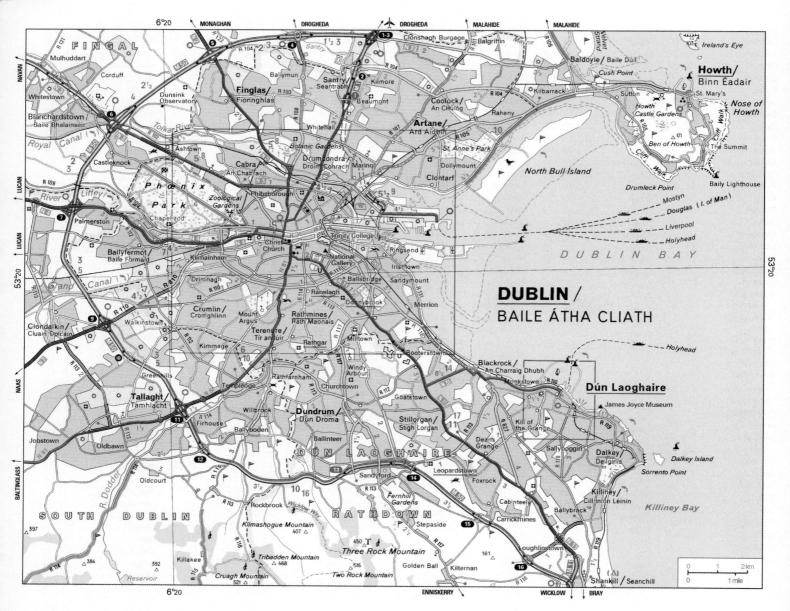

Dromore Lake	94 F10	Drumcong	107 I5	Drumreagh	110 B5	Dunaff Head	117 J2	Dungarvan Harbour	91 J11	Dunmore Head (near
Dromore West	112 F5	Drumcree	108 K7	Drumshanbo	107 H5	Dunaghy	118 M2	Dungiven	118 L3	Portnoo)	116 G3
Dromtrasna	93 E10	Drumcullen	114 M3	Drumsna	107 H6	Dunagree Point	118 L2	Dungonnell Dam	119 N3	Dunmurry	115 N4
Drones (The)	118 M2	Drumduff	113 J4	Drumsurn	118 L3	Dunamase (Rock of)	101 K8	Dungourney	90 H12	Dunnamaggan	96 K10
Drowes	112 H4	Drumena Cashel	115 O5	Duagh	93 D10	Dunamon	106 H7	Dunguaire Castle	99 F8	Dunnamanagh	117 K3
Drum (Monaghan)	108 K5	Drumfea	96 L10	Dually	95 I10	Dunany	109 N6	Dunhill	91 K11	Dunnamore	114 L3
Drum (Roscommon)	101 H7	Drumfin	112 G5	Dublin Bay	103 N7	Dunany Point	109 N6	Duniry	100 G8	Dunnycove
Drum (Sligo)	112 G5	Drumfree	117 J2	Duff	112 H4	Dunbel	96 K10	Dunkellin	99 F8	Bay	89 F13
Drum Hills	91 I11	Drumgoft	103 M9	Duffy	102 L7	Dunboyne	103 M7	Dunkerrin	101 I9	Dunowen Head	89 F13
Drum Manor Forest Park	114 L4	Drumintee	109 M5	Duleek	109 M7	Dunbrody Abbey	96 L11	Dunkineely	112 G4	Dunree Head	117 J2
Drumahoe	117 K3	Drumkeary	99 G8	Dumha Éige / Dooega	104 B6	Dunbulcaun Bay	99 F8	Dunkitt	96 K11	Dunsany	108 M7
Drumandoora	99 F8	Drumkeen	117 I3	Dún Aengus	98 C8	Duncannon	96 L11	Dunlavin	102 L8	Dunshaughlin	108 M7
Drumaness	115 O4	Drumkeeran	112 H5	Dún A'Rí Forest Park	108 L6	Duncormick	96 M11	Dunleer	109 M6	Dunworly Bay	90 F13
Drumanoo Head	112 G4	Drumlaheen Lough	107 I5	Dún Chaoin / Dunquin	92 A11	Dundalk Bay	109 N6	Dunlewy	117 H2	Durlas /
Drumatober	100 G8	Drumlea	107 I5	Dún Dealgan / Dundalk	109 M5	Dunderrow	90 G12	Dunloe (Gap of)	89 D11	Thurles	95 I9
Drumbane	95 I10	Drumlegagh	113 J4	Dún Garbhán /		Dunderry	108 L7	Dunloy	118 M2	Durrow	101 J9
Drumbeg (Feddyglass)	117 J3	Drumlish	107 I6	Dungarvan	91 J11	Dundonald	115 O4	Dunluce Castle	118 M2	Durrus	89 D13
Drumbeg (Lisburn)	115 O4	Drumlosh	101 I7	Dun Laoghaire	103 N8	Dundrod	115 N4	Dunmanus	89 D13	Dursey Head	88 B13
Drumbo	115 O4	Drummannon	114 M4	Dún Mánmhaí /		Dundrum (Down)	115 O5	Dunmanus Bay	88 C13	Dursey
Drumbologe	117 I3	Drummin	96 L10	Dunmanway	89 E12	Dundrum (Dublin)	103 N8	Dunmore	106 O5	Island	88 B13
Drumcar	109 M6	Drummullin	106 H6	Dún Mór / Dunmore	106 F7	Dundrum (Tipperary)	95 H10	Dunmore Cave	96 K9	Duvillaun Beg	110 B5
Drumcard	113 I5	Drumnakilly	114 K4	Dún na nGall / Donegal	113 H4	Dundrum Bay	115 O5	Dunmore East	96 L11	Duvillaun More	110 B5
Drumcliff	112 G5	Drumone	108 K6	Dunabrattin Head	91 K11	Dunfanaghy	117 I2	Dunmore Head (Dunquin)	92 A11	Dyan	114 L4
Drumcliff Bay	112 G5	Drumquin	113 J4	Dunadry	115 N3	Dungannon	114 L4	Dunmore Head (near		Dysart	107 J7
Drumcondra	108 M6	Drumraney	107 I7	Dunaff	117 J2	Dunganstown	96 L10	Culdaff)	118 K2	Dysert O'Dea	99 E9

DUBLIN

Anne St South . . . . . . JYZ 6
Brunswick St North . . HX 24
Buckingham St. . . . . . KX 25
Bull Alley. . . . . HZ 27
Chancery St . . . . HY 33
Clanbrassil St . . . . . . HZ 40
College Green . . . . . . JY 45
College St . . . . JY 46
Cornmarket . . . . HY 49
Dawson St . . . . JYZ
Dorset St . . . . HX 55
Duke St . . . . JY 58
D'Olier St . . . . JY 51
Earlsford Terrace. . . . . JZ 60
Essex Quay . . . . HY 65
Essex St . . . . HY 66
Fishamble St . . . . . . HY 67
Fleet St . . . . JY 68
George's Quay . . . . . KY 69
Golden Lane . . . . HZ 70
Grafton St. . . . . JYZ
Henrietta St . . . . HX 75
Henry St . . . . JX
High St . . . . HY 78
Ilac Centre . . . . HJX
Irish Life Mall Centre . . JKX
Jervis Centre . . . . . . HJX
Kevin St Upper . . . . . HZ 85
Kildare St . . . . JKZ 87
King St South . . . . . . JZ 88
Marlborough St. . . . . . JX 100
Merchants Quay . . . . HY 103
Merrion St. . . . . KZ 104
Montague St . . . . . . JZ 106
Mount St Upper . . . . KZ 112
Nicholas St . . . . HY 118
North Great George's St JX 119
O'Connell St . . . . . . JX
Parnell Square East. . . JX 126
Parnell Square North. . JX 127
Parnell Square West . HJX 129
St Mary's Abbey St . . HY 148
St Patrick Close . . . . HZ 150
Stephens Green . . . . . JZ
Stephen St . . . . . . HJY 165
Tara St. . . . . KY 171
Wellington Quay . . . HJY 181
Werburgh St . . . . . . HY 183
Westland Row . . . . . KY 186
Westmoreland St . . . . JY 187
Wexford St . . . . HZ 189
Whitefriar St . . . . . . HZ 190
Winetavern St . . . . . HY 193
Wood Quay . . . . HY 196

Hugh Lane Gallery . JX M⁴
Number Twenty-
Nine . . . . KZ D

E

Éadan Doire / Édenderry 102 K7
Eagle (Mount) 92 A11
Eagle Island 110 B5
Eagles Hill 88 B12
Eany 112 H3
Eanymore 112 H3
Easky 111 F5
Easky Lough 112 F5
East Ferry 90 H12
East Town 116 H2
Eddy Island 99 F8
Eden 115 O3
Ederny 113 J4
Edgeworthstown 107 J6
Edgeworthstown /
  Meathas Troim 107 J6

Egish (Lough) 108 L5
Eglinton 118 K2
Eglish 114 L4
Eighter 108 K6
Eleven Lane Ends 114 M5
Ellistrin 117 I3
Elly Bay 110 B5
Elphin 106 H6
Elton 94 G10
Elva (Slieve) 99 E8
Emlagh Point 104 C6
Emly 94 G10
Emmoo 106 H7
Emo 101 K8
Emo Court 101 K8
Emyvale 114 L4
Ennel (Lough) 107 J7
Ennis / Inis 99 F9
Enniscorthy / Inis
  Córthaidh 97 M10

Enniskean 89 F12
Enniskerry 103 N8
Enniskillen 113 J4
Ennistimon / Inis Díomáin ...99 E9
Eochaill / Youghal 91 I12
Erne (Lower Lough) 113 I4
Erne (River) 107 J6
Erne (Upper Lough) 113 J5
Erra 107 I6
Errew Abbey 111 E5
Erriff (River) 105 D7
Errigal Mountain 117 H2
Erril 101 I9
Erris Head 110 B5
Errisbeg 104 C7
Errislannan 104 B7
Errit Lough 106 F6
Ervey Cross Roads 118 K3
Eshnadarragh 113 K5
Eshnadeelada 113 K5

Eske 113 H3
Eske (Lough) 113 H3
Esker 99 F8
Esker South 107 I6
Eskeragh 111 D5
Eskragh 113 K4
Eyeries 88 C12
Eyrecourt 100 H8

F

Faha 91 J11
Fahamore 92 B11
Fahan 117 J2
Fahy 100 H8
Fahy Lough 110 C5
Fair Green 99 F9
Fair Head 88 C13
Fairyhouse 108 M7

Fairymount 106 G6
Fallmore 110 B5
Fanad 117 I2
Fanad Head 117 J2
Fane River 108 M5
Fanore 99 E8
Farahy 94 G11
Fardrum 101 I7
Fardurris Point 98 D8
Farmer's Bridge 93 D11
Farnagh 101 I7
Farnagh 107 I6
Farnanes Cross Roads 90 F12
Farnoge 96 K10
Farran 90 F12
Farran Forest Park 90 F12
Farrancassidy Cross Roads ..112 H4
Farranfore 93 D11
Fastnet Rock 89 D13
Faughan 118 K3

Fawney 117 K3
Fea (Lough) 114 L3
Feagarrid 95 I11
Feakle 99 G9
Feale (River) 93 D10
Fearn Hill 113 J3
Fedamore 94 G10
Fee (Lough) 104 C7
Feeagh (Lough) 105 D6
Feeard 93 C10
Feenagh 94 F10
Feeny 118 K3
Feevagh 106 H7
Fenagh 107 I5
Fenit 92 C11
Fennagh 96 L9
Fennor 91 K11
Feohanagh (Kerry) 92 A11
Feohanagh (Limerick) 94 F10

Feohanagh (River) 92 B11
Ferbane 101 I8
Fergus (River) 99 E9
Fern (Lough) 117 I2
Ferns 97 M10
Ferry Bridge 94 F10
Ferrybank 97 N9
Ferrycarrig 97 M10
Ferta 88 B12
Fethard 96 L11
Fews 95 J11
Feystown 119 O3
Fiddown 96 K10
Fieries 93 D11
Finavarra 99 E8
Finglas 103 N7
Finglass 89 C11
Finn (Lough) 117 H3
Finn (River) 117 J3
Finnea 107 J6
Finnisglin 104 C7
Fintona 113 K4
Fintragh Bay 112 G4
Finuge 93 D10
Finvoy 118 M2
Fiodh Ard / Fethard 95 I10
Fionnaithe / Finny 105 D7
Firkeel 88 B13
Fisherhill 105 E6
Five Corners 115 N3
Fivealley 101 I8
Fivemilebridge 90 G12
Fivemiletown 113 K4
Flagmount (Corlea) 99 G9
Flagmount (Kilkenny) 96 K10
Flat Head 90 G12
Flesk 89 D11
Florence Court 113 I5
Florence Court Forest Park 113 I5
Foaty Island/Fota Island 90 H12
Foilycleara 95 H10
Folk Park 99 F9
Fontstown 102 L8
Forbes (Lough) 107 I6
Fordstown 108 L6
Fore 107 K6
Forkill 109 M5
Forlorn Point 96 M11
Formoyle (Lonford) 107 I7
Formoyle (Mayo) 104 C6
Formoyle (near
  Ballivaghan) 99 E8
Formoyle (near Inagh) 99 E9
Formoyle (Lough) 105 D7
Fort Stewart 117 J2
Forthill 107 I7
Fota Island 90 H12
Foul Sound 98 D8
Foulksmills 96 L11
Fountain Cross 99 E9
Four Mile House 106 H6
Four Roads 106 H7
Fourknocks 109 N7
Foxford 105 E6
Foxhall 105 E7
Foyle (Lough) 118 K2
Foynes 93 E10
Foynes Island 93 E10
Francis' Gap 99 G8
Freemount 94 F11
Frenchpark 106 G6
Freshford 95 J9
Freynestown 102 L8
Frosses 112 H3

Frower Point 90 G12
Fuerty 106 H7
Funshin More 99 F8
Funshinagh (Lough) 106 H7
Funshion 94 G11
Furbogh 99 E8
Furnace 105 D7
Furnace Lough 105 D6
Furness 103 M8
Fyagh (Slieve) 111 D5

G

Gabriel (Mount) 89 D13
Gaddagh 89 C11
Gaillimh / Galway 99 E8
Gainestown 107 K7
Galbally (Dungannon) 114 L4
Galbally (Limerick) 94 H10
Galbally (Wexford) 96 M10
Galbolie 108 K6
Galey 93 D10
Galgorm 118 N3
Gallarus Oratory 92 A11
Galley Head 89 F13
Gallion (Slieve) 114 L3
Galmoy 101 J9
Galty Mountains 95 H10
Galtymore Mountain 95 H10
Galway Bay 98 D8
Galways Bridge 89 D12
Gaoth Dobhair /
  Gweedore 116 H2
Gaoth Sáile / Geesala 110 C5
Gap (The) 95 I11
Gara (Lough) 106 G6
Garadice 102 L7
Garadice Lough 107 I5
Garbally 100 H8
Garinish Island 88 C12
Garnavilla 95 I10
Garnish Point 88 B13
Garrane 89 E12
Garranlahan 106 G6
Garraun (Clare) 98 D9
Garraun (Galway) 100 G9
Garraun (Mount) 104 C7
Garries Bridge 89 D12
Garrison 112 H4
Garristown 109 M7
Garron Point 119 O2
Garrycloonagh 111 E5
Garrycullen 96 L11
Garryduff 118 M2
Garryfine 94 F10
Garrykennedy 100 G9
Garryspillane 94 G10
Garryvoe 91 H12
Gartan Lough 117 I3
Gartree Point 114 N4
Garty Lough 107 J6
Garvagh (Coleraine) 118 L3
Garvagh (Rowan) 107 I6
Garvaghy 114 K4
Garvary 113 J4
Gattabaun 101 J9
Gearagh (The) 90 F12
Gearha Bridge 88 C12
Geashill 101 K8
Geevagh 112 H5
George (Lough) 99 F9
Gerahies 89 D13
Giant's Causeway 118 M2
Giles Quay 109 N6
Gilford 114 M4

Gill (Lough) (near Sligo) 112 G5
Gill (Lough) (nearTralee) 92 B11
Glanaruddery Mountains 93 D11
Glandore 89 E13
Glandore Harbour 89 E13
Glangevlin 113 I5
Glanmire 90 G12
Glanmore Lake 89 C12
Glanoe 93 D10
Glantane 90 F11
Glanworth 94 G11
Glarryford 118 M3
Glasdrumman 109 O5
Glaslough 114 L5
Glasmullan 117 J2
Glassan 107 I7
Glasshouse Lake 107 J5
Glassillaun 104 C6
Glastry 115 P4
Gleann Cholm Cille /
  Glencolumbkille 112 F3
Gleann Domhain /
  Glendowan 117 I3
Gleann na Muaidhe /
  Glenamoy 111 C5
Glen 117 I2
Glen (River) (Cork) 90 F11
Glen (River) (Donegal) 112 G3
Glen Bay 112 F3
Glen Head 112 F3
Glen Lough (Donegal) 117 I2
Glen Lough (Westmeath) 107 J7
Glenaan 119 N2
Glenade 112 H4
Glenade Lough 112 H4
Glenamoy (River) 111 D5
Glenariff 119 N2
Glenariff Forest Park 119 N2
Glenariff or Waterfoot 119 N2
Glenarm 119 O3
Glenavy 115 N4
Glenballyemon 119 N2
Glenbeg Lough 88 C12
Glenbeigh 92 C11
Glenboy 112 H5
Glenbridge Lodge 103 M8
Glenbrohane 94 G10
Glenbrook 90 G12
Glencar 88 C12
Glencar Lough 112 G4
Glencloy 119 O3
Glencolmcille Folk Village 112 F3
Glencree 103 N8
Glencullen 103 N8
Glendalough (Brockagh) 103 M8
Glendalough (Waterford) 95 J11
Glenderry 92 C10
Glendorragha 116 G3
Glendovan Mountains 117 H3
Glendree 99 F9
Glendum 119 N2
Glenealy 103 N9
Gleneely (near Ballybofey) 113 I3
Gleneely
  (near Cardonagh) 118 K2
Glenelly 114 K3
Glenelly Valley 114 K3
Glenfarne 113 I5
Glenflesk 89 D11
Glengad Head 118 K1
Glengarriff (River) 89 D12
Glengarriff Harbour 89 D12
Glengesh Pass 112 G3
Glengormley 115 O3
Glenhead 118 K2
Glenhull 114 K3
Glenicmurrin Lough 98 D8

Glenmacnass 103 M8
Glenmalur 103 M9
Glenmore (Clare) 99 E9
Glenmore (Kilkenny) 96 K10
Glennagevlagh 105 D7
Glennamaddy 106 G7
Glennascaul 99 F8
Glenoe 115 O3
Glenshane Pass 118 L3
Glenshesk 119 N2
Glentaisie 119 N2
Glentane 106 G7
Glenties 116 H3
Glentogher 118 K2
Glentrasna 105 D7
Glenvale 118 M3
Glenvar / Gleann Bhairr 117 J2
Glenveagh National Park 117 I2
Glenville 90 G11
Glin 93 E10
Glin Castle 93 E10
Glinsce / Glinsk 104 C7
Glinsk (Donegal) 117 I2
Glinsk (Mayo) 111 D5
Glounthaune 90 G12
Glyde (River) 108 M6
Glynn (Carlow) 96 L10
Glynn (Larne) 115 O3
Gneevgullia 93 E11
Gob an Choire / Achill
  Sound 104 C6
Gobbins (The) 115 O3
Gokane Point 89 E13
Gola Island / Gabhla 116 G2
Golagh Lough 113 H4
Golam Head 98 C8
Golden 95 I10
Golden Vale 95 H10
Goleen 88 C13
Goold's Cross 95 I10
Goresbridge 96 K10
Gorey / Guaire 97 N9
Gormanston 109 N7
Gort an Choirce /
  Gortahork 117 H2
Gortaclare 113 K4
Gortahill 113 I5
Gortaleam 106 F7
Gortarevan 100 H8
Gortaroo 91 I12
Gortaway 117 J2
Gorteen 106 G6
Gorteen Bridge 101 J8
Gorteeny 100 G8
Gortgarriff 88 C12
Gortgarrigan 112 H5
Gortin 113 K3
Gortin Glen Forest Park 113 K3
Gortletteragh 107 I6
Gortmore
  (near Ballycastle) 111 D5
Gortmore (near Bangor) 111 C5
Gortmullan 113 J5
Gortnadeeve 106 G7
Gortnahoo 95 J9
Gortnasillagh 106 G6
Gortree 117 J3
Gortymadden 100 G8
Gorumna Island 98 C8
Gosford Forest Park 114 M5
Gougane Barra Forest Park 89 D12
Gougane Barra Lake 89 E12
Gouladoo 89 C13
Gowla 104 C7
Gowlan 104 C7
Gowlin 96 L10
Gowna (Lough) 107 J6
Gowran 96 K10

Gracehill 118 N3
Graffy 116 H3
Gráig na Manach /
  Graiguenamanagh 96 L10
Graigue 102 L9
Graigue Hill 96 L9
Graigue More 96 M10
Graigues 88 B12
Granabeg 103 M8
Gránard / Granard 107 J6
Grand Canal 101 I8
Graney 102 L9
Graney (Lough) 99 G9
Graney (River) 99 G9
Grange (Kildare) 102 K7
Grange (Kilkenny) 96 K10
Grange (Louth) 109 N5
Grange (Sligo) 112 G4
Grange (Waterford) 91 I12
Grange (River) 106 F7
Grange Con 102 L9
Grangebellew 109 M6
Grangeford 102 L9
Grangegeeth 108 M6
Granias Gap 117 K2
Grannagh 92 F8
Gransha 115 O3
Granville 114 L4
Greagh 107 I6
Great Blasket Island 92 A11
Great Island 90 H12
Great Newtown Head 96 K11
Great Skellig 88 A12
Great Sugar Loaf 103 N8
Greatman's Bay 98 D8
Greenan 103 N9
Greenanstown 109 N7
Greencastle (Donegal) 118 L2
Greencastle (Newry-
  Mourne) 109 N5
Greencastle (Omagh) 114 K3
Greenfield 105 E7
Greenisland 115 O3
Greenore 109 N5
Greenore Point 97 N11
Gregans Castle 99 E8
Gregory's Sound 98 D8
Grenagh 90 G11
Grey Abbey 115 P4
Grey Point 115 O3
Greysteel 118 K2
Greystone 114 L4
Grianan of Aileach 117 J2
Grogan 101 I8
Groomsport 115 P3
Gubaveeny 113 I5
Gubbaroe Point 113 I4
Gulladoo Lough 107 J6
Gulladuff 118 M3
Gullion (Slieve) 109 M5
Gur (Lough) 94 G10
Gurteen (Cappalusk) 99 G7
Gurteen (Leitrim) 112 H5
Gusserane 96 L11
Gwebarra Bridge 116 H3
Gweebarra 116 H3
Gweebarra Bay 116 G3
Gweestin 93 D11
Gweestion 105 E6
Gyleen 90 H12

H

Hacketstown 103 M9
Hags Head 98 D9

Hamiltonsbawn 114 M4
Hand Cross Roads (The) 99 E9
Hannahstown 115 N4
Hare Island 89 D13
Harristown 96 K10
Harrow (The) 97 M10
Healy Pass 89 C12
Helen's Bay 115 O3
Helvick Head 91 J11
Herbertstown 94 G10
High Island 104 B7
Highwood 112 H5
Hill Street 107 H6
Hillsborough 115 N4
Hilltown (Harristown) 96 L11
Hilltown (Newry and
  Mourne) 115 N5
Hind 106 H7
Hog's Head 88 B12
Holeopen Bay West 90 G13
Hollyford 95 H10
Hollyfort 97 M9
Hollymount 105 E7
Hollywood 103 M8
Holy Cross 95 I10
Holy Island 99 G9
Holycross 94 G10
Holywell 113 I5
Holywell Hill 117 J2
Holywood 115 O4
Hook Head 96 L11
Hore Abbey 95 I10
Horn Head 117 I2
Horse and Jockey 95 I10
Horse Island 89 D13
Horseleap 101 J7
Hospital 94 G10
Hugginstown 96 K10
Hungry Hill 88 C12
Hurlers Cross 99 F9
Hurley 109 M7
Hyne (Lough) 89 E13

I

Ilen 89 E13
Illaunstookagh 92 C11
Illauntannig 92 B11
Illies 117 J2
Illnacullin 89 D12
Inagh 99 E9
Inagh (Lough) 104 C7
Inch 92 C11
Inch (Donegal) 117 J2
Inch (near Whitegate) 90 H12
Inch (near Youghal) 91 I12
Inch (Tipperary) 95 H9
Inch (Wexford) 97 N9
Inch Abbey 115 O4
Inch Island 117 J2
Inchagoill 105 E7
Inchamore Bridge 108 L7
Inchbeg 96 J9
Inchcleraun 107 H7
Inchee Bridge 89 D12
Inchicronan Lough 99 F9
Inchigeelagh 89 E12
Inchiquin 105 E7
Inchiquin Lough (Clare) 99 E9
Inchiquin Lough (Kerry) 89 D12
Inchmore 107 I7
Inchnamuck 95 I10
Inchydoney Island 90 F13
Indreabhán / Inveran 98 D8
Inis / Ennis 99 F9
Inis Bó Finne / Inishbofin 117 H2

Inis Meáin / Inishmaan	98 D8	Keady	114 L5
Inis Mór / Inishmore	98 C8	Keady Mountain	118 L2
Inis Oírr / Inisheer	98 D8	Kealduff	89 C12
Inishannon	90 G12	Kealkill	89 D12
Inishbarra	98 C8	Kearney	115 P4
Inishbiggle	110 C6	Kearney Point	115 P4
Inishbofin	104 B7	Keeagh	99 E8
Inishcarra	90 G12	Keel	110 B6
Inishcarra Reservoir	90 F12	Keel (Lough)	117 I2
Inishcrone	111 E5	Keel Lough	110 B6
Inishdoorus	105 D7	Keeloges	106 G7
Inishfarnard	88 B12	Keem Strand	110 B6
Inishfree Bay	116 G2	Keenagh (Longford)	107 I7
Inishfree Upper	116 G3	Keenagh (Mayo)	111 D5
Inishglora	110 B5	Keeraunnagark	98 D8
Inishkea North	110 B5	Keereen	91 I11
Inishkea South	110 B5	Keimaneigh (The pass of)	89 E12
Inishmaine Island	105 E7	Kells (Ballymena)	115 N3
Inishmicatreer	105 E7	Kells (Kerry)	88 B12
Inishmurray	112 G4	Kells (Kilkenny)	96 K10
Inishnabro	92 A11	Kells (Ceanannus Mor) /	
Inishnee	104 C7	Ceanannas (Meath)	108 L6
Inishowen	117 J2	Kells Bay	88 B11
Inishowen Head	118 L2	Kells Priory	96 K10
Inishshark	104 B7	Kellysgrove	100 H8
Inishtooskert	92 A11	Kenmare River	88 B12
Inishtrahull	118 K1	Kentstown	108 M7
Inishtrahull Sound	118 K1	Kerry (Ring of)	88 B12
Inishturk	104 B6	Kerry Head	92 C10
Inishvickillane	92 A11	Kesh (Fermanagh)	113 I4
Inistioge	96 K10	Kesh (Toomour)	106 G5
Innfield	102 L7	Keshcarrigan	107 I5
Innisfree	112 G5	Key (Lough)	106 H5
Inniskeen	108 M5	Kid Island	110 C5
Inny (River)	107 J6	Kilbaha	93 C10
Inver (Donegal)	112 H4	Kilbaha Bay	93 C10
Inver (Mayo)	110 C5	Kilbane	99 G9
Inver Bay	112 H4	Kilbarry	89 E12
Ireland's Eye	103 N7	Kilbeacanty	99 F8
Irish Agricultural Museum	97 M11	Kilbeggan	101 J7
Irishtown	105 F7	Kilbeheny	94 H11
Iron (Lough)	107 J7	Kilbennan	105 F7
Iron Mountains	113 I5	Kilberry (Bert)	108 L6
Irvinestown	113 J4	Kilberry (Kildare)	102 K8
Island Lake	106 F6	Kilbreedy	94 F10
Island Reavy (Lough)	115 N5	Kilbrickan	105 D7
Islandmore	115 P4	Kilbricken	101 J9
Iveragh	88 B12	Kilbride (near Blessington)	103 M8
		Kilbride (near Ratoah)	103 M7
		Kilbride (near Trim)	108 L7
		Kilbride (near Wicklow)	103 N9
J		Kilbrien	95 J11
		Kilbrin	94 F11
J. F. Kennedy Park	96 L11	Kilbrittain	90 F12
Jamestown (Cloonteem)	107 H6	Kilcaimin	99 F8
Jamestown (Laois)	101 K8	Kilcar	112 G4
Japanese Gardens	102 L8	Kilcarn	108 L7
Jerpoint Abbey	96 K10	Kilcatherine Point	88 B12
Jerrettspass	114 M5	Kilcavan	101 J8
Johnstown (Kildare)	103 M8	Kilchreest	99 G8
Johnstown (Kilkenny)	101 J9	Kilclaran	99 G9
Johnstown (Meath)	108 M7	Kilclief	115 P5
Johnstown (near Arklow)	103 N9	Kilcloher	93 C10
Johnstown (near		Kilclonfert	101 J8
Coolgreany)	97 N9	Kilclooney	116 G3
Johnstown Bridge	107 I6	Kilcock	102 L7
Johnstownbridge	102 L7	Kilcogy	107 J6
Jonesborough	109 M5	Kilcolgan	99 F8
Joyce	105 D7	Kilcolman (Cashel)	90 F12
Julianstown	109 N6	Kilcolman (Dunmoylan	
		East)	93 E10
		Kilcoltrim	96 L10
K		Kilcomin	101 I9
		Kilcommon (near Caher)	95 I10
Kanturk Castle	94 F11	Kilcommon (near	
Katesbridge	115 N5	Milestone)	95 H9
Keadew	107 H5		

Kilcon	111 E5	Kilfinny	94 F10
Kilconly (Galway)	105 F7	Kilflyn	93 D10
Kilconly (Kerry)	93 D10	Kilgarvan	89 D12
Kilcoo	115 N5	Kilglass (Galway)	106 G7
Kilcoole	103 N8	Kilglass (Sligo)	111 E5
Kilcormac	101 I8	Kilglass Lough	107 I6
Kilcornan	94 F10	Kilgobnet (Kerry)	89 C11
Kilcotty	97 M10	Kilgobnet (Waterford)	91 J11
Kilcredan	91 I12	Kilgory Lough	99 F9
Kilcredaun Point	93 C10	Kilgowan	102 L8
Kilcrohane	89 C13	Kiljames	96 K10
Kilcrow	100 H8	Kilkea	102 L9
Kilcullen	102 L8	Kilkeary	100 H9
Kilcummin (Kerry)	92 B11	Kilkeasy	96 K10
Kilcummin (Mayo)	111 E5	Kilkeel	109 N5
Kilcummin Farmhill	93 D11	Kilkeeran High Crosses	95 J10
Kilcurly	109 M5	Kilkenny West	107 I7
Kilcurry	109 M5	Kilkerrin	106 G7
Kildalkey	108 L7	Kilkieran / Cill Chiaráin	104 C8
Kildangan	102 K8	Kilkieran Bay	104 C7
Kildavin	96 L9	Kilkiernan	96 K9
Kilderry	96 K9	Kilkinamurry	115 N5
Kildoney Point	112 H4	Kilkinlea	93 E10
Kildorrery	94 G11	Kilkishen	99 F9
Kildress	114 L4	Kill (Cavan)	108 K5
Kildrum	115 N3	Kill (Waterford)	91 J11
Kilfeakle	95 H10	Killabunane	89 D12
Kilfearagh	98 D10	Killaclug	94 H11
Kilfenora	99 E9	Killacolla	94 F10
Kilfinnane	94 G10	Killadangan	105 D6

Killadeas	113 I4	Killea (Donegal)	117 J3
Killadoon	104 C6	Killea (Tipperary)	101 I9
Killadysert	99 E9	Killeagh	91 H12
Killafeen	99 F8	Killealy	115 N3
Killag	96 M11	Killeany	98 D8
Killagan Bridge	118 M2	Killedmond	96 L10
Killaghteen	93 E10	Killeedy	93 E10
Killahy	95 J9	Killeen (Ardamullivan)	99 F9
Killakee	103 N8	Killeen (Armagh)	114 M5
Killala	111 E5	Killeen (Dungannon)	114 M4
Killala Bay	111 E5	Killeenaran	99 F8
Killallon	108 K6	Killeeneenmore	99 F8
Killaloo	118 K3	Killeenleagh Bridge	88 B12
Killamery	95 J10	Killeevan	113 K5
Killane	102 K8	Killeglan	106 H7
Killanena	99 F9	Killeigh	101 J8
Killann	96 L10	Killen	113 J3
Killard	98 D9	Killenagh	97 N10
Killard Point	115 P5	Killenaule	95 I10
Killarga	112 H5	Killeshil	101 K8
Killarney National Park	89 D11	Killeshin	102 K9
Killarone	105 E7	Killeter	113 I3
Killary Harbour	104 C7	Killeter Forest	113 I3
Killashandra	107 J5	Killevy	109 M5
Killashee	107 I6	Killevy Churches	109 M5
Killasser	105 F6	Killilan Bridge	99 G8
Killavally (Mayo)	105 D6	Killimer	93 D10
Killavally (Westmeath)	101 J7	Killimor	100 H8
Killavil	106 G5	Killinaboy	99 E9
Killavullen	94 G11	Killinaspick	96 K10

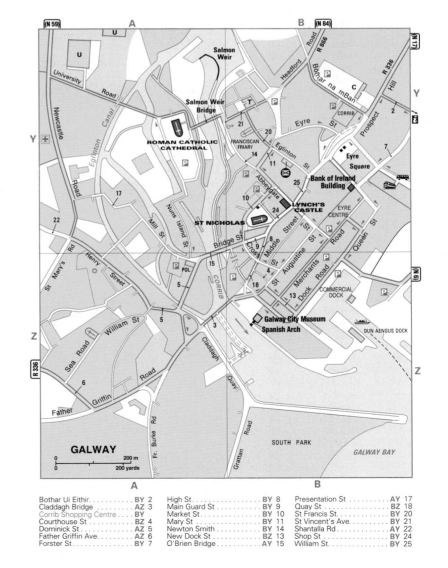

GALWAY

200 m
200 yards

Bothar Ui Eithir	BY 2	High St	BY 8	Presentation St	AY 17
Claddagh Bridge	AZ 3	Main Guard St	BY 9	Quay St	BZ 18
Corrib Shopping Centre	BY	Market St	BY 10	St Francis St	BY 20
Courthouse St	BZ 4	Mary St	BY 11	St Vincent's Ave	BY 21
Dominick St	AZ 5	Newton Smith	BY 14	Shantalla Rd	AY 22
Father Griffin Ave	AZ 6	New Dock St	BZ 13	Shop St	BY 24
Forster St	BY 7	O'Brien Bridge	AY 15	William St	BY 25

Killinchy 115 O4
Killincooly 97 N10
Killiney (Dublin) 103 N8
Killiney (Kerry) 92 B11
Killiney Bay 103 N8
Killinick 97 M11
Killinierin 97 N9
Killinkere 108 K6
Killinny 99 F8
Killinthomas 102 K8
Killinure Lough 107 I7
Killiskey 103 N8
Killkelly 105 F6
Killmuckbridge 97 N10
Killogeary 111 E5
Killogeenaghan 101 I7
Killonecaha 88 B12
Killoran 100 G8
Killoscobe 106 G7
Killough 115 P5
Killough 103 N8
Killowen 109 N5
Killucan 108 K7
Killukin 107 H6
Killurin 96 M10
Killurly 88 B12
Killusty 95 J10
Killwaughter 115 O3
Killyclogher 113 K4
Killyclug 117 I3
Killycolpy 114 M4
Killygar 107 J5
Killygordon 117 I3
Killykeen Forest Park .107 J5
Killylea 114 L4
Killyleagh 115 P4
Killyon 101 I8
Kilmacanoge 103 N8
Kilmacduagh Monastery ..99 F8
Kilmacoo 103 N9
Kilmacow 96 K11
Kilmacrenan 117 I2
Kilmacteige 111 F5
Kilmacthomas 95 J11
Kilmactranny 106 H5
Kilmacurragh 103 N9
Kilmaganny 96 K10
Kilmaine 105 E7
Kilmainham Wood ...108 L6
Kilmakilloge Harbour ..88 C12
Kilmaley 99 E9
Kilmalkedar 92 B11
Kilmanagh 95 J10
Kilmeadan 96 K11
Kilmeage 102 L8
Kilmeedy 94 F10
Kilmeelickin 105 D7
Kilmeena 105 D6
Kilmessan 108 M7
Kilmichael (near
  Castletownbere) ...88 B13
Kilmichael
  (near Macroom) ...89 E12
Kilmichael Point 97 N9
Kilmihil 98 E9
Kilmona 90 G12
Kilmoon 89 D13
Kilmore (Armagh) ...114 M4
Kilmore (Clare) 99 G9
Kilmore (Down) 115 O4
Kilmore (Mayo) 105 E6
Kilmore (Roscommon) .107 H6
Kilmore (Wexford) ...96 M11
Kilmore Quay 96 M11
Kilmorna 93 D10
Kilmorony 102 L9

Kilmovee 106 F6
Kilmurry (Cork) 90 F12
Kilmurry (Limerick) ..94 G10
Kilmurry (near Kilkishen) ..99 F9
Kilmurry (near Milltown) ..98 D9
Kilmurry (Wicklow) ..102 L9
Kilmurry Mac Mahon ..93 E10
Kilmurvy 98 C8
Kilmyshall 96 M10
Kilnagross 107 I6
Kilnalag 106 G6
Kilnaleck 107 K6
Kilnamanagh 97 M10
Kilnamona 99 E9
Kilntown 115 N4
Kilpatrick 90 F12
Kilpeacan Cross Roads ..88 B12
Kilpedder 103 N8
Kilquigguin 97 M9
Kilraghts 118 M2
Kilrane 97 M11
Kilrea 118 M3
Kilrean 116 H3
Kilreekill 100 G8
Kilroghter 99 E8
Kilross (Donegal) ...117 I3
Kilross (Tipperary) ..94 H10
Kilruddery 103 N8
Kilsallagh (Galway) .106 G7
Kilsallagh (Mayo) ...104 C6
Kilsallaghan 103 N7
Kilsally 114 M4
Kilsaran 109 M6
Kilshanchoe 102 L7
Kilshannig 92 B11
Kilshanny 99 E9
Kilsheelan 95 J10
Kilskeer 108 L6
Kilskeery 113 J4
Kiltealy 96 L10
Kilteel 103 M8
Kilteely 94 G10
Kiltegan 103 M9
Kilternan 103 N8
Kiltimagh 105 E6
Kiltober 101 J7
Kiltoom 107 H7
Kiltormer 100 H8
Kiltullagh 99 G8
Kiltyclogher 113 H4
Kilvine 105 F7
Kilworth 94 H11
Kilworth Mountains ..94 H11
Kinale (Lough) 107 J6
Kinard 93 E10
Kinawley 113 J5
Kincasslagh 116 G2
Kindrohid 117 J2
Kindrum 117 I2
Kingarrow 117 H3
Kings River 95 J10
Kingscourt 108 L6
Kingsland 106 G6
Kingsmill 114 M4
Kingstown 104 B7
Kinlough 112 H4
Kinnadoohy 104 C6
Kinnagoe Bay 118 K2
Kinnegad 108 K7
Kinnitty 101 I8
Kinsale (Old Head of) ..90 G13
Kinsale Harbour 90 G12
Kinsalebeg 91 I12
Kinsaley 103 N7
Kinvarra
  (near Camus Bay) .105 D7

Kinvarra (near Kinvarra
  Bay) 99 F8
Kinvarra Bay 99 F8
Kippure 103 N8
Kircubbin 115 P4
Kirkhills 118 M2
Kirkistown 115 P4
Kishkeam 93 E11
Kitconnell 100 G8
Knappagh 105 D6
Knappogue Castle ..99 F9
Knight's Town 88 B12
Knock (Clare) 93 E10
Knock (Mayo) 105 F6
Knock (Tipperary) ..101 I9
Knockaderry 94 F10
Knockadoon Head ..91 I12
Knockainy 94 G10
Knockalla Mount ..117 J2
Knockalongy 112 F5
Knockalough 99 E9
Knockanaffrin 95 J11
Knockananna 103 M9
Knockanefune 93 E11
Knockanevin 94 G11
Knockanillaun 111 E5
Knockanimpaha ...93 E10
Knockanure 93 D10
Knockaunalour 90 G11
Knockaunavoher ..94 G10
Knockaunnaglashy ..92 C11
Knockboy (near
  Dungarvan) 95 I11
Knockboy (near Waterford) ..96 K11

Knockboy (Mount) ..89 D12
Knockbrack 117 I3
Knockbrandon 97 M9
Knockbride 108 L6
Knockbridge 109 M6
Knockbrit 95 I10
Knockcloghrim 114 M3
Knockcroghery ...106 H7
Knockdrin 107 K7
Knockerry 98 D10
Knockferry 105 E7
Knocklayd 119 N2
Knocklofty 95 I10
Knocklomena 89 C12
Knocklong 94 G10
Knockmealdown ...95 I11
Knockmealdown
  Mountains 95 H11
Knockmore 104 B6
Knockmore (Mount) ..104 C6
Knockmourne 90 H11
Knockmoy Abbey ..106 F7
Knocknaboul Cross ..93 E11
Knocknacarry 119 N2
Knocknacree 102 L9
Knocknadobar 88 B12
Knocknagantee ...88 C12
Knocknagashel ...93 D11
Knocknagree 93 E11
Knocknahilan 90 F12
Knocknalina 110 C5
Knocknalower 110 C5
Knockowen 89 C12
Knockraha 90 G12

Knocks (Cork) 89 F12
Knocks (Fermanagh) ..113 J5
Knocks (Laois) 101 J8
Knockshanahullion ..95 H11
Knockskagh 89 F12
Knocktopher 96 K10
Knocktown 96 M11
Knockundervaul ...93 D10
Knockvicar 106 H5
Knowth 108 M6
Kylemore 100 H8
Kylemore Abbey ...104 C7
Kylemore Lough ...104 C7

L

Laban 99 F8
Labasheeda 93 E10
Lack 113 J4
Lackagh 102 K8
Lackan (Carlow) ...96 K9
Lackan (Wicklow) ..103 M8
Lackan bay 111 E5
Lackareagh 89 F12
Laconnell 116 G3
Ladies View 89 D12
Lady's Island Lake ..97 M11
Ladysbridge 90 H12
Ladywell 96 K10
Laffansbridge 95 I10
Lag 117 K2
Lagan (River) 115 N4
Lagan Valley 115 O4

Lagavara 118 M2
Lagganstown 95 I10
Laghey Corner ...114 L4
Laghtnafrankee ...95 J11
Laghy 113 H4
Lahardaun 111 E5
Lakyle 93 E10
Lambay Island 109 N7
Lambeg 115 N4
Lamb's Head 88 B12
Lanesborough 107 I6
Laney (River) 89 F12
Laracor 108 L7
Laragh (Kildare) ..102 L7
Laragh (Monaghan) ..108 L5
Laragh (Wicklow) ..103 N8
Largan (Mayo) 111 D5
Largan (Sligo) 111 F5
Largy 112 G4
Largydonnell 112 H4
Larne 115 O3
Larne Lough 115 O3
Lattin 94 H10
Laune (River) 93 C11
Lauragh 88 C12
Laurelvale 114 M4
Laurencetown 100 H8
Lavagh 112 F5
Lavagh More 117 H3
Lawrencetown 114 N4
Leabgarrow 116 G3
League (Slieve) ...112 F4
League Point 89 D13
Leamaneh Castle ..99 E9

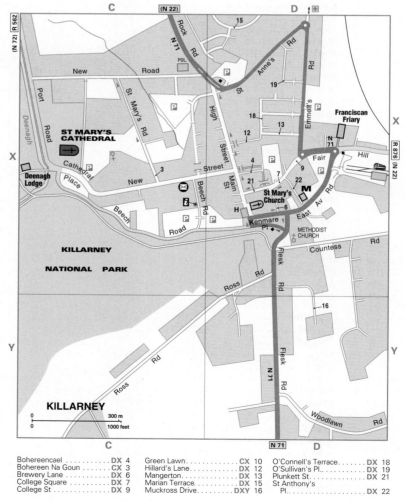

KILLARNEY

Bohereencael ....DX 4
Bohereen Na Goun ....CX 3
Brewery Lane ....DX 6
College Square ....DX 7
College St ....DX 9
Green Lawn ....CX 10
Hillard's Lane ....DX 12
Mangerton ....DX 13
Marian Terrace ....DX 15
Muckross Drive ....DXY 16
O'Connell's Terrace ...DX 18
O'Sullivan's Pl. ....DX 19
Plunkett St. ....DX 21
St Anthony's
  Pl. ....DX 22

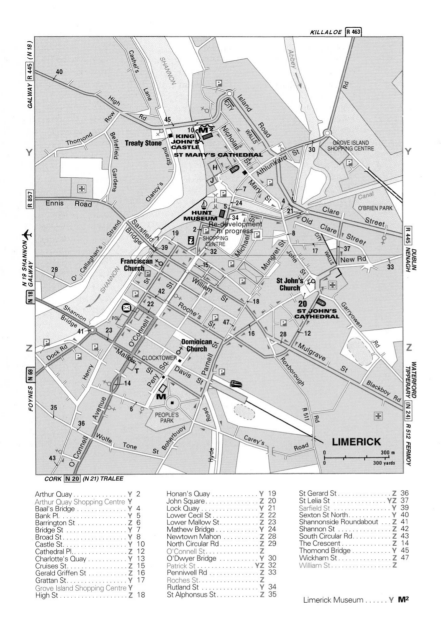

KILLALOE R 463

GALWAY R 445 (N 18)

GALWAY R 857

N 19 SHANNON GALWAY / N 18

FOYNES N 69

Treaty Stone

KING JOHN'S CASTLE

ST MARY'S CATHEDRAL

HUNT MUSEUM

Re-development in progress
SHOPPING CENTRE

Franciscan Church

St John's Church

20 ST JOHN'S CATHEDRAL

Dominican Church

CLOCKTOWER

PEOPLE'S PARK

GROVE ISLAND SHOPPING CENTRE

O'BRIEN PARK

DUBLIN R 445 NENAGH

WATERFORD TIPPERARY (N 24) R 512 FERMOY

CORK N 20 (N 21) TRALEE

LIMERICK

300 m
300 yards

Arthur Quay . . . . Y 2
Arthur Quay Shopping Centre Y
Baal's Bridge . . . . Y 4
Bank Pl. . . . . Y 5
Barrington St . . . . Z 6
Bridge St . . . . Y 7
Broad St . . . . Y 8
Castle St. . . . . Y 10
Cathedral Pl. . . . . Z 12
Charlotte's Quay . . . . Y 13
Cruises St. . . . . Y 15
Gerald Griffen St . . . . Z 16
Grattan St. . . . . Y 17
Grove Island Shopping Centre Y
High St . . . . Z 18

Honan's Quay . . . . Y 19
John Square. . . . . Z 20
Lock Quay . . . . Y 21
Lower Cecil St . . . . Z 22
Lower Mallow St. . . . . Z 23
Mathew Bridge . . . . Y 24
Newtown Mahon . . . . Z 28
North Circular Rd . . . . Y 29
O'Connell St. . . . . Z
O'Dwyer Bridge . . . . Y 30
Patrick St . . . . YZ 32
Penniwell Rd . . . . Z 33
Roches St . . . . Z
Rutland St . . . . Y 34
St Alphonsus St. . . . . Z 35

St Gerard St . . . . Z 36
St Lelia St . . . . YZ 37
Sarfield St . . . . Y 39
Sexton St North . . . . Z 40
Shannonside Roundabout . . . . Y 41
Shannon St . . . . Z 42
South Circular Rd. . . . . Z 43
The Crescent . . . . Z 14
Thomond Bridge . . . . Y 45
Wickham St . . . . Z 47
William St . . . . Z

Limerick Museum . . . . . . Y M²

Leamlara	90 H12	Leighlinbridge	96 L9
Leamore Strand	103 N8	Leinster (Mount)	96 L10
Leane (Lough)	89 D11	Leitir Mealláin / Lettermullan	98 C8
Leannan (River)	117 I2	Leitir Mhic an Bhaird / Lettermacaward	116 H3
Leap	89 E13	Leitrim (Banbridge)	115 O5
Leap (The) (near Enniscorthy)	96 M10	Leitrim (Creegh)	98 D9
Leap (The) (near New Ross)	96 L10	Leitrim (Leitrim)	107 H6
Lecale Peninsula	115 O5	Leixlip	103 M7
Lecarrow (Leitrim)	112 H5	Lemanaghan	101 I8
Lecarrow (Roscommon)	107 H7	Lemybrien	91 J11
Leckanarainey	112 H4	Lenadoon Point	111 E5
Leckanvy	105 C6	Lenan Head	117 J2
Leckaun	112 H5	Lene (Lough)	107 K7
Leckavrea Mountain	105 D7	Lerrig	93 C10
Leckemy	118 K2	Leslie Hill	114 L5
Lee	93 C11	Letterbarra	112 H3
Lee (River)	90 G12	Letterbreen	113 I5
Lee Reservoir	90 F12	Lettercallow	98 C8
Leek Point	93 C10	Lettercraffroe Lough	105 D7
Leenane	104 C7	Letterfinish	88 C12
Legan or Lenamore	107 J7	Letterfrack	104 C7
Legananny Dolmen	115 N5	Letterkelly	99 E9
Leggah	107 J6	Letterkenny / Leitir Ceanainn	117 I3
Legoniel	115 O4	Letterleague	117 I3
Lehardan	117 J2		

Lettermore	98 D8	Lisdowney	101 J9
Lettermore Island	98 C8	Lisduff (Cavan)	108 K6
Levally	106 F7	Lisduff (Leitrim)	107 I6
Levally Lough	105 E6	Lisduff (Offaly)	101 I8
Licketstown	96 K11	Lisgarode	100 H9
Liffey (River)	102 M8	Lisgoold	90 H12
Lifford	117 J3	Lislea (Magherafelt)	118 M3
Light House Island	115 P3	Lislea (Newry-Mourne)	114 M5
Limavady	118 L2	Lismacaffry	107 J6
Limerick / Luimneach	94 G10	Lismoghry	117 J3
Limerick Junction	95 H10	Lismoyle	106 H7
Lios Dúin Bhearna / Lisdoonvarna	99 E8	Lisnacree	109 N5
Lios Mór / Lismore	91 I11	Lisnageer	108 K5
Lios Póil / Lispole	92 B11	Lisnagleer	114 L4
Lios Tuathail / Listowel	93 D10	Lisnagry	94 G9
Lisacul	106 G6	Lisnagunogue	118 M2
Lisbane	115 O4	Lisnamuck	118 L3
Lisbellaw	113 J5	Lisnarrick	113 I4
Lisburn	115 N4	Lisnaskea	113 J5
Liscannor	98 D9	Lisnavagh	102 L9
Liscannor Bay	98 D9	Lispatrick	90 G13
Liscarney	105 D6	Lisroe	99 E9
Liscarroll	94 F11	Lisronagh	95 I10
Liscolman	118 M2	Lisryan	107 J6
Liscooly	117 J3	Lissadell House	112 G4
Lisdoart	114 K4	Lissalway	106 G6
		Lissamona	89 D13

Lissatinnig Bridge	88 C12	Lyre	90 F11
Lissavaird	89 F13	Lyrenaglogh	95 H11
Lisselton	93 D10		
Lissinagroagh	112 H5		
Lissiniska	112 H4		
Lissycasey	99 E9	**M**	
Listellick	93 C11		
Listerlin	96 K10	Maas	116 G3
Listooder	115 O4	Mac Gregor's Corner	119 N3
Lisvarrinane	94 H10	Mac Laughlins Corner	118 M3
Little Bray	103 N8	Mac Mahon's Town	114 K4
Little Island	90 G12	Mac Swyne's Bay	112 G4
Little Skellig	88 A12	Mace	105 D6
Littleton	95 I10	Mace Head	104 C8
Lixnaw	93 D10	Macgillycuddy's Reeks	89 C12
Loanends	115 N4	Machugh (Lough)	116 G3
Lobinstown	108 M6	Mackan	113 J5
Loch Garman / Wexford	97 M10	Macnean Lower (Lough)	113 I5
Loghill	93 E10	Macnean Upper (Lough)	113 I5
Lombardstown	94 F11	Macosquin	118 L2
Londonderry	117 K3	Macroom/Maigh Chromtha	89 F12
Lonehort Point	88 C13	Maddan	114 L5
Long Island	89 D13	Maddockstown	96 K10
Longford	101 I8	Maganey	102 L9
Longhill	101 K9	Magee (Island)	115 O3
Longwood	108 L7	Maghaberry	115 N4
Loo Bridge	89 D12	Maghanlawaun	89 C12
Loobagh	94 G10	Maghera (Clare)	99 F9
Loop Head	92 C10	Maghera (Donegal)	116 G3
Lorrha	100 H8	Maghera (Down)	115 O5
Loskeran	91 J11	Maghera (Magherafelt)	118 L3
Losset (Cavan)	107 J6	Magherabane	117 J2
Losset (Donegal)	117 I2	Magherafelt	114 M3
Lough Bradan Forest	113 J4	Magheragall	115 N4
Lough Gowna	107 J6	Magheralin	114 N4
Lough Key Forest Park	106 H6	Magheramason	117 J3
Lough Navar Forest	113 I4	Magheramorne	115 O3
Loughanavally	107 J7	Magheraveely	113 K5
Loughanillaunmore	98 D8	Maghery (near Dungannon)	114 M4
Loughanure	116 H2	Maghery (near Dunglow)	116 G3
Loughbrickland	114 N5	Magilligan	118 L2
Lougher	92 C11	Magilligan Point	118 L2
Loughermore	118 K3	Magilligan Strand	118 L2
Loughfad Hill	113 I4	Maguiresbridge	113 J5
Loughgall	114 M4	Mahee Island	115 P4
Loughglinn	106 G6	Mahon	95 J11
Loughguile	119 N2	Mahon (Lough)	90 G12
Loughinisland	115 O4	Mahoonagh	93 E10
Loughlinstown	103 N8	Maigh Chromtha / Macroom	89 F12
Loughmoe	101 I9	Maigh Cuilinn / Moycullen	105 E7
Loughmorne	108 L5	Maigh Nuad / Maynooth	103 M7
Loughros More Bay	116 G3	Maigue (River)	94 F10
Loughros Point	116 G3	Main	118 N3
Loughsalt Mount	117 I2	Maine (River)	93 C11
Loughshinny	109 N7	Mainham	102 L8
Louisburgh	104 C6	Mainistir Fhear Mai / Fermoy	90 H11
Loup (The)	114 M3	Mainistir na Búille / Boyle	106 H6
Louth	108 M6	Mainistir na Corann / Midleton	90 H12
Lower Ballinderry	114 N4	Máistir Gaoithe / Mastergeehy	88 B12
Lower Lake	103 N8	Mal Bay	98 D9
Lowertown	89 D13	Mala / Mallow	94 G11
Lowerymore	113 I3	Málainn Bhig / Malin Beg	112 F3
Lowtown	115 N5	Malin	118 K2
Lucan	103 M7	Malin Bay	112 F3
Luggacurren	101 K9	Malin Head	117 J1
Lugnaquillia Mountain	103 M9	Malin More	112 F3
Luimneach / Limerick	94 G10	Mallusk	115 N3
Lukeswell	96 K10	Mamore (Gap of)	117 J2
Lullymore	102 L8	Manger	112 H4
Lurgan (Craigavon)	114 N4	Mangerton Mountain	89 D12
Lurgan (Frenchpark)	106 G6		
Lurganboy (Donegal)	117 J2		
Lurganboy (Leitrim)	112 H5		
Lusk	109 N7		
Lyle	115 N3		
Lyracrumpane	93 D10		

Mannin Bay 104 B7
Mannin Lake 105 F6
Manorcunningham 117 J3
Manselstown 95 I9
Mansfieldstown 109 M6
Mantua 106 H6
Manulla 105 E6
Manulla (River) 105 E6
Maothail / Mohill 107 I6
Marble Arch Caves ..113 I5
Marble Hill 117 I2
Mardyke 95 J10
Markethill 114 M5
Marshalstown 96 M10
Martin 90 G12
Martinstown
(Emlygrennan) 94 G10
Martinstown
(Grennanstown) ..108 L7
Martinstown (South
Somerset) 119 N3
Mask (Lough) 105 D7
Massford 115 N4
Masshill 112 F5
Masterstown 95 I10
Matehy 90 G12
Matrix (Castle) 94 F10
Mattock (River) 108 M6
Mauherslieve 95 H9
Maum 105 D7
Maumakeogh 111 D5
Maumeen Lough 104 B7
Maumtrasna 105 D7
Maumturk Mountains ..104 C7
Mauricesmills 99 E9
Mayo 105 E6
Mayo (Plains of) 105 E6
Mayobridge 114 N5
Mazetown 115 N4
Mealagh 89 D12
Meanus 94 G10
Meathas Troim /
Edgeworthstown ..107 J6
Meela (Lough) 116 G3
Meelick 100 H8
Meelin 93 E11
Meenaclady 116 H2
Meenacross 116 G3
Meenanarwa 117 H3
Meenaneary /
Mín na Aoire 112 G3
Meenatotan 116 H3
Meenavean 112 F3
Meencorwick 116 H3
Meenglass 113 I3
Meenlaragh 117 H2
Meenreagh 113 I3
Meentullynagarn 112 G3
Meenybraddan 112 H3
Meeting of the Waters ..103 N9
Mellifont Abbey 109 M6
Melmore Head 117 I2
Melvin (Lough) 112 H4
Menlough 106 G7
Mew Island 115 P3
Michelstown Caves ..95 H11
Middletown 116 H2
Middletown (Armagh) ..114 L5
Midfield 105 F6
Mile 117 J2
Milebush 115 O3
Milehouse 96 M10
Milemill 102 L8
Milestone 95 H9
Milford (Armagh) 114 L5
Milford (Cork) 94 F10
Mill Town 114 L5

Millbay 115 O3
Millbrook (Derry) 118 K3
Millbrook (Larne) 115 O3
Millbrook (Oldcastle) ..108 K6
Milleen 93 E11
Millford 117 I2
Millisle 115 P4
Millroad 96 M11
Millstreet (Cork) 89 E11
Millstreet (Waterford) ..91 I11
Milltown (Armagh) ..114 L5
Milltown (Ballymoney) ..118 M2
Milltown (Banbridge) ..114 N5
Milltown (Cavan) 107 J5
Milltown (Craigavon) ..114 M4
Milltown (Dublin) 103 M8
Milltown (Kildare) 102 L8
Milltown (near Dingle) ..92 B11
Milltown (near Mount
Bellew) 106 G7
Milltown (near Tralee) ..93 C11
Milltown (near Tuam) ..105 F7
Milltown (Omagh) 114 K4
Milltown (Wexford) ..97 M10
Miltownpass 107 K7
Minane Bridge 90 G12
Minard Head 92 B11
Mine Head 91 J12
Minerstown 115 O5
Minterburn 114 L4
Mizen Head 88 C13
Moanmore 98 D9
Modelligo 91 I11
Modreeny 100 H9
Mogeely 90 H12
Moglass 95 I10
Moher (Cliffs of) 98 D9
Moher Lough 105 D6
Mohil 96 K9
Móinteach Mílic /
Mountmellick 101 K8
Moira 115 N4
Moll's Gap 89 D12
Monard 95 H10
Monaseed 97 M9
Monaster 94 G10
Monasteraden 106 G6
Monasteranenagh Abbey ..94 G10
Monasterboice 109 M6
Monasterevin 102 K8
Monavullagh Mountains ..95 J11
Mondello Park 102 L8
Monea 113 I4
Moneen (Clare) 95 C10
Moneen (Galway) 105 F7
Money Point 93 D10
Moneydig 118 M3
Moneygall 101 I9
Moneyglass 114 M3
Moneygold 112 G4
Moneylahan 112 G4
Moneymore 114 L3
Moneyneany 118 L3
Moneyreagh 115 O4
Monilea 107 K7
Monivea 106 F7
Monkstown (Cork) 90 G12
Monkstown
(Newtownabbey) ..115 O3
Monroe 107 J7
Montpelier 99 G9
Mooncoin 96 K11
Moone 102 L9
Moord 91 I12
Moore Bay 98 C9
Moorfields 115 N3

More (Island) 105 D6
Morenane 94 F10
Morley's Bridge 89 D12
Morningstar 94 G10
Mornington 109 N6
Mosney 109 N7
Moss-Side 118 M2
Mossley 115 O3
Mothel 95 J11
Motte Stone 103 N9
Mount Falcon 111 E5
Mount Garret 96 L10
Mount Hamilton
or Sperrin 114 K3
Mount Melleray
Monastery 95 I11
Mount Norris 114 M5
Mount Nugent 107 K6
Mount Stewart Gardens ..115 P4
Mount Talbot 106 H7
Mount Temple 107 I7
Mount Uniacke 91 H12
Mount Usher Gardens ..103 N8
Mountbolus 101 J8
Mountcastle 117 J3
Mountcharles 112 H4
Mountcollins 93 E11
Mountfield 114 K4
Mounthenry 105 E7
Mountjoy (Dungannon) ..114 M4
Mountjoy (Omagh) ..113 J4
Mountrath 101 J8
Mountrivers Bridge ..98 D9
Mountshannon 100 G9
Mourne (Lough) (near
Ballybofey) 113 I3
Mourne (Lough) (near
Carrickfergus) 115 O3
Mourne Beg 113 I3
Mourne Mountains ..109 N5
Mourne River 113 J3
Moveen 98 C10
Moville / Bun an Phobail ..118 K2
Mowhan 114 M5
Moy (River) 114 L4
Moy (River) 111 E5
Moyagh 117 J3
Moyallan 114 M4
Moyard 104 B7
Moyarget 118 N2
Moyasta 98 D9
Moydow 107 I7
Moygashel 114 L4
Moyglass 99 G8
Moylough (Galway) ..106 G7
Moylough (Sligo) 106 F5
Moynalty 108 L6
Moynalvy 108 L7
Moyne (Roscommon) ..106 G6
Moyne (Tipperary) ..107 J6
Moyne (Wicklow) 103 M9
Moyne Abbey 111 E5
Moyrus 104 C7
Moyteoge Head 110 B6
Moyvally 102 L7
Moyvore 107 J7
Moyvoughly 107 I7
Muck (Isle of) 115 O3
Muckamore 115 N3
Muckanagh Lough ..99 F9
Muckish Mountain ..117 H2
Mucklon 102 L7
Muckno Lake 108 L5
Muckros Head 112 G4
Muckross 89 D11
Muff 117 K2

Muggort's Bay 91 J11
Muinchille / Cootehill ..108 K5
Muine Bheag /
Bagenalstown 96 L9
Muineachán / Monaghan ..114 L5
Muing 111 D5
Muingnabo 111 C5
Mulhuddart 103 M7
Mulkear 94 G10
Mullach Íde / Malahide ..103 N7
Mullagh (Cavan) 108 L6
Mullagh (Galway) 100 G8
Mullagh (Mayo) 104 C6
Mullagh (Meath) 103 M7
Mullaghanattin 88 C12
Mullaghanish 89 E12
Mullaghareirk Mountains ..93 E10
Mullaghash 118 K3
Mullaghbane 109 M5
Mullaghboy 115 O3
Mullaghcarn 113 K3
Mullaghcleevaun 103 M8
Mullaghclogha 114 K3
Mullaghmore (Cliffony
North) 112 G4
Mullaghmore
(Magherafelt) 118 L3
Mullaghmore Head ..112 G4
Mullaghroe 106 G6
Mullan (Coleraine) ..118 L2
Mullan (Figullar) 114 L4
Mullany's Cross 111 F5
Mullartown 109 O5
Mullen 106 G6
Mullenbeg 96 K10
Mullet Peninsula 110 B5
Mullinahone 95 J10
Mullinasole 112 H4
Mullinavat 96 K10
Mulroy Bay 117 I2
Multeen 95 H10
Multyfarnham 107 J7
Mungret 94 F10

N

Na Cealla Beaga /
Killybegs 112 G4
Na Clocha Liatha /
Greystones 103 N8
Na Dúnaibh / Downies ..117 I2
Na Sceirí / Skerries ..109 N7
Nacorra (Lough) 105 D6
Nacung (Lough) 117 H2
Nad 90 F11
Nafooey (Lough) 105 D7
Nagles Mountains 90 G11
Nalughraman (Lough) ..116 G3
Naminn (Lough) 117 J2
Namona (Lough) 88 B12
Nanny 108 M7
Naran 116 G3
Narraghmore 102 L8
Narrow Water Castle ..109 N5
Naul 109 N7
Neagh (Lough) 114 M4
Neale 105 E7
Nealstown 101 I9
Neidín / Kenmare 89 D12
Nenagh 100 H9

Nephin 111 D5
Nephin (Glen) 105 D6
Nephin Beg 111 D5
Nephin Beg Range ..111 C5
New Birmingham 95 J10
New Buildings 117 J3
New Inn (Cavan) 108 K6
New Inn (Galway) ..100 G8
New Kildimo 94 F10
New Quay / Bealaclugga ..99 E8
New Twopothouse Village ..94 G11
Newbawn 96 L10
Newbliss 113 K5
Newbridge (Fingal) ..109 N7
Newbridge (Limerick) ..94 F10
Newbridge (near Tuomard) ..106 G7
Newbridge / An Droichead
Nua 102 L8
Newcastle (Down) ..115 O5
Newcastle (Dublin) ..103 N8
Newcastle (Galway) ..99 F7
Newcastle (Tipperary) ..95 I11
Newcastle (Wicklow) ..103 N8
Newcestown 90 F12
Newchapel 95 I10
Newferry 114 M3
Newgrange 109 M6
Newinn 95 I10
Newmarket (Cork) 93 F11
Newmarket (Kilkenny) ..96 K10
Newmarket on Fergus ..99 F9
Newmills (Donegal) ..117 I3
Newmills (Dungannon) ..114 L4
Newport (Tipperary) ..100 G9
Newport Bay 105 C6
Newport Trench 114 M4
Newry 114 M5
Newtown (Cork) 94 G11
Newtown (Galway) ..99 F8
Newtown (Kildare) ..102 L7
Newtown (Laois) 101 K9
Newtown (Limerick) ..94 G10
Newtown (near Knock) ..101 I9

LONDONDERRY

Barrack St .... X 2
Clooney Terrace .... X 5
Creggan St .... X 6
Custom House St .... X 7
Duke St .... X 9
Dungiven Rd .... X 8
Foyle Rd .... X 10
Foyle St .... X 12
Francis St .... X 13
Glendermott Rd .... X 14
Harbour Square .... X 15
Infirmary Rd .... X 17
John St .... X 18
Lecky Rd .... X 19
Limavady Rd .... X 20
Little James
St .... X 22
Long Tower St .... X 23
Sackville St .... X 26
Simpsons Brae .... X 29
Strand Rd .... X 30
Water St .... X 32
William St .... X 34

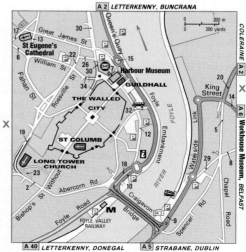

Newtown (near Nenagh) 100 H9
Newtown (Offaly) 100 H8
Newtown (Roscommon) 100 H7
Newtown (Tipperary) 95 H10
Newtown (Waterford) 95 J11
Newtown (Wexford) 96 M11
Newtown Cashel 107 I7
Newtown Cloghans 111 E5
Newtown-Crommelin 119 N3
Newtown Cunningham 117 J3
Newtown Forbes 107 I6
Newtown Gore 107 I5
Newtown Mount Kennedy 103 N8
Newtown Sandes 93 D10
Newtownabbey 115 O4
Newtownards 115 O4
Newtownbreda 115 O4
Newtownbutler 113 J5
Newtownhamilton 114 M5
Newtownlow 101 J7
Newtownlynch 99 E8
Newtownshandrum 94 F10
Newtownstewart 113 J3
Nier 95 J11
Ninemilehouse 95 J10
Nobber 108 L6
Nohaval 90 G12
Nore 101 J9
Nore (River) 96 K10
North Channel 119 O2
North Ring 90 F13
North Sound 98 C8
Nose of Howth 103 N7
Noughaval (Doora) 99 F9
Noughaval (Noughaval) 99 E8
Nowen Hill 89 E12
Nuns Quarter 115 O4
Nurney (Carlow) 96 L9
Nurney (Kildare) 102 L8
Nutt's Corner 115 N4

O

Oaghley 93 D10
Oatfield 99 F9
Oatquarter 98 C8
O'Brien's Tower 98 D9
O'Flynn (Lough) 106 G6
Oghil (Clare) 100 H8
Oghil (Galway) 98 C8
Ogonnelloe 99 G9
O'Grady (Lough) 99 G9
Oileán Ciarraí / Castleisland 93 D11
Oilgate 97 M10
Oily 112 G4
Old Court 89 E13
Old Head (Ballymackean) 90 G13
Old Head (Louisburgh) 104 C6
Old Kilcullen 102 L8
Old Kildimo 94 F10
Old Ross 96 L10
Old Town (Donegal) 117 I3
Old Town (Laois) 101 J9
Old Town (Roscommon) 100 H8
Old Town (Wexford) 96 L10
Old Twopothouse 94 G11
Oldleighlin 96 K9
Oldmill Bridge 93 E10
Oldtown (Dublin) 109 N7
Oldtown (Roscommon) 101 I7
Omagh 113 K4
Omeath 109 N5
Omey Island 104 B7

Onaght 98 C8
Oola 94 H10
Oorid Lough 105 D7
Oranmore 99 F8
Oriel (Mount) 108 M6
Oristown 108 L6
Oritor 114 L4
Ossian's Grave 119 N2
Ougther (Lough) 107 J6
Oulart 97 M10
Ovens 90 G12
Owel (Lough) 107 J7
Owenascaul 92 B11
Owenator 116 H3
Owenavorragh 97 M10
Owenbeagh 117 H3
Owenbeg 111 F5
Owenbeg (River) 112 G5
Owenboliska 99 E8
Owenboy 90 G12
Owenbristy 99 F8
Owencarrow 117 I2
Owendalulleegh 99 G8
Owenea 116 G3
Owengarve (Clew Bay) 105 D6
Owengarve (River Moy) 106 F5
Owenglin 104 C7
Oweniny 111 D5
Owenkillew (Glenelly) 114 K3
Owenkillew (Lough Swilly) 117 J2
Owenmore Bridge 105 D6
Owennacurra 90 H12
Owenreagh Hill 117 J3
Owenriff 105 D7
Owentaraglin 93 E11
Owentocker 116 H3
Owenur (River) 106 H6
Ower 105 E7
Owning 95 J10
Owroe Bridge 88 B12
Owvane 89 D12
Oysterhaven 90 G12

P

Palace 96 L10
Palatine 102 L9
Pallas 101 J8
Pallas Cross 100 I9
Pallas Green 94 G10
Pallaskenry 94 F10
Paps (The) 89 E11
Park (Bellavary) 105 E6
Park (Derry) 118 K3
Parke's Castle 112 H5
Parkgate 115 N3
Parkmore 99 F8
Parkmore Point 92 A11
Parknasilla 88 C12
Parteen 99 G9
Partry 105 E6
Partry Mountains 105 D7
Passage 106 H7
Passage East 96 L11
Passage West 90 G12
Patrickswell 94 F10
Patterson's Spade Mill 115 N3
Paulstown 96 K9
Peake 90 F12
Peatlands 114 M4
Peterswell 99 F8
Pettigoe 113 I4
Phoenix Park 103 M7
Piercetown 97 M11
Pigeons (The) 107 I7

Pike 100 H8
Pike (The) (near Boola) 91 I11
Pike (The) (near Lamybrien) 91 J11
Pike (The) (Tipperary) 100 H8
Pike Corner 108 L7
Pike of Rush Hall 101 J9
Piltown 95 K10
Pluck 117 J3
Plumbridge 113 K3
Pollagh 101 I8
Pollan Bay 117 J2
Pollatomish 111 C5
Pollnalaght 113 J4
Pollshask 106 G7
Pomeroy 114 L4
Pontoon 105 E6
Port 116 F3
Port Ballintrae 118 M2
Port Durlainne / Porturlin 111 C5
Port Láirge / Waterford 96 K11
Port Laoise / Portlaoise 101 K8
Port Omna / Portumna 100 H8
Portacloy 111 C5
Portadown 114 M4
Portaferry 115 P4
Portaleen 118 K2
Portavogie 115 P4
Portbradden 118 M2
Portglenone 118 M3
Portland 100 H8
Portlaw 96 K11
Portmagee 88 A12
Portmagee Channel 88 A12
Portmarnock 103 N7
Portmuck 115 O3
Portnablagh 117 I2
Portnoo 116 G3
Portrane 109 N7
Portroe 100 G9
Portrush 118 M2
Portsalon 117 J2
Portstewart 118 L2
Poulaphouca Reservoir 103 M8
Poulnamucky 95 I10
Poulnasherry Bay 98 D10
Power Head 90 H12
Power's Cross 100 H8
Powerscourt Demesne 103 N8
Powerstown 96 K10
Poyntz Pass 114 M5
Priesthaggard 96 L11
Prosperous 102 L8
Puckaun 100 H9
Puffin Island 88 A12
Punchestown 103 M8

Q

Quarrytown 119 N3
Querrin 93 D10
Quigley's Point 118 K2
Quilty 98 D9
Quin 99 F9
Quoile 115 O4

R

Rabbit Islands 89 E13
Race End 117 I2
Raffrey 115 O4
Raghly 112 G5
Raghtin More 117 J2
Rahan 101 J8

Rahanagh 93 E10
Rahara 106 H7
Raharney 108 K7
Raheen 96 L10
Raigh 105 D7
Railyard 101 K9
Rake Street 111 D5
Ram Head 91 I12
Ramor (Lough) 108 K6
Ramore Head 118 M2
Rams Island 114 N4
Ramsgrange 96 L11
Randalstown 114 N3
Rapemills 101 I8
Raphoe 117 J3
Rasharkin 118 M3
Rashedoge 117 I3
Ráth Caola / Rathkeale 94 F10
Ráth Droma / Rathdrum 103 N9
Rathangan 102 L8
Rathaspick 107 J7
Rathbrit 95 I10
Rathcabban 100 H8
Rathconrath 107 J7
Rathcool 89 F11
Rathcoole 103 M8
Rathcor 109 N6
Rathcore 102 L7
Rathcormack (near Fermoy) 90 H11
Rathcormack (near Sligo) 112 G5
Rathcroghan 106 H6
Rathdangan 103 M9
Rathdowney 101 J9
Rathduff 90 G11
Rathedan 96 L9
Rathfeigh 108 M7
Rathfriland 115 N5
Rathfylane 96 L10
Rathgarogue 96 L10
Rathgormuck 95 J11
Rathkeevin 95 I10
Rathkenny 108 M6
Rathlackan 111 E5
Rathlee 111 E5
Rathlin Island 119 N2
Rathlin O'Birne Island 112 F4
Rathlin Sound 119 N2
Rathmelton 117 J2
Rathmines 103 N8
Rathmolyon 108 L7
Rathmore 89 E11
Rathmullan 117 J2
Rathnew 103 N9
Rathnure 96 L10
Rathoma 111 E5
Rathowen 107 J7
Rathvilla 101 K8
Rathvilly 102 L9
Ratoath 108 M7
Raven Point (The) 97 M10
Ravensdale 109 M5
Ray (near Dunfanaghy) 117 H2
Ray (near Rathmillan) 117 J2
Ray (River) 117 H2
Rea (Lough) 99 G8
Reaghstown 108 M6
Reanagowan Cross Roads 93 D11
Reananeree / Rae na nDoirí 89 E12
Reanascreena 89 E13
Rear Cross 95 H9
Red Bay 119 N2
Redcastle 118 K2
Redcross 103 N9

Redgate 97 M10
Redhills 107 K5
Ree (Lough) 107 I7
Reelan 117 H3
Reen 89 D12
Reens 94 F10
Reevanagh 96 K9
Relaghbeg 108 L6
Rerrin 88 C13
Rhode 101 K7
Richhill 114 M4
Ridge 96 K9
Ridge Point 110 C5
Rine (River) 99 F9
Rineanna Point 99 F9
Ringabella Bay 90 H12
Ringarogy Island 89 D13
Ringaskiddy 90 H12
Ringboy 115 P4
Ringfad Point 115 P5
Ringsend 118 L2
Ringstown 101 J8
Ringville / An Rinn 91 J11
Rinmore Point 117 I2
Rinn (River) 107 I6
Rinn Lough 107 I6
Rinneen (Clare) 98 D9
Rinneen (Cork) 89 E13
Rinroe Point 110 C5
Rinville 99 F8
Rinvyle 104 C7
Rinvyle Castle 104 B7
Rinvyle Point 104 B7
River 110 B6
Riverchapel 97 N10
Riverstick 90 G12
Riverstown (Cork) 90 G12
Riverstown (Sligo) 112 G5
Riverstown (Tipperary) 101 I8
Riverville 93 D11
Roadford 98 D8
Roaninish 116 G3
Roaringwater Bay 89 D13
Robe 105 E6
Robert's Head 90 H12
Robertstown 102 L8
Robinstown 108 L7
Roche's Point 90 H12
Rochestown 96 K11
Rochfortbridge 101 K7
Rock (The) 114 L4
Rock Island 98 C8
Rockabill 109 N7
Rockchapel 93 E11
Rockcorry 108 K5
Rockhill 94 F10
Rockmills 94 G11
Rodeen 107 H6
Roe 118 L3
Roe Valley 118 L2
Roney Point 97 N10
Rooaun 100 H8
Roonagh Quay 104 C6
Roonah Lough 104 C6
Roosky (Leitrim) 112 H4
Roosky (Mayo) 106 F6
Roosky (Roscommon) 107 I6
Ropefield 112 G5
Ros an Mhil / Rossaveel 98 D8
Ros Comáin / Roscommon 106 H7
Ros Cré / Roscrea 101 I9
Ros Láir / Rosslare 97 M11
Ros Mhic Thriúin / New Ross 96 L10
Rosapenna 117 I2
Rosbercon 96 L10

Rosegreen 95 I10
Rosenallis 101 J8
Rosguill 117 I2
Roskeeragh Point 112 F4
Rosmuck 105 D7
Rosmult 95 I9
Rosnakill 117 I2
Ross (Lough Leane) 89 D11
Ross (Lough Sheelin) 107 K6
Ross Abbey 105 E7
Ross Lake 105 E7
Ross Port 111 C5
Ross West 105 E6
Rossan Point 112 F3
Rossbeg 116 G3
Rossbeigh Creek 92 C11
Rossbrin 89 D13
Rosscahill 105 E7
Rosscarbery 89 E13
Rosscarbery Bay 89 E13
Rosscor 113 H4
Rossdohan Island 88 C12
Rosserk Abbey 111 E5
Rosses (The) 116 G2
Rosses Bay 116 G2
Rosses Point 112 G5
Rossgeir 117 J3
Rossglass 115 O5
Rossinver 112 H4
Rosslare Bay 97 M11
Rosslare Point 97 M11
Rosslea 113 K5
Rossmore (Cork) 89 F12
Rossmore (Laois) 102 K9
Rossmore Forest Park 114 L5
Rossmore Island 88 C12
Rossnowlagh 112 H4
Rostellan 90 H12
Rostrevor 109 N5
Rosturk 105 C6
Rough Point 92 B11
Roughty 89 D12
Roundfort 105 E7
Roundstone 104 C7
Roundwood 103 N8
Roury 89 E13
Rousky 114 K3
Rowallane Gardens 115 O4
Rower (The) 96 L10
Royal Canal 107 I7
Royaloak 96 L9
Ruan 99 F9
Rubane 115 P4
Rue Point 119 N2
Runabay Head 119 N2
Runnabackan 106 H6
Rushen (Slieve) 113 J5
Russborough House 103 M8
Rutland Island 116 G3
Ryefield 108 K6
Ryehill 106 F7
Rylane Cross 90 F12

S

Saddle Head 110 B5
Saggart 103 M8
St. Finan's Bay 88 A12
St. John's Lough 107 I5
St. John's Point 115 P5
St. John's Point 112 G4
St. Johnstown 117 J3
St. Macdara's Island 104 C8
St. Margaret's 103 N7
St. Mochta's House 108 M6